WHAT (ABO... ...BOOK

"I have known Greg for over 15 years and have watched God use him in amazing ways with students. Here is a book gathered from years and years of 'In the trenches' youth work with teens. There are too few true veteran Youth Pastors who are still impacting this generation of teenagers. I would recommend this book to the Youth Pastor starting a new position, to a discouraged Youth Pastor who has been serving his heart out for a number of years, and to the veteran Youth Pastor who is looking for great resources to train up the next generation for those walled to stand in the gap for teenagers." Dan Howard, Youth Pastor, California.

"If you want a guide from someone who has spent decades ministering to youth in a variety of settings, then this is the book for you. I've had the privilege of ministering to youth with Greg in the trenches and can say first hand that his talk definitely matches his walk. Greg is serving Jesus Christ by ministering to thousands of teenagers around the world." Karen Grant, Professor of Youth Ministries, Columbia International University.

"To count how long Greg has been effectively serving students and Youth Pastors, you'd have to count in decades and not years. Because of his example and wealth of experience, Greg is uniquely qualified to share 'thoughts' with those of us actively involved in student ministries." Brian Farka, Youth Pastor, Wisconsin

"Greg has been a good friend and mentor to me in youth ministry. I have enjoyed the times we have been able to sit and talk about youth ministry. Greg has been used by God to change the lives of teenagers for many years, and I have never met anyone more effective at it than him. If you work with teenagers you need to read this book." Randy Larson, Youth Pastor, New Mexico

"This book for me has been the time I've always wished I had to sit down with you and just talk about youth ministry. Greg is a man who loves God and simply wants to be the most for His Heavenly Father. I admire Greg for this and believe his unique experiences will teach and help you." Scott Groff, Youth Pastor, Minnesota

"If you are in youth ministry or even thinking about it, this book is a must read." Craig Sanborn, Youth Speaker, Minnesota

"When I started out in youth ministry I was blessed to have some older and wiser youth ministry people I could lean on. Many do not have this so Greg's book is like having a veteran Youth Pastor in the office next door that you can look to for advice and counsel. It should be required reading for everyone working with teenagers." Al Schuck, Youth Pastor, Minnesota

MUSTARD SEEDS ON YOUTH MINISTRY
Small Thoughts That Can Lead to Big Change

GREG O. SPECK

For video and additional media content please visit
www.gregspeck.com

Copyright © 2018 Greg Speck
Book design by Julia Attalla
Editing by Lori Westman
Cover design by Debi Yu
Cover photo courtesy of Jeremy Bishop

All Rights Reserved

ISBN: **978-1984996114**

This book is dedicated to Dr. Bob MacRae, Jim Goding, Marty Larsen, Dave Stuart, Dave Creek, Brandon Early, Craig Sanborn, and David Westman. These are men that have helped shape my life and faith. I am a better man, husband, father, grandfather, and Christ follower because of them!

TABLE OF CONTENTS

THE OPENING SEED	1
DON'T DO YOUTH WORK	3
IF THE HORSE IS DEAD DISMOUNT	8
HELP YOUR STUDENTS GROW UP SPIRITUALLY	15
TRY A RADICAL APPROACH TO YOUR PHILOSOPHY OF YOUTH MINISTRY	27
YOU NEED TO PRAY	30
TAKE TIME OFF	35
ARE YOUR STUDENTS PHYSICALLY SAFE?	39
YOUTH MINISTRY IS NOT A STEPPING STONE	43
PARENTS MAKE GREAT ALLIES	50
YOU MUST KNOW YOUR FLOCK	53
THERE ARE WRONG WAYS TO LOVE THE OPPOSITE SEX	60
WE MUST REMAIN SEXUALLY PURE	65
IF YOU HAVE TO CHOOSE BETWEEN MINISTRY OR SPOUSE—PICK SPOUSE	79
THE FOUR 'MUSTS' FOR YOUTH PASTORS	87
BECOME A MORE EFFECTIVE LEADER	92
YOU CAN'T BE A LONE RANGER	103
BUILD YOUR VOLUNTEER STAFF	111
YOU CAN BE BETTER ORGANIZED	121
AVOID SOME ROOKIE MISTAKES	127

DISCIPLINE IS NOT A DIRTY WORD	134
YOU CAN BE A BETTER COMMUNICATOR	145
LET THEM HEAR SOMEONE BESIDES YOU	158
KNOW THE ISSUES HURTING OUR STUDENTS	164
WE NEED TO HELP OUR STUDENTS DEAL WITH THE ISSUES IN THEIR LIVES	168
WATCH OUT FOR BURNOUT	173
GET INTO YOUR PUBLIC HIGH SCHOOL AND MIDDLE SCHOOL CAMPUSES	187
IT'S GOOD TO GET ALONG WITH YOUR SENIOR PASTOR	195
WHEN YOU CANDIDATE–YOU BETTER CHECK OUT THE SENIOR PASTOR	200
BEING IN YOUTH MINISTRY FOR THE LONG HAUL IS A GOOD THING	203
BE AWARE OF THE BASIC NEEDS OF TEENAGERS	208
STAY AWAY FROM WHAT GOD HATES	214
GET INVOLVED IN SHORT TERM MISSIONS	223
CHARACTER AND TOLERANCE DO NOT MIX	237
START YOUR YOUTH MINISTRY RIGHT	242
START STRONG	250
ALWAYS ASK, HOW ARE WE DOING?	259
DON'T JUST DO SOMETHING, TO DO SOMETHING	266
DO NOT FEAR	269
FINAL THOUGHT	275

THE OPENING SEED

For a very long time I have worked with teenagers because it is what God has called me to do. I love it, and I wouldn't want to do anything else. Along the way I have learned many lessons and have a lot of thoughts on youth ministry. This is my chance to pass on some of those thoughts to you.

For you to understand some of my thoughts it would be good if you understood a little about myself. I became a Christian as a senior in high school growing up in Walnut Creek, California. I graduated from Bethel University in St. Paul, Minnesota with a major in sociology and minors in social work and Biblical and Theological studies.

God called me to Illinois where I have worked with teens. I have served as:

- a caseworker for delinquent and emotionally disturbed teenage boys
- been a Youth Pastor in two different churches
- was founder and president of Youth Ministries International
- worked as the youth specialist for Moody Bible Institute
- led mission trips to Europe and the British Isles with Reign Ministries-Royal Servants International
- served on the speaker team with Family Life and have traveled around the world speaking to teenagers and families

I am married to a beautiful woman, Bonnie, she has put up with me, loved me and encouraged me to do what God has called me to do. She is my wife, mother of our children, my love and best friend. I have four children, Justin Joseph, Julia Camille, Kelley Cameron and Garrett Gregory. Their love for Jesus has been an inspiration for me and I am excited for what God will continue to do in and through their lives. I delight in my family and they have been my closest friends and biggest supporters.

But nothing or no one is more important to me than Jesus Christ. I fall short but I so desire to love and serve Him. I am so excited to be

His man and live for Him. To bring Him glory and to live for Him is my desire. I am able to do what I am doing because of what Jesus had done in my life.

After Jesus and the Speck family my passion is youth ministry. I can't believe God has allowed me to privilege to work with and invest my life in the lives of teenagers. I love…

- Speaking to them
- Laughing with them
- Listening to them
- Leading them
- Learning from them
- Crying with them
- Encouraging them
- Correcting them, and
- Challenging them

This book is all about the things I have learned over the years of working with students and some thoughts I have in response to what I have learned. This is me writing about what I love to do. I am still in the midst of the adventure but I wanted to share some of what God has taught me.

I don't know specifically what I will be doing ten years from now but I know I am committed to youth ministry and it is what I want to do for the rest of my life. I am truly blessed by the Lord and I am so thankful He has called me to work with teens.

Come join me as we explore some thoughts on youth ministry.

THOUGHT:
"DON'T DO YOUTH WORK"

"We can't compete with the world when it comes to entertainment. We must touch their souls." Al Schuck

- ➢ "My son is bored with youth group."
- ➢ "You need more activities."
- ➢ "My daughter would come more if you played more games."

How many of us have heard these kinds of comments one or more times? We feel under pressure to entertain, amuse and preoccupy those entrusted to us, and there lies the problem. Instead of doing youth ministry, there are far too many of us caught up in youth work.

Have you ever gone on a bigger-better scavenger hunt as an activity? Everyone gathers at the church and you break them into teams that will fit SAFELY in a vehicle. You give each group a penny and a time they need to be back. Be sure you put an adult driver behind the wheel. Off they go into the different neighborhoods. They stop anywhere, run up to a door, ring the bell, and say, "Hi, we are from 1st church on the corner and we are on a bigger and better scavenger hunt. Do you have anything bigger or better than a penny?" The person goes into their house and gets anything bigger or better than a penny and trades it with you. You say, "Thank you," and run off to the next house. "Hi, we are from 1st church on the corner and we are on a bigger and better scavenger hunt. Could we trade this dead hamster for something bigger or better?" That's how it goes for the next three hours. In the end, whichever group brings back the biggest or best thing, wins!

"Students today are not looking for bigger and better; they desire consistency, depth, unconditional love and acceptance. If they find it, they will keep coming, that's youth ministry." Scott Brown

That's what youth work has become. Doing activities and trying to entertain your students so they keep coming out. Youth work has to do with activities, programs and events. We think we can capture teens by entertaining them. We fall into the "bigger and better trap." Meaning, if I am going to keep students coming out I had better do a lot of cool activities and those activities better get more exciting as time goes by. Each month you try to do something bigger or better.

- 1st Month: You - "Come on out this weekend because we are going to play Ultimate Frisbee."
  Your students respond - "OK but it better get better than this."

- 2nd Month: You - "This weekend will be great! We are having a progressive dinner including prime rib and lobster tail"
  Your students - "I don't eat meat, I'm a veterinarian."

- 3rd Month: You - "Hey, everybody this weekend we are going on a cruise to the Bahamas!"
  Your students - "I get seasick and I don't want to room with Sue."

- 4th Month: You - "This month I have a great surprise. We are going to Disney World, Japan!"
  Your students - "I don't like sushi"

Now there is tremendous pressure to top that. What do I do next month?

- 5th Month: You - "Are you ready for this? I have booked us on the space shuttle."
  Your students - "Do they serve refreshments? I look fat in a space suit."

Then you finally reach the point where you can't make it any bigger or better. You are emotionally exhausted and so you go back to Ultimate Frisbee. What happens? They complain more than usual. "Ultimate Frisbee? Are you kidding me? I've just been on the space shuttle, I've just been to Japan, and I don't want to play Ultimate Frisbee. This is stupid!" Then their parents begin to complain. You have developed a group of spectators. They want to be entertained. You are exhausted and tired of doing youth work at that church so you pack up your bag of tricks and move to the next church and repeat the cycle. No wonder the average stay of a Youth Pastor is around two years. You were not called to be a cruise director or Pastor of activities. If the church wants someone to play games with the teens let them hire Ronald McDonald.

Here is a quick quiz, no looking this up, just off the top of your head answer these questions.
1. Who are the five richest people in the world?
2. Who are the past three Miss American winners?
3. What film won the academy award for best picture in the years 2010 and 2011?
4. Name the American Idol winners over the past five years?
5. Name the who won the Pulitzer prize for the past three years?

How did you do? Probably pretty poorly but now answer these questions.
1. Name two teachers that influenced you in positive ways?
2. Name three good friends who have encouraged you?
3. Name two Christian speakers that have inspired you?
4. Name one person that has been a mentor to you?
5. Name two of your heroes of the faith?

What is the point? The people who made a difference in your life, the people you remember, were the ones who cared about you. This is something we can do really well as Youth Pastors.

"We can't compete with the world when it comes to entertainment. We must give them a reason beyond entertainment to keep them coming back." David Boyd

You've been called to youth ministry. Youth ministry has its focus on the students and seeing their life changed. You want to see them become fully devoted followers of Christ! This is what fuels your passion for the ministry. God has called you to something far greater than games and activities. He has called you to witness Him, the living God, working in and through the lives of teenagers. Will parents still complain if you are doing youth ministry? Yes. Why? Because some of your teens won't like the direction you are heading. A teen doesn't always know what is best for them. They want what feels good. For some, it feels a lot better playing games than getting their lives right before God. Your numbers will probably drop but that is OK, Jesus kept trimming the crowds. Sometimes numbers need to decrease before they begin to increase.

Do you ever play games? Do you ever plan activities? Yes, but it should not be the focus of your ministry and then the pressure is removed to entertain them. How do you get that pressure off your shoulders?

> ➢ You teach them that...
>   - All Joy is found in the person of Jesus Christ.
>   - If you are a Christian then Jesus lives within you.
>   - That means the source of all Joy is in you.

Programs, activities and events are not there to give you joy. They are there so you can give them joy. In other words, you are developing participators and not a bunch of spectators. If some guy came to me and said, "This event is boring," I would say, "Whose fault is that? This event was never planned to give you joy. This was planned so you could come and give it joy." "Now get away from me!" Oops, OK, I didn't say that. But I am saying to them they need to be participators and to get off their big fat...couches and stop whining!

Show them James 1:2, "Consider it pure joy, my brothers, whenever you face trials of many kinds," Where is the joy coming from? It's not coming from the trial itself. You don't have a teen fall out of a tree, on his head; break his neck and say, "This is great! I am the only kid in the neighborhood that can spin his head around." No, the joy comes from within, from the knowledge that God is sovereign, He is in control and I can trust Him. Concerts get old, capture the flag gets boring but their relationship with Jesus Christ gets better and better!

Do what God has called you to do and that is youth ministry. Let Him use you to change the lives of teenagers. It never gets old, it doesn't drain you, it keeps you on the cutting edge and close to Jesus.

THINK ABOUT IT:
1. Are you doing youth work or youth ministry?
2. If you are going to make it for the long haul what do you need to change?
3. Are your students, for the most part, participators or spectators?

THOUGHTS FROM OTHERS:
"Find out how much God has given you and from it take what you need; the remainder is needed by others." Saint Augustine

"An unshared life is not living." Stephen S. Wise

"Simply give others a bit of yourself; a thoughtful act, a helpful idea, a word of appreciation, a lift over a rough spot, a sense of understanding, a timely suggestion. You take something out of your mind, garnished in kindness out of your heart, and put it into the other fellow's mind and heart." Charles H. Burr

"We cannot hold a torch to light another's path without brightening our own." Ben Sweetland

THOUGHT
"IF THE HORSE IS DEAD, DISMOUNT"

"After you've done a thing the same way for two years, look it over carefully. After five years, look at it with suspicion. And after ten years, throw it away and start all over." Alfred Edward Perlman

It is very hard to ride into battle on a dead horse. It won't get you where you want to go and it will be totally ineffective. No one will follow you on a dead horse because you aren't going anywhere. It is pretty hard to inspire the troops from atop a dead horse. Too many of us are riding dead horses. We are hanging onto programs because they worked 20 years ago but now they're no longer effective in ministering to teens. Why do we do this? Perhaps we don't know what else to do or maybe we are under pressure to maintain the program. We have a Senior Pastor or a board member who found the program effective when they were teens or youth workers. Now they are out of touch when it comes to youth ministry and still think it is effective.

What we need to be doing on a weekly, monthly and yearly basis is evaluating. What's working and what isn't working? As the youth pastor, you are either maintaining or you are building. If you are maintaining then you are actually slipping backwards because everything else around you is changing. The world is changing, styles change, likes and dislikes, who wins and who loses, the teenagers themselves and their needs change. But you try to maintain the same program. What happens? It is no longer relevant to the student and they leave.

I am not talking about entertaining them. I am talking about being culturally relevant, doing things that are going to minister to the needs and be applicable to the student. You need to be evaluating, building and making necessary changes; taking the next step as you seek to honor God and make a difference in the lives of teens. Change is important so we stay current and fresh. We are leading today and at the same time preparing for tomorrow. We are creating our future and not just surviving the present.

**"When you're through changing, you're through."
Bruce Barton**

Scripture is written in ink but everything else should be in pencil. Scripture is the inerrant Word of God almighty. We always teach the Word of God and we never stray from that basic. Programs do not change lives, God changes lives and we never get away from presenting the Word of God to our students. We can change a lot of things but we never change from preaching the Word. Continue to major on the majors and the number one major is God's Word.

- ➢ But how we teach it...
  - Through Drama
  - Dance
  - Multi Media
  - Song
  - Preaching
  - Small groups

- ➢ Where we teach it...
  - Outside
  - By candle light
  - At a grave yard
  - In a bus
  - On the roof

And when we teach it changes.

I personally think Sunday School is a dead horse. It is one of the worst times to try to communicate truth to a teenager. Teenagers are usually nocturnal beings by nature. Come Sunday morning they are usually tired from being up late Saturday night. They don't like getting up in the morning and are uncomfortable and many them do not want to be there in the first place. The student is there because the parent has forced them to be there.

So, lets dismount and say this was a great program in the past but it is no longer effective with teenagers. Let's look at a better time to communicate the truths of God's word. I think evening is a better time for teenagers.

When I was Youth Pastor I decided to pull the teens out of Sunday evening church and start our own youth service. You would have thought I had said, "Jesus is no longer God." Many of the older saints became very upset with me. They remembered how much they loved Sunday evening church and how the church was always full. A former Senior Pastor came back to preach and criticized me from the pulpit without ever talking to me face to face. He expressed "How sad and wrong it was to no longer have teenagers in the evening service." I received angry and rude notes, some of them without a signature.

But with the support of my Senior Pastor, the board, parents and teens I started that Sunday evening service. Before there were less than 10 teens in the evening service and we almost immediately jumped to 100 in the youth service. It hurt me emotionally to get all the attacks but it was the right thing to do. Remember the right thing to do is not always the easy thing to do or is it necessarily the path of least resistance. 1 Corinthians 16:9, "Because a great door for effective work has opened to me, and there are many who oppose me."

"Nothing will ever be attempted if all possible objections must be first removed." Samuel Johnson

Now I realize not many of us have the authority to decide we will no longer have Sunday School. I can't imagine what they would have done if I had tried to do away with Sunday School. Boil me in oil, tar and feather me are two things that came to mind. If we can't do away with it then at least make some changes when it comes to purpose and structure. You might decide this will no longer be a primary teaching time. Instead make it an introduction time to your Youth Ministry, a first step to encourage them to get more involved in the other ministries. Make it enjoyable for them so that they want to become connected.

> ➢ Have refreshments (teens love food).

- ➢ Let them hang out and talk with their friends longer.
- ➢ Facilitate more relational activities.
- ➢ Make it more discussion and less lecture but still sharing God's truth.
- ➢ Get together with your youth staff and do some evaluating.

If you are going to move ahead then there will need to be some changes. To stay relevant, to impact lives and to stay on the cutting edge of ministry you need to be evaluating. Make the changes that need to be made. Make a list of all the changes you and your staff would like to see happen. Now put them in order of priority. But before you make the change make sure you have taken these steps.

- ➢ **Step 1** - make sure this is fulfilling your vision statement. Don't just do something because someone else is doing it and it is working. Just because something works at another church doesn't mean it is going to work at your church. Bathe the change in prayer and get the wisdom of Godly counsel.

- ➢ **Step 2** - make sure you have a plan and you know what you are doing. List all the advantages and disadvantages in making this change. The advantages need to outweigh the disadvantages. Have I counted the cost and do I have the resources I will need to make it happen? Things like money, space, materials, staff, etc. You don't want to get part way into the change and then realize you don't really have what you need to make it happen. What do you think will happen the next time you want to make a change? Think through the timing. Do I have a time line? When will this start? Timing is crucial. You must plan ahead and give people the opportunity to respond to the changes you want to make.

"Courage is the power to let go of the familiar."
Mary Bryant

- ➢ **Step 3** - make sure you have the support of all the key individuals. Pastors, the board, parents and student leaders are all on board. You have given them information and you have allowed them input so they feel like they have been part of the process. Meet with key families and leaders to share your vision and answer their questions. Remember the old saying, "People don't resist change as much as being changed." Your church history fights against change. People think what helped them and was significant ministry must still work today.

- ➤ **Step 4** - get the information out. You make everyone aware of the change, what is going to happen, when it is going to happen and the purpose behind it. Over communicate with announcements, e-mail, text, meetings and one-on-one time with key players. Let them ask questions. People will want to see how it benefits them. They are going to be weighing the pros and cons for them and their families. So, don't just tell them how this will benefit the ministry as a whole but how will this benefit them as individuals. It is also very important you have considered how this change will impact the other church ministries. For example, if you are going to change your mid week meeting from Wednesday to Tuesday but the adults and children meet on Wednesday than the change may not benefit the church as a whole.

If students, parents and volunteer staff perceive you love them, have taken time to develop a relationship and they can trust you then they will be more open to the change. That is why it can be very hard to walk in brand new and make significant changes. You haven't built the relationships and people don't really know if they can trust you. If the people do not like the person that is representing the change then they will usually not like the change. So, if you have some parents who are upset at you they will probably oppose the change.

Time is a huge factor when considering the change. People want to know how this will affect my time. If it is more of a time commitment then people will resist it. This doesn't mean you don't do it but you must take the time to win their hearts. Also, when you propose change you are asking people to step into the unknown. We are moving them out of their comfort zone. Some people are comfortable with the ineffective, irrelevant and dead, because they have always done it that way.

It takes courage to make the changes you need to make. But you must pick your battles carefully. What are you willing to go to the wall for and what isn't worth it? Change should not be like a bull in a china shop. Meaning you are going to do this and it doesn't matter how much chaos it causes. I have seen the Youth Pastor who comes in brand new and decides to make all these changes. This is what they did at their last church and if it worked there than it must work at this church. However, the people resist, they haven't weighted the pros and cons, they haven't counted the cost, they haven't developed relationships and they end up leaving because of all the resistance. That doesn't mean you don't make changes just be smarter and think it through ahead of time.

Make the changes God is calling you to make. Tradition is a lousy excuse for no longer being relevant. Are you riding any dead horses? Then dismount! You'll like the view better and it won't stink so badly.

THINK ABOUT IT:
1. Are you riding any dead horses?
2. What isn't happening in the youth ministry that needs to happen?
3. What can you do to make things more relevant?

THOUGHTS FROM OTHERS:
"Everything passes; everything wears out; everything breaks." French proverb

"Things alter for the worse spontaneously, if they be not altered for the better designedly." Francis Bacon

"Everything flows, nothing stays still." Heraclitus

"Even if you're on the right track, you'll get run over if you just sit there." Will Rogers

"The art of progress is to preserve order amid change, and to preserve change amid order." Alfred North Whitehead

"If you board the wrong train, it is no use running along the corridor in the other direction." Dietrich Bonhoeffer

"You can't steal second base and keep one foot on first." Frederick B. Wilson

"There are two kinds of fools. One says, 'This is old, therefore it is good.' The other says, 'This is new, therefore it is better'." James Gibbons Huneker

THOUGHT
"HELP YOUR STUDENTS GROW UP SPIRITUALLY"

"While building relationships with students is crucial we must go beyond the role of a buddy and enter into the world of spiritual shepherding." David Boyd

I have had the privilege of working with so many outstanding students as a Youth Pastor. Todd Bizel was a pretty typical teen. A little awkward, got along with his father like oil mixes with water, struggled with self-image, was not good at school, and he had the temptations and problems of most teens. Today Todd loves Jesus, works with teens, and is making a difference in the lives of students. How did Todd get from then to now? He took some steps and we can help our students spiritually and see them go from a spectator to participator as they take these five steps.

1. A personal relationship with Jesus Christ! If we build on anything besides this then we are building on quicksand. The ultimate answer for the needs of our teenagers is a close, personal, relationship with Jesus Christ. I read a statistic which said over 80% of all teenagers believe in God. Wow, that must be the reason we all love each other, are remaining sexually pure and packing out the churches. (OK that was sarcasm). But we are tempted to read a statistic like this and feel pretty good. Until we read James 2:19. "You believe that there is one God. Good! Even the demons believe that--and shudder." One hundred percent of the demons believe in God and not one of them is going to Heaven. So, there needs to be more than just empty beliefs. We need to bring the student face to face with the living God and help them to understand and experience His passion for them. Then we give them the chance to decide whether they want to love and follow Him. As they fall in love with Jesus and discover His love for them we disciple them so they understand the basics of their faith. We want to develop within them a passion for God as they understand His passion for them.

"You called, you cried, you shattered my deafness, you sparkled, you blazed, you drove away my blindness, you shed your fragrance, and I drew my breath, and I pant for you." Saint Augustine

You don't need to be their savior. This takes a lot of pressure off us. We are faithful to do what God has called us to do, we lift Jesus up and He draws these students to Himself.

2. Healthy Personhood. I define this as, seeing yourself through the eyes of God. For teens to understand who they are in Christ and their birthright.

> Things like...
- John 1:12- I am a child of God
- John 15:15- I am Jesus' friend
- John 15:16- Jesus chose me to bear fruit
- Colossians 1:22- I am holy and acceptable to God.
- Romans 8:35-39- Nothing can separate me from the love of Christ.
- I Corinthians 3:16- I am the Temple of the Holy Spirit
- II Corinthians 6:1- I am God's co-worker
- Ephesians 1:5- I am adopted as God's child
- Ephesians 2:6- I am seated with Christ in Heaven.
- Ephesians 2:10- I am God's handiwork, created by Him.
- Ephesians 2:19- I am a citizen of Heaven.
- Philippians 4:13- I can do all things through Christ
- Colossians 2:10- I am complete in Christ
- Colossians 2:13- All my sins are forgiven

This is who we are. Not what we are becoming! Whether we feel like it or not it is who we are. Too many teens see themselves through the eyes of the world and they are horribly manipulated. The world never allows the teen to arrive. They can never come to their closet and say, "There, I finally have everything I need to be stylish!" Because the world says to them, "Did you think that outfit was in? No, that was last week." They are always changing the styles and our teens feel ugly, fat, worthless and unsatisfied. They become bound and enslaved to those feelings. That is why Jesus said, in John 8:32, "Then you will know the truth, and the truth will set you free."

When I talk to teens about having a healthy Personhood I seek to communicate these four truths to them. Feel free to borrow, tweak and use these four points when you are sharing with your students about seeing themselves through the eyes of God!

A. What you look like on the outside is not what is most important.

The world says just the opposite. To have a slim body, white teeth, full hair and a clean complexion is the ultimate! Teens buy into this and begin to compare themselves to others. When they compare themselves, they can always find people they think are better looking than they are. This leads to depression and self-destructive behaviors. It is like they are on an emotional roller coaster. Up and down they go depending on how they feel about themselves on any certain day or in some cases how they feel about themselves at any certain hour. Sometimes they might feel superior to others but in most cases, they are feeling inferior. Your student needs to know they are neither inferior or superior. They are just themselves and that is something good to be.

What they look like on the outside isn't what is most important! I Samuel 16:7, says: "But the Lord said to Samuel, 'do not consider his appearance or his height, for I have rejected him. The Lord does not look at the things man looks at. Man looks at the outward appearance, but the Lord looks at the heart." God doesn't focus on the outside and neither should we.

**"Beauty is altogether in the eye of the beholder"
General Lew Wallace**

Do your students understand there is no standard for beauty? Beauty is in the eye of the beholder. How do I know this? Take ten high school guys to another high school, they have never been to, in another state. Bring all the teenage girls from the school into the gym and identify them by power stapling a number to their shoulder. Then have the ten guys spread out, give them each a pen and a piece of paper. They can't talk to each other but they need to write down the number of the best-looking woman. They will pick ten different women. Why? Because each has their own idea of what is beautiful.

The world tries to tell you there is a standard for beauty. A certain hair style or body type but this is a lie. Now take ten teenage women and bring them to a high school they have never been before. Bring all the guys from the school into the auditorium and identify them by gently hanging a number around their neck (Hey, I am a guy and I don't want to be stapled). Now have the girls pick the best-looking man. They will pick ten different men. The great news for your students is some members of the opposite sex will think they are one of the best-looking people alive no matter how they look on the outside.

Take the teens to Isaiah 53:2 and talk about Jesus physical appearance. "He grew up before him like a tender shoot, and like a root out of dry ground. He had no beauty or majesty to attract us to Him, nothing in his appearance that we should desire him." Jesus could have been handsome beyond words, the best-looking man to have ever lived. But he wasn't and I believe, by his very physical appearance, he was saying what you look like on the outside is not what is most important.

B. God's desire for us is to have inward beauty.

I Samuel 16:7c, "But the Lord looks at the heart." The heart and what is happening on the inside is what is most important. How can they begin to work on their insides?
- Draw near to God.
- Hear the truth taught.
- Be a seeker of the truth.
- Get counseling and help for the pain inside their lives.
- Start making good choices.

I tell teens when they are beautiful on the inside it shows itself on the outside. As people get to know you, you become more and more beautiful to them because of your commitment to Jesus Christ, character, personality, etc. How else do you explain someone like me, looking like a cross between Winnie the Pooh and the Cowardly Lion on the *Wizard of Oz*, having such a beautiful wife? When you are younger, looks are really important. But when you mature and get older you become tired of shallow people who only have pretty faces. You want someone with depth, someone who is beautiful on the inside.

"Many beautiful people become ugly when they open their mouth and let what's inside come out." David Malouf

C. God was actively involved in their creation.

Psalm 119:73a, says: "Your hands made me and formed me," Also check out Psalm 139. Than say to your students… God does not make garbage, He doesn't hold garage sales. He made you and you are someone wonderful, unique and beautiful. Look at your eyes, ears, nose, check out your chin, look at your other chin. You are different from other people and that is good. Who decides one person's nose is more attractive than another person's nose? That is ridiculous. Noses are different, some have pug noses; others look like ski jumps but they are all beautiful - hand made by God.

Let's say I make a little clay figure which then comes alive. It begins to dance for joy. I am also happy because it took me a lot of time and loving care to make them and it is good to see them rejoicing. The little figure dances in front of a mirror; they stop and stare at themselves. All of a sudden they say, "I am so ugly, gross, disgusting and worthless." What happens? My heart is broken. Why? Because the clay figure isn't cutting itself down, it's slamming me because I made it. When you look at yourself in the mirror and put yourself down, who are you really criticizing? Jesus Christ, your creator! When's the last time you saw a flower and ran away in terror? When's the last time you saw a sunset and felt like vomiting? When's the last time you have been grossed out by a tree? Never! You look at everything God has made, it's all different and it's all beautiful. You are part of His creation and you are beautiful!

When I was in middle school students use to call me "basset hound" because I had droopy eyes. They would always say to me, "Hey, why don't you open your eyes." I would respond by saying, "Hey, why don't you shut your mouth." For years I hated my eyes. I would always think, "Why do I have to look like a dog?" Then I became a Christian as a senior in high school and discovered God was actively involved in my creation. For the first time, I was thankful for my eyes and it became such a freeing experience for me. I tell students I want them to stand at the mirror, look at themselves and say out loud, "Jesus, thank you for making me...me!" Some of our students have never done this. Maybe you have never done it!

D. Christ died for You!

Years ago my wife went to the refrigerator to begin to prepare a meal. As she started pulling things out she discovered a container which was buried under other stuff. Now it was supposed to be a clear container but for some reason she couldn't see what was inside. So, she opened it and immediately it smelled like eight dogs had died and decayed in our kitchen. It was this old chicken that looked like we had saved it from our honeymoon.

I took it out to the garbage can, which sits in our garage, on Wednesday, our garbage pickup is on Tuesday. This was during the summer, in the Midwest, high temperatures and high humidity. Monday, I came home from work and the smell almost knocked me out. I decided to carry the can down to the street. We have a plastic container with many holes in it because our garbage person takes such good care of our container. I place the can on the street and walk back into the garage, only to discover hundreds of maggots crawling around. I wasn't grossed out - yeah right!

Now what if I came to your house and poured out some of the grossest and sickest garbage in your driveway. Then I take a 357 Magnum, a very powerful hand gun, so powerful, that if I shot you with it, it would probably hurt you. I point the gun at your head and ask you, "Would you be willing to die for that pile of garbage?" My hope is you would reply, "No!" That would be a good choice. See neither would Jesus have died for that garbage and He died for you.

Because you are so precious to Him he was willing to lay down his life for you. He did this because he loves and values you. You are not some gross, ugly, mistake!
- ➢ You are a creation of God,
- ➢ Made for a purpose.
- ➢ A child of the King.
- ➢ Dearly loved.
- ➢ Saved by the very blood of Jesus.

God made you and you will not grow up spiritually until you receive this good gift and be thankful for YOU. Get your eyes off everyone else and focus in on your creator. See yourself through His eyes.

3. Healthy Relationships

I Corinthians 15:33, says: "Do not be misled: 'Bad company corrupts good character'."

The key word is healthy. Our students have a lot of relationships but not all of them are healthy. One of the fastest ways to destroy what God does on a mission's trip, during camp or retreat is to have them go back to a bunch of unhealthy relationships. I have had the experience of going up to some of my students and saying, "I don't think you ought to be hanging with this person or dating this person." Now sometimes it was received but sometimes it wasn't, depending on my relationship with them. I thought, "How can I help them to see and discover whether their relationship is healthy or not?" I came up with five questions. I asked the teens to think of their best friends, the person they are dating and answer these questions honestly. Afterwards they will be able to tell me whether the relationship is healthy or not.

A. When you are with this person or people what do you do? Does it honor God?

B. What comes out of your mouth? Is there profanity, gossip; are you tearing down or building up?

C. How do you feel about your parents and authority? Do you obey or do you disobey? Are you deceptive? Do you lie? Do you break the law?

D. What is this relationship doing to your healthy personhood? When you are all by yourself, in your room, and you look in the mirror, do you like what you are becoming? Do you like the direction you are heading? If you continue in this direction where are you going to end up in 5 years, 10 years, and 20 years?

E. How is it impacting your relationship with God? Are these relationships drawing you closer to God or pushing you farther away?

If the answer to one of these questions is negative you may have an unhealthy relationship. If the answer to two or more of the questions is negative then you can be pretty assured you have a negative, unhealthy relationship.

So, what does the student need to do if it is unhealthy? End the relationship! Students then say to me, "Jesus spent time with the tax collectors and prostitutes." True, but he didn't rip people off with the tax collectors and he didn't sleep with any prostitutes. The problem is you are compromising. "Yea, well what kind of friend would I be if I left my friend or broke up?" A much better friend than you are right now. If you get out of their life then maybe God can bring someone who can impact them in a positive way.

If our students are going to grow up spiritually then we need to teach them to develop healthy relationships in a lot of different areas. With…
- ➢ Parents
- ➢ Dating relationships
- ➢ Co-Workers
- ➢ School and church friends
- ➢ Adults

Teach them how to make friends. There are numbers of teens who are lonely and awkward. They want friends but they don't know how to develop healthy relationships.

Teach them how to combat peer pressure. What do they need to say and do when they are confronted with sin and compromise? I believe the three biggest factors that combat peer pressure are...
- ➢ Close relationship with Jesus Christ.
- ➢ Healthy personhood.
- ➢ Strong family relationships.

Teach them about conflict resolution. How do you deal with someone who has hurt you? How do you work through all the anger and aggression you feel?

Jesus spent a lot of time ministering to those in the world but His closest friends were His disciples. So, teach your students their closest friends need to be those that love Jesus Christ and desire to follow Him.

4. Growth Experiences

How do we get Jesus Christ to go from being a couple of words in a book to a reality in their hearts? Get them involved in growth experiences, where they are out of their comfort zone and they need to trust the Lord.

Every student in your youth ministry should have the opportunity to go out on short term missions, to give them a vision for what God is doing around the world to open the door to the possibility of them becoming missionaries and to create images and memories they will never forget and will help to shape their character. Short term missions take a lot of work. I don't understand why we are always looking to do something unique in this area. Why not team with a mission's organization?

Get your students involved in growth experiences in their own city. There are all kinds of things you can do locally that will stretch them spiritually.
- ➢ Go downtown and share your faith with someone on the street.
- ➢ Work the morning at a soup kitchen.

- ➢ Help out at a homeless shelter.
- ➢ Rake your neighbor's leaves.
- ➢ Spend the day picking up trash in your city.
- ➢ Have a car wash and wash cars for free.
- ➢ Visit some senior citizens.
- ➢ In the winter deliver food and blankets to people on the street.
- ➢ Go to single moms and volunteer to baby-sit their kids for free.

There are hundreds of things you can do to serve others. When we get them on the cutting edge and allow them to step out in faith to serve Jesus Christ then they will come face to face with the living God and their lives will be changed. They will see God working in and through them and know the joy that comes from being used by the Lord. In other words, we want to see them come to Christ, train them up as disciples and send them to do what God is calling them to do.

5. Give students opportunities

Youth ministry needs to be adult directed but student led. Get the students involved in the ministry. Then they begin to own the ministry. No longer is it yours but it becomes ours. What can they do? They can do it all!
- ➢ Welcoming from the front and being the MC for the program.
- ➢ Do sound
- ➢ Multi Media
- ➢ Play in the band
- ➢ Give their testimony
- ➢ Follow up with guests and new students
- ➢ Lead worship
- ➢ Drama
- ➢ Plan the whole program
- ➢ Etc, etc, etc. A student can do it!

Believe in the teenagers and express your belief to them. They will meet your expectations. Affirm and build them. Let them know exactly what they are doing right. Then give them the freedom to fail. That is how they will learn. If they could do everything right without mistakes then they wouldn't need you as their leader. You make mistakes and they will do the same thing.

Now remember, it needs to be adult directed. We need to keep students accountable to follow through. We need to be there and keep everything under control. We help with quality control before the meeting and crowd control during it.

The exception would be the teaching. I think the students need to hear from their Pastor on a regular basis. Would I ever allow one of my Godly seniors to teach? Yes, but only if I had met with them ahead of time and I knew what they were going to say.

"The Christian is a person who makes it easy for others to believe in God." Robert M. McCheyne

Be careful you don't put carnal students up front. Make sure those leading the ministry are those who love Jesus Christ and are seeking to live for Him. Teens need to know not only is it a privilege to lead but it is also an awesome responsibility. In our country, we have said character doesn't really matter. What you do in private or during your off time is no concern to anyone if you do what you need to do in public. That is ridiculous. What you do in the dark, what you do when you don't think anyone sees is who you really are. Plus, if you are a carnal Christian, living in sin, you are missing out on God's power, blessing and favor. So, I do not want to put those students in a leadership position.

Is it OK if the student up front is not as talented as some of the adults? Yes. With time, they will get better. Plus, they become an inspiration to their peers.

Help them take the steps they need to grow up spiritually. Each student will be at a different level so challenge them to take the next step. Help them to deal with whatever they need to deal with and work on whatever they need to work on. We are calling them to become everything that Jesus Christ has created them to be and refusing to settle for anything less than God's very best.

THINK ABOUT IT:
1. Are your students seeing themselves through the eyes of God?
2. What can you do to get students involved in growth experiences?
3. Are you adult directed but student led?

THOUGHT
"TRY A RADICAL APPROACH TO YOUR PHILOSOPHY OF YOUTH MINISTRY"

"I had a moment of revelation where God told me to stop thinking of good ideas and start seeking out what He was already doing and join with Him." Scott Groff

"What is your philosophy of youth ministry?" It's a question I would always get when I candidate somewhere. So, I would engage in "youth speak" and tell them my philosophy, plan, direction and vision, all very impressive. Then one day it hit me, "Greg who are you really depending upon, yourself or God?" The answer was...me. All my education and experience was going to carry me and we would do great things for God, but what about doing things with God?

What if we answered the question about philosophy this way?
- I am going to love Jesus Christ.
- I am going to love students.
- Then I am going to get down on my knees, with my face to the floor, and ask God, "What do you want to do?" Then whatever He said I would do.

Sure, I think there would be some churches that would say, "Don't call us, we'll call you." Do you really want to minister at that church? But I think other churches would find that exciting and refreshing.

I remember talking to a search committee from the Church of The Open Door in the Twin Cities. They asked me, "What would you do if you came?" I said, "I don't know, I would pray and see what God wanted to do." You know what their response was? "Great!" That's the kind of church you want to minister with. They give you the freedom to be a God pleaser and to do what God wants you to do and to go where God wants you to go.

Does that mean education isn't important? Can we skip that step? No, education is very important because you want to prepare yourself to be the best possible tool for God to use. Depending on God also involves depending on His Word and the philosophy that comes through it. Loving God goes hand in hand with clear Biblical methods.

For example, I decide to build a house but I am not sure what kind of house I should build so I seek the Lord. "What kind of house would be best for this setting and would best meet the needs of my family." Than I wait on Him and I am willing to move in the direction He leads. This all sounds good except for one little problem, I can't build a house. It doesn't make much sense for me to pray about what kind of house I should build if I don't have the ability to build the house in the first place. It really doesn't matter what God says to me because I am not going to be able to build a house.

So, we need to have the skills, understanding and ability to build a youth ministry. We study hard and get the degrees but that is not where we put our hope for changed lives and successful ministry. Our only hope is in Jesus Christ and we depend upon the Spirit. Psalm 20:7 says, "Some trust in chariots and some in horses, but we trust in the name of the Lord our God." We can make the horse ready for battle but the victory is in God's hands, Proverbs 21:31.

"I try to avoid looking forward or backward, I try to keep looking upward." Charlotte Bronte

You focus on what is really important and that is God. Ministry is about doing God's will! The students at your Church are unique, the circumstances are different, the needs vary and so you seek God and what He wants to do and then you do it. Listen for the still small voice. He still speaks but we are so busy we never take the time to listen. Wait for the Lord.

We come into a new church and do what we did at our old church because it worked and we were successful. But what worked at church is not necessarily going to work at this church. Some of us never even considered the possibility God doesn't want us to do what we did at the old church. We are comfortable with what we know. But this journey is all about faith, taking different paths and trusting God to use us to accomplish what He wants to accomplish, not necessarily what we want to accomplish. Youth ministry is a great adventure. It is about you following Him and becoming what He wants you to be and doing what He wants you to do.

Why be like everyone else when you can do something new and exciting as you follow the Lord? When you step out in faith then life becomes a great adventure. You and Jesus walking hand in hand as you discover all that He wants to do. Don't ask Jesus to come and join you, you go and join Him!

THINK ABOUT IT:
1. Are you depending on the Spirit or you?
2. What is your philosophy of youth ministry?
3. Is there anything that you are doing in which you are so dependent upon the Lord, that if He didn't show up, it would fail?

THOUGHTS FROM OTHERS:
"Nothing hath separated us from God but our own will, or rather our own will is our separation from God." William Law

"I would rather walk with God in the dark than go alone in the light." Mary Gardiner Brainard

"I've been amazed over the years at the number of Pastors who stubbornly hold on to the patterns and programs of the past refusing to change the way they do things. Jesus is not an 'in the box' character. He's God. He's huge! He's awesome! He's uncontainable! When we let God out of the ministry box we've constructed, we understand that changing the way we lead is part of our response to the culture we're in, as well as a response to the Holy Spirit growing and maturing us." J. T. Bean

THOUGHT
"YOU NEED TO PRAY"

"It's so easy to get caught up in programming that we forget to pray. Some of the best youth nights we had was when we skipped the 'ice breaker,' skipped the game, skipped the announcements and spent time praying for one another." Craig Sanborn

Notice it's not should, or ought or it would be good to pray but you <u>NEED</u> to pray. Prayer is not a preparation for a greater work, it is the greater work. We have a Friday night evangelistic rally and five minutes before we start we have a quick word of prayer and ask God to bless what we have decided to do. Our priorities are messed up. You give your time to whatever you think is most important. How much time did you spend planning the outreach? Then how much time did you spend in prayer? Just give this a try. Spend less time on the program itself and more time in prayer. See what happens when we get our priorities set correctly. What is most important is not the planning of program but the petitions of prayer. What is most important is not wowing the teens but bringing them into the presence of God.

> ➢ I spoke for an outreach that didn't come off real slick and smooth.
>   - The band wasn't very good.
>   - We were in a gym.
>   - The students, about 200, were sitting on the floor.
>   - There was a game that involved water and it was all over the stage and floor.
>   - There were spotlights and I couldn't see one person in the crowd.
>   - The program went long.
>   - Some kid in the back, I couldn't see him, heckled me the whole time.
>   - The sound system wasn't very good.

I gave a gospel presentation and then invited students to come forward to receive Christ. Over <u>seventy</u> came forward!! Why did it happen? Because this church had committed to praying weeks before the event and God showed up! You can tell the difference between a program that is bathed in prayer and one that isn't. Too often we spend hours putting together a program and then minutes praying about it.

My favorite verse is Exodus 33:11a "The Lord would speak to Moses face to face, as a man speaks with his friend..." It's my favorite because that's the kind of relationship I want with God. At times to sit in an easy chair and talk to Him face to face as a friend. But then at other times I want to get on my knees and worship Him as King of Kings and Lord of Lords. I believe that God is waiting and wanting to pour out His Spirit. He is ready to work beyond anything you could ask or imagine but you need to ask.

"To be a Christian without prayer is no more possible than to be alive without breathing." Martin Luther

Can I suggest that your first hour in the office, as Youth Pastor, be spent with God? Just put Him down as your first appointment of the morning. Then tell your secretary to hold all your calls. Study the Word, not for teaching preparation, but for life application.

Then pray and meet face to face with your friend and King! There is nothing more important than your relationship with Jesus Christ. Do you believe that? If I followed you around, saw how you spent your time, would I believe Jesus is most important in your life? Does your spouse believe it? Do the teens see it?

Do something crazy right now! How about spending time in prayer? Lock the door, turn your phone off, set aside the tyranny of the urgent and do what is most important. "Come to me all that are weary and I will give you rest." Come rest in the arms of Jesus...NOW!

Let me walk you through a time with your friend, father and King. You have the privilege of coming face to face with the King of

Kings and Lord of Lords and talking with Him! I want to suggest, if you are physically able, you get down on your knees and humble yourself.

Are there any sins you need to confess? Agree with God it is a sin and then tell Him that you are sorry. It is good to be broken before the Lord and if tears begin to come, let them. To weep because of your sin is a good thing. It was for that sin that Jesus willingly gave up his life. Is there anyone you need to apologize to and make a relationship right? Then get on the phone right now and do it so you are free to continue to fellowship with God. You need to always maintain a clear conscience with others and God.

Now you are free to worship Him. Worship is saying, "You are worthy of my life, service and commitment." You are remembering He isn't just your friend but He is your LORD. To help you get started, finish this sentence, "God you are............!" Fill in that blank with holy, righteous, all powerful, all knowing, eternal, the great I AM, love, the Alpha and Omega, everywhere at once, great, wonderful and on and on it goes. Often, I am brought to tears as I worship because I am so happy and in awe of the fact I can have a relationship with God. Put on a worship CD, lift your hands to heaven like a child wants to be picked up by their daddy or rest your head on a chair like a child resting their head in the lap of their father. Call out to the Great King over all the earth, for He is worthy of your adoration and praise.

Are you thankful? Is the cup half empty, does life stink, are you caught in despair? Take time to be thankful. Things we take for granted - car that runs, clothes, good food, water, blue sky, rain, friends, laughter, pets, green grass, life, ministry, mountains and oceans, teenagers, pleasant smells, warm fire, peace of mind, family, salvation, forgiveness, and the chance to spend time talking to you Lord! You could literally spend hours just thanking God for everything He has done and provided.

What do you want Him to do? Ask Him because He delights in answering your prayers. This isn't about what you want or some "name it, claim it, get rich quick" garbage. This is what you need or someone else needs. Then approach Him and ask. Things like, physical healing, dollars for a mission trip, a car that runs, money for bills, a soft heart, favor as you speak, relationships to be mended, salvation, etc. What if tonight Jesus Christ would appear before you and ask, "What do you want me to do for you?" What would you say? That is what it means to ask God. The great news is, God always answers prayer, yes, no or slow. Slow, meaning, it is a good request but you need to grow or the person you are praying for needs to grow or other things need to occur. Remember God's delays are not His denials.

Finally, I want you to listen. Prayer is about you talking and then actively listening. We hardly ever take time to listen. We are in such a hurry. We have so many important things to do. But nothing is more important than sitting at the feet of Jesus and just listening.

Is there someone in your life that you love? If there is, then I bet you talk to them because a lack of communication is a lack of love. You naturally communicate with someone you love. Do you love Jesus Christ? Then PRAY!

"Pray for great things, expect great things, work for great things, but above all, pray." R.A. Torrey

The more you pray the more you will want to pray. If you do it enough it becomes a habit for you. There is someone who will fight very hard to stop you from praying. Satan hates it when you pray. Which ought to say to us how important and significant it is to pray. You can do a lot of things which will help you to be a better Youth Pastor or youth sponsor but nothing is more important than coming face to face with God. Take advantage of time to pray. While you are driving in the car, pray but don't close your eyes. When you are taking a shower, while you are waiting for an appointment to show up, as you watch a sporting event, before you get out of bed and before you fall asleep…pray.

THINK ABOUT IT:
1. Do you put more time into a program or prayer?
2. Does tyranny of the urgent rob your prayer time?

3. When is the best time for you to devote to prayer?

THOUGHTS FROM OTHERS:
"The one concern of the devil is to keep Christians from praying. He fears nothing from prayerless studies, prayerless work, and prayerless religion. He laughs at our toil, mocks at our wisdom, and trembles when we pray." Samuel Chadwick

"We look upon prayer as a means of getting things for ourselves; The Bible idea of prayer is that we may get to know God Himself." Oswald Chambers

"The value of consistent prayer is not that He will hear us, but that we will hear Him." William McGill

"Prayer honors God, acknowledges His being, exalts His power, adores His providence, secures His aid." E. M. Bounds

"Tomorrow I plan to work, work, from early until late. In fact, I have so much to do that I shall spend the first three hours in prayer." Martin Luther

"God is not a cosmic bellboy." Harry Emerson Fosdick

"Unless I had the spirit of prayer, I could do nothing." Charles G. Finney

"Prayer does not change God, but it changes him who prays." Soren Kierkegaard

THOUGHT
"TAKE TIME OFF"

"Have courage for the great sorrows of life and patience for the small ones; and when you have laboriously accomplished your daily task, go to sleep in peace. God is awake." Victor Hugo

The first Senior Pastor I served with was Gordon Hanstead. He said something to me that God has used to refresh and prolong my stay in youth ministry. He said, "Greg, break each day down into three parts, morning, afternoon and evening. Never work more than two of those." I believe this is one reason I have lasted so long in youth ministry. There are too many youth Pastors who are trying to work all three and they burn out, their marriage falls apart and their children rebel. You need to take time off because working with teenagers is draining. You are always in crisis because teenagers are emotional and everything becomes more intense for them. From broken hearts to broken homes, from the silly to the serious.

Few people understand if you are a high school Pastor you are losing one quarter of your congregation every year. If you are a middle school Pastor you can be losing half your congregation. So over two to four years you are losing your entire congregation. That means new leaders and leadership development. You are putting in a lot of time and there can be a lot of stress.

Your youth ministry runs in cycles. You graduate a strong senior class and move up a weak junior class. Schools see this all the time. But we seem to forget it applies to our youth group as well. How would Senior Pastors do if every year one quarter of their congregation left? Then every four years they had an entirely new congregation. It would be tough on them. Welcome to the world of youth ministry.

No one takes more shots and criticism than the youth and music Pastors. Everyone has very strong opinions in these areas. Everyone thinks they know what is best for the youth of the church. They remember what it was like when they were a teen and don't understand why you aren't doing the same things. "Hey, it worked in the 1960's!" Parents want what is best for their teen but really don't think of the group as a whole and what is best for everyone. In the same week, I had two sets of parents come to me. One said, "My son doesn't like small groups. Why can't you just keep them together in a large group?" The other said, "My daughter doesn't like being in the large group. She feels like she is lost. Why can't you keep them in small groups?"

"The devil is easy to identify. He appears when you're terribly tired and makes a very reasonable request which you know you shouldn't grant." Fiorello La Guardia

Let's face it, youth ministry is emotionally, physically and spiritually draining. You need time off. Here are some suggestions.

1. Break the day into three parts and only work two of them. If you feel guilty in taking time off then it is false guilt.

2. Take at least one day off a week. This does not include Sunday. Take the entire day off. Turn off your cell phone and don't check your E-mails. Don't answer the phone. Let voicemail pick it up and then you can decide when to call back. I would say to my student, "Don't call me on my day off unless it is an extreme emergency. Someone breaking up with you, your gold fish dying and getting a bad report card are not extreme emergencies." If you feel guilty about that then, once again, let me say you are suffering from false guilt. If you can't do this and you need to always be available for the teens then let me suggest we are now talking about you meeting needs in your own life and not the lives of the teens. That is not healthy. You must take time off. You are in trouble when you become emotionally, physically and spiritually drained. You are more susceptible to temptations, it leads to bad decision making, and you treat people poorly. Being tired makes cowards of us all.

"Taking a Sabbath was one of the hardest things for me to do as a Youth Pastor. There was so much to be done! As the Lord began to convict me I took the Sabbath seriously

and took that time off. Much to my surprise I was more efficient and felt healthier the rest of the week." Craig Sanborn

3. Take one day off each quarter to just get away and seek God's face. Spend the day fasting, praying and studying the Word. You will find it wonderfully renewing plus you will gain some great insights from the Word. This is in addition to your regular days off.

4. Get away for at least one week of conferences per year. This is to sharpen your skills, gain fellowship, network with those who are like minded and to be refreshed.

5. Don't become the hang out. Do not let your house become the place students
hang out anytime, day or night. Protect your spouse, family and personal times. You can have special times when they come over to the house. Our house became the place to go for Monday night football and SuperBowl Sunday.

6. Take vacation every year and get away. You don't have to spend a lot of money mostly because you don't have a lot of money to spend. But it gives you one or more weeks to relax and be with your family. I had a board member say to me, "the devil doesn't take a vacation." To which I replied, "we don't want to follow his example do we?"

7. Date your spouse once a week. Youth Ministry puts a lot of pressure on marriages. In a relatively short amount of time you can feel like two strangers living together in the same house. Doing this once a week keeps you connected and makes your spouse a priority in your life.

If you are going to make it for the long haul then you need to take time off. Youth Ministry isn't a sprint, although it can feel like it, it's a marathon.

THINK ABOUT IT:
1. How are you feeling emotionally?
2. Are you taking enough time off?
3. Are you in this for the long haul? Then what changes do you need to make?

THOUGHT
"ARE YOUR STUDENTS PHYSICALLY SAFE?"

"When deciding whether or not to do some activity I picture myself trying to explain to the parents how their child got hurt. If it sounds ridiculous or negligent than I don't do it." Karen Grant

We care about our student's spiritual well being and we want to make sure we don't hurt them emotionally. But do we ever consider what is happening to them physically?

I was the Director of Student Ministries with the responsibility to oversee the Senior High and Middle school students. I had full time Pastors working in both areas. We were having an all-night outreach for middle school. Between two and three hundred teens had showed up.

- The evening started with a band and evangelistic message.
- Then we load them in a fleet of buses to go bowling.
- After that they were off to a deluxe pizza place for all the pizza they can eat, soda they can drink and free tokens for all the games they want to play.
- Next, they headed for miniature golf or laser tag or something like that, I don't really remember.
- Finally, they were to come back to the church for breakfast, something healthy like donuts and then their parents pick them up. At this point my middle school Pastor and his lay staff could slip into a coma.

I made a token appearance at the evangelistic rally and then I headed home to sleep in my bed. In the wee hours of the morning my phone rings. It is my middle school Pastor and he tells me one of the teens had gotten hurt playing in the plastic balls at the pizza parlor. He had called 911, contacted the parents and wanted to know what he should do. I told him to stay with the teens and I would meet the parents at the hospital.

The parents were walking in just as I arrived. I introduced myself to them and shared all the information I had. We sat together in the waiting room making small conversation; their only son was a visitor to our church. I am trying to think ahead. I need to call the senior and executive Pastors to let them know what has happened. We will need to cover the cost for ambulance; emergency room and they may want to keep him overnight for observation. I am thinking through all this when the emergency room doctor walks up to us. We are the only ones in the waiting room. I look up and the doctor says, "I am sorry but your son is gone." It was like someone slugged me. I was stunned. The mother started to cry and I turned to her and said, "I am so sorry." I didn't know what else to say so we sat in silence and cried.

After a while I went to the doctor and asked him, "What happened?" He said, "We aren't sure and won't know until after the autopsy." When the report came back it said, "Extreme whiplash." They think he was playing in the balls and someone came down the little slide and hit him, with their foot, on the side of his head. Not hard enough to leave a bruise but hard enough to spin his head around and kill him instantly.

The wonderful part of the story is that this young man had gone forward at the beginning of the evening and asked Jesus into his heart. But if I can lose a student at a Pizza Parlor then I can lose a student anywhere. After that experience, I realized in the past, I had been putting students in harm's way for the sake of "having fun". We had played games at camp which had the potential of hurting the students. I decided it wasn't worth it. We started rethinking everything we did and we eliminated many the games we played. We still did white water rafting, high ropes course, repelling, etc. but we made sure we had taken every precaution, safety wise.

"Persons are to be loved; things are to be used." Reuel Howe

I don't care how fun the game is, if it has the potential of hurting our students we get rid of it. Some will say "Every game has the potential of hurting a student." But you and I both know there are some games that definitely put our teens at risk. Get rid of those.

Things like putting cardboard boxes over our teenagers' head and having them run relays where they're running into other people and tripping over the other students. Running relays, inside, in the dark, with a strobe light going off. Piling eight students on an inner tube and sending them down a snow-covered hill into a grove of trees. Towing students, behind a boat, on an inner tube and going way too fast. A high ropes course can be a lot safer than some of the games we play at church. I know students can and have gotten hurt playing capture the flag. But eliminate anything that is "a disaster waiting to happen."

The whole experience reminded me of the importance of having lay staff who are medically trained. Nurses, doctors, paramedics are all a great help and comfort to you and the parents.

Be sure you have responsible drivers for your church sponsored events. Having teenagers drive teenagers is not a good idea. Having college students drive may be a bad idea. Better to have parents drive.

You love your students and you want what is best for them, you're building them spiritually and helping them emotionally. Now I want you to make their physical safety a priority. With leadership comes responsibility. Never take that lightly.

THINK ABOUT IT:
1. Do you put your students in harm's way?
2. Do you have any medical professionals on your lay staff?
3. What games or activities do you need to stop doing?

THOUGHTS FROM OTHERS:
"Men and women everywhere must exercise deliberate selection to live wisely." Robert Grant

"Full maturity…is achieved by realizing that you have choices to make." Angela Barron McBride

"Decisions determine destiny." Frederick Speakman

"To be a man is, precisely, to be responsible." Antoine De Saint-Exupery

"The ability to accept responsibility is the measure of the man." Roy L. Smith

"Few things help an individual more than to place responsibility upon him, and to let him know that you trust him." Booker T. Washington

THOUGHT
"YOUTH MINISTRY IS NOT A STEPPING STONE"

"Looking around in a room of volunteers, who are former students, gives me such a feeling of gratitude for what God is doing through the ministry, through the years." Scott Groff

In the past, if you wanted to be a "real" Pastor then you started out working with teenagers. It was a stepping stone to get involved in something better and more significant. I remember, as a youth Pastor, back in the dark ages, visiting an adult in the hospital. After we talked for a while she asked me "Is the Pastor from the church going to visit me?" I said, "I am a Pastor from the church." And she replied, "I mean a real Pastor." I laugh about it now but back then I was a little offended. Back then the only "real" Pastor was the senior Pastor. If you stayed in youth ministry it was because you were lacking and couldn't cut it as a "real" Pastor. Well, I am happy to say, that has all changed. Youth Ministry is not a stepping stone to something better, it is the BEST!

People still say to me, "How can you work with teenagers? Don't they scare you?" I say, "If you could only see teenagers the way I see them. The way they open up and their commitment to Jesus Christ. Then you would have the same passion." Teenagers get so much bad publicity but most of them are great! If you reach out to them in love then they will reach back. I feel so honored and thankful the Lord allows me to invest my life in the lives of teenagers and I can call them friends. I don't believe there has been a greater time in all history to be working with teens than right now.

Let me give you some reasons why I still work with teenagers.

1. Because they are excited, open, and responsive to God! Over eighty percent of all people who receive Christ do so before the age of 19. They are open to the gospel and excited about serving Jesus Christ.

- Nobody loves Jesus like a teenager loves Jesus.
- Nobody worships like teenagers worships.
- Nobody shares their faith like a teenager does.

There is an enthusiasm and joy I don't see much among adults. Today the Spirit of God is moving in powerful ways among teenagers. But Satan is also massing his demons and targeting teens. Some of the darkest places I have been are on certain public-school campuses across the US. It is a battle ground. When you are involved in the lives of teenagers you are on the cutting edge of Ministry. You are advancing on the gates of Hell and you might as well paint a target on your chest because the enemy wants you out of the picture.

But don't fear because greater is Jesus Christ in us than Satan in the world, 1 John 4:4. Each morning we get up and put on the whole armor of God. Then we stand on the wall and in the gap on behalf of teenagers. I confess, I love *Lord of the Rings.* So...
- With the wisdom of Gandalf.
- The courage of Aragon.
- The agility of Legolas.
- The strength of Gimli.
- The determination of Frodo.
- The faithfulness of Sam.
- And with the joy, not the immaturity, of Merry and Pippin, all given to us by the Spirit of God, we do battle.

It's not always easy, it's not always fun and sometimes it is down right discouraging. But it is never boring. My feeling is, why would you want to do anything else but Youth Ministry?

"Carve your name on hearts and not on marble." Charles H. Spurgeon

2. The teenage years are when they are making life changing decisions. The choices they are making now are sending them in a direction, for either good or evil, which some will never turn from. They are making serious decisions about:
- God

- Sex
- Drugs
- Drinking
- Career direction, etc.

Now is the time when we need to comfort, correct, encourage and challenge them with the truths of God's Word. A Youth Pastor has the unique opportunity to pour into the lives of teenagers. They become significant others to the students and a support for the parents. The youth Pastor can say the same things the parents are saying but because it isn't a parent they will listen.

I had a few parents approach me and say we shouldn't be talking about sex in church because it is the responsibility of the family. My response was, "Wouldn't it be wonderful if every family was like yours but unfortunately they aren't." There are a significant number of teens who will never hear God's view of sex if we don't communicate it.
- Some families just don't want to talk about it.
- Some come from non-Christian homes.
- Some come from homes where the parents are more messed up than the teen.

I had a girl come to me for advice. Her mom wanted her to bring guys home and have sex with them so she could become more popular. If I hadn't brought the topic up from the front she might never have sought me out. We speak truth and give teens hope. We let them know their yesterdays don't determine their tomorrows. They can be different because Jesus will give them the power to be different. They can be forgiven and have a brand-new beginning.

3. Teenagers are the greatest reservoir for future leadership and leadership right now. I have never liked this statement, "Teenagers are the church of tomorrow." I understand what they are saying but I want to make sure they understand teenagers are also the church of today. God is ready, willing and able to work through the lives of teens to serve the church and make a difference in their world.

God is raising up heroes of the faith right now. Today we have

young men and women who are radically committed to Jesus Christ. They are going to serve the Lord now and then they will become:
- Youth Pastors
- Missionaries
- Other Pastors
- Musicians
- Theologians
- Authors
- Presidents
- CEO's, etc. who will stand with us on the wall for the cause of Christ.

We have the chance to impact future generations. To pour our lives into the lives of these students and the great news is age doesn't matter. Some people still say to me, 'What are you going to do if you grow up?" I say, "I want to work with teenagers." A while ago a group came to me and said I was prime for the senior Pastorate because I was old! Would I be interested? I said not even a little bit. As long as God gives me favor there is no one I would rather work with or invest my life in than teenagers. I remember when they use to say, "You need to be in your twenties to work with teens." That is baloney. The older you get the better job you do because you are maturing emotionally and spiritually. I do a far better job leading, loving, communicating and caring for teens now than when I was younger.

It's true I can't play with them like I use to when I was younger. I had the privilege of speaking for an all Korean, high school, summer camp. What a great group of teenagers. They were fun and very responsive to the Word of God. The last day they asked me to play in their big football game. Now I am very relational and love hanging out with students during free time. But my days of effectively competing athletically are behind me. But because I used to play football my mind deceived me into thinking I can still do it. So, there I was playing defensive end. Obviously, my team thought that is probably the spot where I can do the least damage. The quarterback rolled to my side. Now in my prime I could not have caught him, but again my mind deceives me and says, "You can do it, you have the speed to catch him." Right, I have the speed of a pregnant hippo running in the mud. I went after him, "He is not going to get around me!" I took about three steps at a full sprint. Keep in mind that my full sprint is equivalent to an 18-month-old child running. After the third step, my hamstring went bye-bye. My momentum carried me for another step and then I went down...hard...really hard! I hit my head which knocked me out for a moment. When I came to, I discovered I was in a lot of pain. After being checked out I headed for home.

That evening I got to tell my wife. "On the same play I...
- ➢ Pulled my hamstring,
- ➢ Cracked two ribs,
- ➢ Partially tore my rotator cup and
- ➢ bruised my tail bone while playing football and NOBODY touched me."

How pathetic is that? I have realized they have plenty of people who can play with them. They need someone with wisdom and maturity to lead them.

4. I believe this is the generation God is raising up to fulfill the Great Commission. With all the tattoos, piercing, colored hair and brokenness God is calling them. He will send them around the world to every tribe, tongue and nation. Some will be martyred for their faith. They will be greatly used by the Lord. Even now He is beginning to raise up heroes of the faith.

In January 1956 Jim Elliott, Nate Saint, Pete Fleming, Ed McCully, and Roger Youderian were called (by God) to Ecuador to bring the gospel to the Auca Indians. It was there these five committed, young, missionaries laid down their lives for the sake of the Gospel. They were killed by the very people they were trying to love. Was it a waste of life? Not even close. Because of the missionaries' obedience, God raised up young men and women across the United States to go around the world to share the Good News. Rachel Saint, Nate's sister, lived and worked among the Auca Indians for over 30 years. During that time, many gave their lives to Jesus Christ. Steve Saint, Nate's son, was even baptized by some of the men who killed his father.

I was speaking in Ecuador when Wycliffe finished the Bible to the Auca Indians. Because Jim Elliott is one of my heroes of the faith I asked them if I could just get the page with John 3:16 on it. Wycliffe said they would see what they could do. After I had returned home I received a package in the mail with the entire Bible to the Auca Indians. It sits on my shelf as one of my most prized possessions.

It was Jim Elliott who said, "He is no fool that gives up what he cannot keep to gain what he can not lose." That is one thing we must teach our teens. You are not a fool to give up your life to gain all the wonder and glory of heaven. They can be heroes of the faith. A hero is someone who is available to go where God calls them to go and is faithful to do what God wants them to do.

We get the privilege of preparing them to go. To teach, develop and mold them into fully devoted disciples of Jesus Christ. To encourage them to lay their lives on God's alter as living sacrifices, holy and pleasing to Him.

There are many perks associated with being in youth ministry for the long haul. One is being able to work with the children of your past students. I remember the shock of hearing this from a teenage girl for the first time. "You don't know me but when my mom was in high school you were her youth Pastor." or "When my dad was in middle school he heard you speak at a retreat." How great is that! I now have the opportunity to work with a whole new generation of teenagers. A girl came to me at a youth convention and said, "When my mom was a teenager she asked Jesus into her life at a church retreat you spoke for." Wow, it doesn't get any better than that.

I understand some of you will be called out of youth ministry and that is fine. You would never want to stay in youth ministry if God is calling you to something else. But make sure it is God and not you listening to the lies saying you're too old or you should be doing something more significant.

"Become a person who listens to God and follows His leading." Al Schuck

For me, Youth Ministry is a life long calling. Come join me!

THINK ABOUT IT:
1. Do you hear God calling you to Youth Ministry for life?
2. Have you looked at getting older as a negative?
3. Do you find my story of the football game pretty pathetic? Thank you for your sensitivity.

THOUGHT
"PARENTS MAKE GREAT ALLIES"

"I have found that explaining why we do what we do helps parents like what we do." David Malouf

Most parents want to be on your side and see you do well because their children are in your Ministry. Once they see your heart and understand the vision they will make wonderful allies and supporters. You need to always be seeking to draw parents to teens and teens to parents. You want to be God's instrument to see this happen. You will gain your biggest insights into the teens you are working with by talking to, spending time with, and listening to parents of those teens. This isn't just nice or polite but absolutely necessary.

Parents will be coming with different priorities that shape their agenda, because they are coming from so many different backgrounds. Home school, Christian school, public school, prep school, single parents, healthy, dysfunctional, first born, only child, one of eleven, etc. They all have expectations and think, what is important to them ought to be important to you and what works with their child ought to work with all children. They will most definitely let you know when you aren't meeting those expectations. Bottom line, you must listen, seek to be sensitive, but you must be a God pleaser. To try to please everyone is to please no one and cause yourself a nervous break down.

"A thick skin is a gift from God." Konrad Adenauer

For you who are young and not yet a parent it can be hard to understand where parents are coming from. At this point you need to depend on significant others in your life. Ask for help and go to parents that are your supporters. Ask them to help you to understand and see things from a parent's perspective. They will be delighted to do it, you will learn a lot and avoid some mistakes which could get you into hot water.

Most parents have good hearts. They can make wonderful, committed, supportive staff. They have a lot of wisdom and understanding. Because of this, I wanted parents to be a part of the volunteer staff. So, I handed out paper to each of my students and said, "Write the names of people you would like to see on youth staff. If you feel OK about it, include your parent's names." Then I could approach the parents and say, "See, your own child wants you on staff." It was much harder for them to say, "No"!

There are three broad areas in which you can get parents involved.

1. Relational Ministry. This involves leading small groups, speaking, counseling, music, worship, drama, dance, etc.

2. Task Oriented. Decorating the room, providing food, opening their homes, overseeing multi-media, setting up transportation, booking camps, helping to set up and tear down, sound system, organize trips, help with budget and finances, etc.

3. Visionary. They can be on an advisory board for the direction of the youth Ministry. They then give insight and direction into the values, purpose, vision and strategy of the ministry.

Remember, every church has parents who are going to be rude and obnoxious. I have had many dealings with rude parents. Let me tell you a story. At this point I had been the director of student ministries for close to four years. I started with a youth group that was having a lot of problems. My first week on the job a couple of girls tried to set fire to the youth room because they hated the youth group. Before I got there a girl was sexually assaulted at a social in the church. We had about 30 teens coming out on a Wednesday night. The former youth Pastor had lasted less than one year.

Now four years later we had about 200 senior high and 100 middle school coming out on a Wednesday night. Two dads asked to meet with me for breakfast. Now they said many stupid things but this was the number one dumb statement. One of them said to me, "In the four years you have been here I haven't seen any positive changes." Let me tell you what my flesh wanted to do. I wanted to reach across the table and..... OK, never mind. I listened to them and tried to maintain a Christ like attitude but it really upset me. He had two children that were not doing well spiritually. So instead of taking responsibility for their lack of spiritual interest he wanted to blame someone else. I realize the amount of pain a parent inflicts on you is usually the amount of pain they feel. That is no excuse for them being rude but it does give you some insight and understanding on why they are behaving the way they are.

This was a tough time in my life and the enemy used this to rock me. I did consider stepping down and moving on. This was such a dysfunctional youth ministry when I started and I had given my life, which was a mistake, to this ministry. As I look back I can see I was emotionally exhausted. It was the support of my youth staff, volunteers and students that helped me get through this time. I had individuals that were willing to listen to me and God used those people to speak truth into my life. As I look back I can see the Lord using this in my life and the tremendous growth taking place but it was no fun at the time.

Every church has these people. Thank goodness, they are in the minority. Don't let this scare you away from getting parents on board as part of your lay staff. They will be your biggest supporters and stand with you when other parents take shots at you!

THINK ABOUT IT:
1. How many parents do you have on your volunteer staff? When is the last time you have expressed your appreciation to them?
2. Are you insecure around parents? What can you do to overcome that?
3. Do you pursue spending time with parents?

THOUGHTS FROM OTHERS:
 "Be brave enough to accept the help of others." Melba Colgrove, Harold H. Bloomfield, Peter McWilliams

"The smartest thing I ever said was, 'Help Me'!" Anon.

"Friendship requires great communication." Saint Francis de Sale

THOUGHT
"YOU MUST KNOW YOUR FLOCK"

"The Youth Pastor must never become like a CEO, several layers removed from the students." Brian Float

I Peter 5:2 says, "Be shepherds of God's flock that is under your care, serving as overseers - not because you must, but because you are willing, as God wants you to be."

How can you shepherd your flock if you don't know them? How can you really know them without knowing their hearts? And how can you know their hearts unless you are spending time listening to them? Today youth ministry can become like big business with huge youth groups. The youth Pastor starts to become a CEO several levels removed from the students, developing people who are going to develop people who are going to work with teens. As a youth ministry grows the Youth Pastor must prioritize the development of other leaders while continuing to spend time with teens.

If you have become like a CEO I would like to draw you back to one of the basics of youth ministry, the one thing that drew you to this ministry in the first place and that is spending time with students. It's amazing how the tyranny of the urgent keeps us from doing what is most important.
- Spending time with God.
- Spending time with your spouse.
- Spending time with your children.
- Spending time with teens.

How do you get to know your flock? You must take the time to love them. Your students will know whether you love them or not. They will know whether spending time with them is a joy or a burden to you. They will understand very quickly whether you care about them as a person or whether they are just a number to help you look good.

The greatest lover that ever lived was not Don Juan or Casanova but Jesus Christ. We need to follow that example and love teens in the purest sense of the word. How do we love our teens? Dr. Gary Chapman has done an excellent job identifying five love languages that are appropriate for us to show to our teenagers.

1. Words. With your words, you bring life or death. You can either build them up or tear them down. Be careful when it comes to sarcasm. I am the King of sarcasm and sometimes it's funny but sometimes it wounds others. When Bonnie and I were first married I would say things to her meaning to be funny and I would hurt her. She would say to me, "that wasn't funny." I discovered sometimes sarcasm is a wall I hid behind so I didn't have to be vulnerable. Have you wounded any students by the words that come out of our mouths? Remember, a joke is only funny if it is funny for everyone. A joke is not funny at the expense of someone else.

I started my ministry right out of college, working as a caseworker with delinquent and emotionally disturbed teens. We had a motto I carried with me to the Youth Pastorate, "catch them being good." It was easy to catch them being bad; they were a bunch of delinquents. If I walked into the den and Bobby was sitting quietly, reading a book, that is when I would go up and encourage him. I would say, "Bobby, this is great. I am so glad to see you reading." Today our Motto is, "No news is good news. If you do what I want you to do then you won't hear from me. But the first time you mess up I will be right there in your face." If we do this, we are stressing the negative. Do not fall into the trap that ignores positive behavior and pays attention to negative behavior. Look for opportunities to build and encourage your teens. They need to hear you say to them things like this...
- You are the best
- I love you
- I'm so impressed
- I wouldn't trade you for any other group

Say this from the front and say it to individual students, one to one. It is like giving a cup of cold water to a thirsty person. Many of our teens come out of homes where little or no encouragement is expressed to them. Sometimes it is just the opposite and they are being verbally abused. When they come to youth group are you building them up or slamming them?

We quickly notice when a student does well physically. They score a touchdown, get the lead in the play or sing a solo. It is good that we notice and compliment them for doing a good job but it is important to be developing your students emotionally and spiritually. You do this by noticing what is happening on the inside. At your next meeting why don't you give your students compliments based on the fruit if the spirit from Galatians 5:22?
- Love: "You are always reaching out to the visitors."
- Joy: "Your sense of humor is the best."
- Peace: "Always trusting and never worrying, that is you."
- Patience: "You never give up."
- Kindness: "I saw you sit with that lonely girl"
- Goodness: "Your lifestyle honors the Lord."
- Gentleness: "Thanks for being a good listener."
- Faithfulness: "I can always count on you." Or, "I trust you."
- Self-Control: "Your commitment to Jesus inspires me."

To say to your student, "You are someone of great character and integrity," will mean much more than, "I really like your shirt." If you want to build the fruit in their lives than notice the fruit in their lives. If you want to see something developed in the life of a teen then emphasis it, point it out and show them you notice. Whether they show it or not, I will guarantee you God will use your words to minister to their hearts and He will remind them of it for weeks and maybe the rest of their life.

I played football. My position was tight end. They used to time me with a sun dial but I could catch the ball. One summer we were in the middle of two-a-day practices. The whistle blew to signal that practice was over. I began to drag my body off the field. I had my helmet in my hand, sweat was pouring off me and my whole body ached. My coach walked past me and smacked me on the rear, (I don't know why coaches do that) but he smacked me on the rear, looked at me and said, "Good job Speck." All of a sudden, I realized all my hard work had been worth it because someone noticed. A simple gesture and three words changed my day. Are you noticing your students? Catch them being good and look for opportunities to encourage them.

When I was working at Sunny Ridge home, with all these delinquent and emotionally disturbed teens, I had a poster that hung in my office and I would read it every day. The poster said, "Love can break the hardest heart so that faith can grow." What can stand up to God's love if it is shown with a tough, unconditional determination? Nothing! Our students need to experience that kind of love. God's love, through us, will change lives.

2. Gifts. A gift can be anything. A note, coke, order of fries, etc. When you give them something you are saying to them, "while we are apart, I am thinking about you." Each week I would dictate off several letters to teens in the group. Just to build, encourage and express my love and care. One evening I was dining at a church family's home. They gave me a tour of the house and when we walked into the daughter's room I saw the letter I had written her, weeks ago, up in the middle of her bulletin board. It hit me how important the letter had been to her. They delete a text, get rid of an e-mail but a note or card can be kept for the rest of their life. Write into your budget a fund that allows you to take teens out and treat them. The church might think, "What is the big deal? It is only $3.00 for a couple of cokes." Sure, but then multiply that times 50 students and you are getting into some serious money, especially on a Youth Pastors salary.

"When your students experience the unconditional love of God through you, it is in that moment that the Kingdom of God is experienced here on earth, and that moment will never be forgotten." Scott Brown

3. Service. By serving them you are seeking to make their load lighter. You are looking to help them and encourage them through some act of love. What can you do to serve the students?
- Helping prepare a speech for school.
- Taking care of their dirty dishes at camp.
- Coaching a teen on how to share their faith with a friend.
- Giving students a ride home.
- Teaching them how to shoot a basketball.

You are seeking to sacrifice and give to them. No greater love is this, than a man lays down his life for his friend. When you serve you are laying down your life. It is important men be gentlemen. Some of our girls have never had anyone open a door for them, pull out a chair, help them on with a coat and treat them with that kind of respect. Have you been to rough with the girls in the youth group, have you treated them like one of the guys? Be a gentleman and treat your girls with respect.

4. Time. Spending time and listening to them. This can happen in the midst of a hundred other teens all talking and laughing around you. You give the person focused attention, you are making eye contact and you aren't looking around to see what else is happening. You make them feel like they are special. As Youth Pastors, we are usually really good at talking. Let me take it a step farther, some of us talk too much. We show love when we keep our mouths closed and listen to them. It is great for them when you come to their sporting events, plays and musicals but it means even more to them when you take the time to listen to them.

I became a Christian as a senior in high school. I knew very little about God or the Bible. Some friends, who were instrumental in seeing me come to Christ, sent me to Mt. Hermon Christian camp in the Santa Cruz Mountains. It was beautiful and I had a great time. The speaker was a guy named Bill. He was really funny and I remember thinking, "I would love to do what he does." One day he sat down, talked and listened to me for about one hour. This made such a huge impression on my life. The fact this man would take time out of his schedule to talk to me just blew me away. God used him to encourage me in my walk with Him. I have never forgotten the impact that had on me. I desire the Lord to use me in the lives of teenagers, as I am willing to spend time with them.

5. Touch. If you want to do an interesting study go through the gospels and note all the times Jesus touched someone. When you touch someone you are saying, "You are someone significant and worth while." Giving someone a high five, patting them on the back or hugging them communicates love. When I was Youth Pastor, if you followed me around on a Wednesday night, you would see me touching as many students as I could. For some of your students the only kind of touching they experience is one done in anger or lust. For them to be touched in purity and love will be wonderful and deeply meaningful.

Do you know your flock? You get to know them by loving them. That is the second greatest commandment and it needs to be a priority in our ministry. If we aren't taking the time to love students then our priorities are messed up. We better rethink what we are doing in youth ministry. Build them up, give them gifts, serve them, listen to them and touch them in purity. As you love your students God will give you favor and draw them to you.

THINK ABOUT IT:
1. Are you spending time with students?
2. Are you loving the flock?
3. Do you pray for your students by name?

THOUGHTS FROM OTHERS:
"I took up that word love, and I do not know how many weeks I spent in studying the passages in which it occurs, till at last I could not help loving people. I had been feeding on love so long that I was anxious to do everybody good I came in contact with. I got full of it. It ran out my fingers. You take up the subject of love in the Bible! You will get so full of it that all you have to do is to open your lips, and a flood of the love of God flows out." D. L. Moody

"Love is a product of habit." Lucretius

"Three things in human life are important: The first is to be kind. The second is to be kind. And the third is to be kind." Henry James

"If you judge people, you have no time to love them." Mother Teresa

"Behold! I do not give lectures on a little charity. When I give, I give myself." Walt Whitman

"A wise lover values not so much the gift of the lover as the love of the giver." Thomas A Kempis

"A part of kindness consists in loving people more than they deserve." Joseph Joubert

THOUGHT
"THERE ARE WRONG WAYS TO LOVE THE OPPOSITE SEX"

"Satan separates; God unites; love binds us together." D. L. Moody

A word of warning about seeking to love members of the opposite sex. You must be very careful or you end up sending the wrong message. Let me go back to the five ways to love and talk about things you need to do and not do.

1. Words. When you are verbally building up a member of the opposite sex stay away from the physical and focus on their character. That is true for any of your students but it is especially true for the opposite sex. If you compliment them on the physical, their perfume, muscles, clothes, face, hair, etc. you are saying to them, "I notice your body, I notice how you look on the outside and those things are attractive to me." That is not a message we want to send. What they look like on the outside is not what is most important. We want them to focus on what they are like on the inside. So, encourage this by talking about what they're like on the inside. Is it OK to mention the outside if they're all dressed up? Yes, but don't make it your focus.

2. Gifts. Sending a birthday card, note of encouragement, buying them a coke is fine. You want to stay away from personal gifts. You wouldn't buy a girl perfume or get her a sweater. That would come across as strange and cause them to either feel creepy about you or be attracted to you. Women you wouldn't want to give a man jewelry or clothes. Remember, when you give a student a gift you are telling them you are thinking about them when they aren't around. That is OK because we are thinking about them even when they aren't around. Make sure all your students are receiving gifts and not just a chosen few.

3. Service. When you lay down your life for someone by seeking to meet their needs and treating them with respect, you win their hearts and they will be drawn to you. Men, when you act like gentlemen you will win the hearts of the girls. That is fine if you're pointing them toward the person of Jesus Christ. In the past, people in youth ministry have used that for evil. They have won the hearts of teens and then used them. Women you are teaching the men to be gentlemen and communicating to the women what they look for in a man.

4. Time. This is key to our Ministry. We need to spend time with students. But with members of the opposite sex we seek to be alone in a crowd. You never, ever want to be alone and isolated with a member of the opposite sex. If I caught any of my full-time youth staff alone in a car with a member of the opposite sex I would fire them immediately, unless it was some kind of life or death emergency. All students need access to their Pastor. To say a girl or a guy can't talk to the youth Pastor in charge is ridiculous. We have swung the pendulum much too far to the opposite extreme. We have allowed a few sick and evil individuals to dictate how we will treat one another in youth ministry.

"Let's allow pure examples to lead us and not evil examples to drive us." GS

However, you should not do ongoing counseling with members of the opposite sex. Meet with them once and then refer them to a Godly member of the same sex or professional counseling. I have a Youth Pastor friend who will meet three times with the opposite sex and than refer them to a counselor. There is not exact number you can or can't meet with them, just don't be stupid.

In the large group, instead of pulling them out of the room, just move into a corner and talk in the midst of the group. If you are in an office then there needs to be a big window in the door or the door needs to be open. Your secretary needs to be very close at hand as well. It is extremely important that you don't isolate yourself with a member of the opposite sex, even for a short time. All they have to say is that you touched them in an improper way. Then it becomes your word against theirs and who are people going to believe, you or a teenager? Even if they are lying your ministry is probably finished.

5. Touch. Obviously, this is a huge area of concern. You must be very, very careful as to whom you touch and how much you touch. There are individuals in our groups who are rape and incest survivors. They may be very uncomfortable and even scared of a touch by you. You can't be touching certain members of your group more than others. The teens will notice real fast. If you hug them then you do it from the side and not a full-frontal hug. Jesus touched the leper, the outcast and the reject. If all we ever do is touch the "popular" people then there is something very wrong with our motives. Like Jesus, we reach out to all people and which includes the heavy, awkward, and socially inept.

You may struggle with lust of the flesh and you need to stay away from touching the opposite sex except for a high five or a pat on the back. If you sense one of your students has a crush on you then do not touch them. It is always better to be safe than sorry. Err of the side of touching too little rather than too much. Give your staff permission to speak truth into your life. If they say some student likes you or you are touching too much then listen to them.

"Would the boy you were - be proud of the man you are?" Charles Caleb Colton

You don't want to be on the other extreme of touch, which is abuse. Never touch a student in anger. Hitting, slapping or grabbing a student in anger is wrong and will get you in big, big trouble. There are some teens who deserve a spanking because they are acting like two-year-olds but don't do it. You may need a time out if you are mad at them. Go to a different room so you can calm down emotionally. If you don't get away for a few minutes you will end up saying and doing things you regret. Remember, those who are the least loveable often require the most love.

Touch is a powerful way to communicate love or the lack of love. How do you welcome the new freshmen? When I started as Youth Pastor the youth group had a tradition of abusing the new freshmen as kind of an initiation or right of passage at camp. As I travel and speak I have been with other groups that do the same thing. They duct tape them to different things, cover them with food products and then throw them in a lake. I was speaking for a youth group's winter retreat where the upper-class guys would poop on pieces of plastic and then put them on the sleeping bags of the freshmen. What is this all communicating to your incoming freshmen? How much do they want to be a part of that camp? As Youth Pastor, I stopped the tradition of abusing freshmen. Were my seniors mad? Yes. What was their argument? "Hey, we got abused so now it's our turn to abuse someone else." That is exactly the word they used, "abuse." This had become a sick tradition no one had the courage to end. I even had some parents of seniors who were upset with me. But getting it stopped was worth it and I would do it again.

Look, the world and the enemy will seek to abuse and use us. It ought to be different within the Body of Christ. We need to be building each other up. If you want to have a tradition of welcoming the new freshmen then do it with love and kindness. You can still have fun with it! We would have a kidnap breakfast for the incoming freshmen. We would go to their houses at 5:00am and take them to a breakfast where we would honor and welcome them.

What have your relationships with the opposite sex been like? Don't set yourself up to fail. Do not put yourself in positions where you have the potential of falling. You have an adversary who knows he can get rid of you by getting you to fall in this area. It is a wonderful privilege to love our students but it is also an awesome responsibility. We never want to do anything to hurt them emotionally, spiritually or physically. God takes this very seriously and so should we.

THINK ABOUT IT:
1. Are you showing love to ALL your students?
2. Do you have staff you have given permission to speak truth into your life?
3. How do you welcome the new middle and high school students?

THOUGHTS FROM OTHERS:
"I visited the 110-story, 1,454-foot Sears Tower. It is a fantastic

architectural feat, but someday its tons of concrete will be broken and its designer's name will be forgotten. And yet a cup of cold water, given in love, will break on the shores of eternity. In a world gone mad with greed and hate, how wonderful to know that love never dies! Love is never obsolete." George Sweeting

"For where love is wanting, the beauty of all virtue is mere tinsel, is empty sound, is not worth a straw, nay more, is offensive and disgusting." John Calvin

"Love is friendship set on fire." Jeremy Taylor

"Yes, love is the magic key of life-not to get what we want but to become what we ought to be." Eileen Guder

"There are more people who wish to be loved than there are willing to love." S. R. N. Chamfort

"Live so that your friends can defend you, but never have to." Arnold Glasow

"The call to love is not for the halfhearted. It is a full-time, life-long vocation." George Sweeting

THOUGHT
"WE MUST REMAIN SEXUALLY PURE"

"When we long for life without difficulties, remind us that oaks grow strong in contrary winds and diamonds are made under pressure."
Peter Marshall

We have all heard the horror stories of men and women who have fallen into sexual sin. Affairs and adultery are devastating to everyone. Hardly a week goes by I don't hear of someone has fallen into sexual sin. It hurts God's reputation, throws the Church into turmoil and negatively impacts those involved for the rest of their lives. When teenagers are being caught up in this sexual abuse, there is pain, damage and distress beyond anything we can even imagine. How long before they ever trust another Pastor? In some cases, never. Please, please, please stay sexually pure.

Let me suggest eight things you need to begin to do now.

1. Discern the difference between spiritual gifts and spirituality.
We all have spiritual gifts and we manifest those as we minister, but that is no indication of our spirituality. Spiritual gifts are how man perceives us and spirituality is how God sees us. People see the outward manifestation of our gifts but God sees us on the inside and our true spirituality. You can be demonstrating your gifts on the outside and be totally messed up on the inside. We have all heard the stories about a person having an affair that has been going on for weeks, months and sometimes years. All the time the affair is happening they continue to preach, teach, counsel and minister to others. We ask, "How can this be?" Because they were manifesting their spiritual gifts but this was no indication of their spirituality.

We must always be more concerned about our spirituality and how God sees us. Our first priority is to seek after God. Psalm 119:9-11 says, "How can a young man keep his way pure? By living according to your Word. I seek you with all my heart, do not let me stray away from your commands. I have hidden your Word in my heart that I might not sin against you." We must be men and women who study, meditate, memorize and live out the Word of God. A healthy, close, personal relationship with Jesus Christ isn't inherited, it is cultivated. It takes time, energy and commitment. There is NOTHING more important than your relationship with God. The Word of God and the Holy Spirit will keep you from sin or sin will keep you from the Holy Spirit and the Word of God. Make the basics of Bible study and prayer a priority and make the development of your spiritual gifts a secondary concern. As you develop your spirituality and surrender to the control of the Holy Spirit, He will bring forth your spiritual gifts and use them for the good of the Body. Don't depend upon your gifts. Seek the giver over the gift!

2. Don't deny your sexuality. We were all created as sexual beings. Sex is something wonderful, beautiful and good. Only an awesome God could have thought of something as exciting as sex. But it must be controlled. It is like fire. In the fireplace, where it belongs, it is warm, wonderful and inviting. But, out of control, in the middle of the living room, it becomes terrifying, destructive and deadly. I Thessalonians 4:3-5, Paul says, "It is God's will that you should be sanctified. That you should avoid sexual immorality, that each of you should learn to control his own body in a way that is holy and honorable, not in passionate lust like the heathen who does not know God."

How can you begin to control your body?

> **Be surrendered to, controlled and empowered by the Holy Spirit.** This is a daily choice.

> **Bring your struggles and temptations into the light.** Sin grows in the darkness. Share the struggles with a mentor or accountability partner.

> **Don't try to deny it.** To deny you have sexual feelings, thoughts and temptations is absurd. Plus, it doesn't work. If I said to you, "Don't think about ice cream. Don't think about chocolate fudge chunk or pralines and cream or rich and creamy strawberry. Don't think about ice cream!" The more you say it the more you think about it. So, it doesn't

work to try to deny sexual feelings by saying "don't think about sex." The more you say, don't think about sex, the more you think about it.

- ➤ **Don't try to repress it.** Remember sin grows in secrecy. To try to ignore the sin is to allow the temptation to build in your life. It will build, and build and build until the pressure is so great, it explodes. That leads to you acting out sexually and becomes very unhealthy and destructive for you. You run in cycles where you do well for periods of time and then give into the sexual desire. So you have these cycles of doing well and then doing poorly and then doing well and then doing poorly.

- ➤ **Try redirecting it.** When you are tempted sexually redirect it to your heavenly Father. Say, "God, thank you for sex and for making me a sexual being. I desire to honor you with this area of my life. So, I give you these feelings and thoughts." Now, the first day you try this, you may be praying that prayer 800 times. That would be awesome to talk to God 800 times in one day! By doing this, you are constantly reminding yourself of the personal presence of God in your life.

- ➤ **Treat the temptation like spiritual warfare.** If this is a weakness then satan is probably targeting this area in your life. Try taking the offensive. When the enemy attacks we become reactive and defensive. I want to suggest you bypass this attack and take the offensive against the enemy. How do you do that? Think of one person who is a carnal Christian and one person who is a non-Christian-person who could do satan severe damage if they gave their lives to Jesus Christ. Now, when you are tempted, instead of focusing in on the sexual temptation, begin to pray for these two people. Ask the Lord to bring them to Himself. If this is spiritual warfare, then the enemy will pull back from their attack because they won't like the fact that you are praying for two people they are controlling. It is not worth it to the enemy to lose two individuals they control just for the chance to tempt you.

Learn to warfare pray. I would recommend the books by Neil Anderson to get more insight into this area like the Bondage Breaker or Stomping out the darkness. What I appreciate most about his books is that he is Christ-centered and not demon-centered.

- ➢ **Choose not to look a second time.** We all see things that are sexually stimulating every single day. A member of the opposite sex walks by, driving past a billboard, seeing a magazine cover, channel surfing, etc. But do you look a second time? We can't always help seeing it the first time but we choose whether we will look at it a second time. If you look again then you are feeding your lust. The next step is sexual fantasies, then masturbation and after that.... you tell me. It is a road that leads to perversion and depravity. Make good choices in this area. The old saying goes, "You can't prevent a bird from flying over your head but you can stop it from making a nest in your hair."

- ➢ **Watch what you are taking into your life.** Your lifestyle choices are either helping or hindering you in this area. TV, movies, music, CD's, magazines, books, the internet, etc., are all having an impact on your life for good or for evil! Charles Spurgeon talked about the battle inside his life between his old and new natures. He described it like two big dogs fighting. Someone asked him, "Which dog wins?" And he said, "Whichever dog I feed the most." Which dog are you feeding? (Matthew 6:22-23)

"For me to be completely in touch with my own humanness and the darker side, of who I am, keeps me fixated on my daily need for Christ and my healthy dependence on Him for my very existence." Scott Brown

3. Never say never. Never say, "Oh, this would never happen to me. I would never fall sexually!" Proverbs 16:18 says, "Pride goes before destruction, a haughty spirit before a fall." When we say, "This will never happen to me," then we aren't preparing ourselves for the possibility which makes us more susceptible and vulnerable.

I was speaking at a large youth conference in Minnesota. They had bought out all the rooms at a hotel and that's where I was staying. It was Friday evening; I had finished speaking and was in the gift shop buying a newspaper. A young woman approaches me and says, "Hi!" She looks like she is in her mid-twenties, real cute and has this great smile. Here is out basic conversation:

- Girl: "You look bored."
- Greg: "No, I'm just kind of tired. I thought I would get a paper to read later in my room."
- Girl: "Is your wife here?"
- Greg: "No, she usually doesn't come with me on these weekend trips. I fly in on Friday and then leave on Sunday so it goes by pretty fast."
- Girl: "Do you have a room by yourself?"
- Greg: "Oh yea, it's a great room, looks out over the pool and is really nice." (I am totally oblivious to what is happening). She is just staring at me with this big smile on her face. I am thinking she is a youth sponsor and I'll ask her what group are you with, where are you from, how are you doing, etc? But before I can ask these things she says...
- Girl: "SO do you ever mess around?" It so caught me off guard. This was the last thing I expected. I felt like someone had slugged me in the stomach. My mouth was wide open, I could feel my face turning bright red and it was like someone turned on two faucets in my arm pits.
- Girl: "Come on not even a little bit?"
- Greg: I finally managed to squeak out... "No."
- Girl: "Well, I just thought you were kind of cute." Then she reached up, pinched my cheek and walked away.

Here I am a married man, four children, loving Jesus, travel around the world preaching the gospel, on the speaker team with Family Life Ministries, past youth specialist for Moody Bible Institute, youth Pastor for 10 years, mission leader to Europe for over 20 years, author and youth communicator. When she asked me, "do you ever mess around," do you know what my first thought was? "Who will know? I am hundreds of miles away from home; she is good looking, who will ever know." Then the second thing that jumped into my mind was the Word of God. "Do not be deceived, God is not mocked, for what a man sows so shall he reap." If you don't acknowledge this as a possibility then you are not prepared if it happens. Instead of saying "Never" we need to say, "Jesus I know how sick I can be and I need you." In your weakness, there is strength as you become more and more dependent upon the Lord.

4. Don't set yourself up to fail. Proverbs 4:13-15 says, "Hold on to instruction do not let it go; guard it well, for it is your life. Do not set foot on the path of the wicked or walk in the way of evil men. Avoid it, do not travel on it; turn from it and go on your way."

We want to love and serve the Lord but then we put ourselves in stupid situations and we set ourselves up to fail. Here are some examples:

- **Showing poor judgment.** I look back at some of my decisions and I cringe. I did some really stupid things that set me up to fail. "Thank you Jesus for protecting me in my stupidity." I was a single Youth Pastor. This is my first church; I am young, eager and clueless. That is a dangerous situation. It was 2:00am when there was a knock at my apartment door. I get up; I was in my boxers, so I threw on a robe. When I opened the door, I saw one of my senior girls sobbing. She had a huge fight with her parents and left. She had no where to go. So, are you ready for this, I invited her into my apartment to talk with her till 4:00am. She then went home, patched things up with her parents and the Dad even called to thank me. I look back and I am amazed at my lack of wisdom. Not only was I alone with her but I was alone with her for two hours. All she would have had to say is Greg kissed me or touched me and my ministry would have been over.
  - What should I have done?
    - ✓ Have her wait in the hall.
    - ✓ Get fully dressed.
    - ✓ Call her parents, with her permission, and let them know I am with her.
    - ✓ Drive separately to an all-night restaurant and talk there.

- **Don't isolate yourself with a member of the opposite sex.** Do not be alone in a car, their house, your place, the office, taking a walk, anywhere. Don't do it! You put your ministry, future, and Christ's reputation all at risk. It is not that hard to get somewhere public where you have witnesses and accountability.

- **Do not flirt, even in jest.** Never make any kind of suggestive comments as to how they look. One student came to me and said that her Youth Pastor said, "If I was young and single I would want to date you." That is totally out of line and that guy needs to lose his job over such a comment. He is playing with her feelings.

- **Be careful about physical contact.** If touch is the primary love language for a person then it may be opening them to temptation and thoughts about you they should not be thinking. Just be careful about who, where and how much you touch.

- **Make eye contact.** They will notice if your eyes move to other parts of their body. Then what are you communicating to them? My wife is so offended when she is talking to a guy and he looks at her chest. Does he think my wife won't notice that? If my wife tells me when this happens to her then you can be sure a teenage girl will tell her friends if your eyes wander. What kind of reputation will you be building in the youth group?

- **Marital problems will open you up to more temptation.** You need to maintain a strong and healthy relationship with your spouse. That includes an exciting sexual relationship with him/her. Talk to each other about sex. How can you please one another if you aren't talking about it? Marriage takes hard work and effort. You won't stay close just because you said, "I do", seven years ago. I highly recommend you attend a Family Life Weekend to Remember marriage conference. It is a great tune up for your marriage.

- **On-going counseling.** Again, this was my first youth Pastor position and I was doing on-going counseling with a teenage girl. She had been very sexually active, had a bad home situation and had recently become a Christian. We had met several times and I had been very loving, kind and encouraging. I wanted to see her fall in love with Jesus and live for Him. My motives were pure but I was so naive. One day my senior Pastor, Gordon Hanstead, calls me into his office. He asks me, "Did you know this girl is in love with you?" To which I responded..."Huh?" This teenage girl had more sense than I did. She went to the Pastor and confessed she was falling in love with me. I learned it was O.K. to meet with my girls but any on-going counseling needed to be with a woman or professional counselor. Remember, when you are involved in counseling...

- You are beginning to fill an important void in their life.
- You give comfort, love, understanding and compassion. All these qualities are highly valued in a spouse.
- They begin to need you and that is a nice feeling for you, it is also a very dangerous position for you.

"One reason sin flourishes is that it is treated like a cream puff instead of a rattlesnake." Billy Sunday

> **Stay away from pornography.** It is a cancer that will eat you alive. Pornography's biggest lie to us is, "next time." Just one more video, magazine, internet site and then you'll be satisfied. That leads to lust and masturbation and the porn begins to control you. No matter how much time you spend pursuing the desire it is never enough and it becomes insatiable. If you do it enough the unthinkable begins to happen. You start thinking about your students or staff sexually. Then there will be the temptation to act on those fantasies. You <u>must</u> get help now. Get some controls on your computer and get yourself under accountability. Bring it out in the light.

5. Think about it objectively. When we are tempted sexually our emotions are in control and we aren't thinking through any of the consequences. So, let me walk you through this process.

> You meet someone very good looking.

> They confess they really like you.

- You have great sex for a year, six months, three weeks, two days, one hour?

- Now imagine the feelings of guilt and regret. The fear and worry about being caught and the depression which comes from living a lie.

- Consider what it will be like as God removes His blessing from your life.

- Even though they promised not to say anything, they share it with a close friend.

- The close friend tells others about what you have done.

- Now imagine having to stand before the Pastors and board and be confronted with this.

- How does your spouse respond when you have to confess it to them? How will your children respond? Imagine looking into their eyes and seeing the hurt.

- See the facial expressions of the teens when you confess it before them.

- Then you go before the whole congregation.

- The community finds out, the media catches wind of it and maybe even the police are called.

- How about your parents, her parents, other Youth Pastors?

- When people talk about you they just shake their heads. Do they remember all the good things you did? No, your legacy will be the affair.

- Now imagine going to jail and being labeled a child molester.

> You get out of jail and sell shoes for the rest of your life.

I don't care how good looking they are or how great the sex was. It isn't worth it, not even close. So, keep this in mind when you come under attack. I want you to stand firm and think through all the consequences. When you fall, you don't fall alone. There will be a number of students who will fall with you. Because they believed in you and you are Jesus with flesh to them. Here is a sobering reminder from God's word, Luke 17: 1&2, "Jesus said to His disciples: 'Things that cause people to sin are bound to come, but woe to that person through whom they come. It would be better for him to be thrown into the sea with a millstone tied around his neck than for him to cause one of these little ones to sin'."

6. Watch for the danger signs. I Peter 5:8 says, "Be self-controlled and alert. Your enemy the devil prowls around like a roaring lion looking for someone to devour." Wake up and look for these signs the relationship is in trouble.

> They have a growing dependence upon you. They need you, your wisdom and insight. They begin to call you for advice and direction. Teenagers will feed your ego.

> This person praises and affirms you a lot. In their eyes, you are wonderful. Do you want to go home to your spouse who knows the real you and to a relationship which has gotten kind of boring or stay with this exciting person?

> They have never had a friend like you. Before meeting you, there was a lot of loneliness. You have become an escape from emotional pain.

> You start to receive gifts from them. Notes, cards and letters arrive. Now they are making conscious efforts to please you. You might even begin to feel obligated.

> Do they touch you? How much do they touch you? Where do they touch you? Is it increasing? Do they want to give you back rubs? Are they snuggling with you? When they

talk to you are they getting real close and do they touch you while they talk?

- How do they dress? Is it tight, suggestive, and revealing?
- Listen to what they are saying to you. Do they talk about things having to do with sex? Do they joke about how attractive you are? Do they let you know when their spouse or parents are going to be gone?

While all this is going on outwardly, something begins to happen inside of you.

- You start to think about them when they aren't around. At first you are thinking about positive things like their spiritual condition, problem, how you can help, etc.
- After a while you begin to compare them to your spouse, which isn't fair because this other person is always at their best, dressing nice, smelling good and acting great. Your spouse seems to be lacking compared to them.
- You begin to look forward to seeing them. Your heart races in anticipation. You make excuses to see them and you start to touch them more. Initially you are just seeing each other in group settings or when they come into the office. This is where the emotional affair begins.

"If…you can't be a good example, then you'll just have to be a horrible warning." Catherine Aird

- You start to share some of your needs, frustrations and desires with them. Some may have to do with the disappointment you feel toward your spouse. No longer do they see you as just a Youth Pastor but as a needy person. This now raises compassion and a desire in them to help meet your needs.
- Then you begin to have sexual fantasies about them. This

will usually lead to masturbation. You rationalize as long as it isn't really happening it is OK. You convince yourself this is a way to release pressure and it is better then having an affair. But the enemy is so deceptive and he is actually moving you toward the affair.

➤ You begin to compare your fantasy to reality and what looks better? Fantasy always looks better than reality. Instead of questioning your fantasy you begin to question reality.

➤ Now you try to set up times to be alone together. This may involve deception and lies. At first it is just to talk, in private, so you don't have to be disturbed by other people or the phone. You think, "There is nothing wrong with this, we're just friends." The enemy is a deadly viper and he is about to strike you. You are moving closer, deception has you in its grip and you are being pulled deeper into the trap.

➤ You start to hold the person in your arms, giving them long hugs. You just want to encourage them. You think, "There is nothing wrong with a hug." But hugging excites you.

➤ When you get home, you start to feel bad. This is God reaching out to you trying to speak truth. But you are not listening. You become irritable and angry with your spouse. You're trying to justify your actions so you look for opportunities to criticize your spouse. You are totally lost spiritually. You're not thinking clearly and you really don't care. You want to be with this person and besides, you deserve better then what you are getting from your spouse. And then the viper strikes!

➤ One day you take, what is now, a very small step and it becomes a physical, sexual affair. Then, if you love the Lord at all, you regret it for the rest of your life.

7. Listen to your spouse. God will speak to you through your spouse. If you don't accept corrections, advice, warnings and insight then you are stupid! How do I know that? Because Proverbs 12:1b says, "He who hates correction is stupid." Don't you love how God just says it and doesn't beat around the bush?

For the men reading this: No one knows a woman like another woman. If your wife says to you, "That girl likes you," then I am willing to bet my house she is absolutely right. But what is your first reaction? You immediately want to dismiss it as not being true. You are really saying you know women better than your wife and that my friend, says you are stupid.

For the women reading this: No one knows the mind of a man like another man. How much he is thinking about sex, what he thinks when he looks at you, how what you wear affects him. If your husband says, "That guy has a crush on you or is sexually excited by you," listen to him. Otherwise, you are stupid.

8. Get an accountability partner now. James 5:16 says, 'Therefore confess your sins to each other and pray for each other so that you may be healed. The prayer of a righteous man is powerful and effective." Find a Godly, same sex, individual and begin to meet regularly. Give them permission to ask you all the tough questions, especially when it comes to purity and sexual temptations. We need each other and for you to have a person in your life to help keep you and the right track is a good thing.

This isn't necessary but you might want to consider an accountability partner who does not go to your church. I don't think your Senior Pastor makes a good accountability partner because of your working relationship and the fact this is your boss. Your accountability partner must be someone you trust and could share anything with. Now the trust will take time to build but this person needs to have the potential of being someone you can be totally honest with. I have a great accountability partner; his name is Bob MacRae. I trust him completely and I can and have told him everything. He can be understanding and encouraging and at other times he gives me a spiritual kick in the rear. He knows all the good, bad and ugly about me.

A number who have fallen had accountability partners but lied to them. Sin corrupts and as you begin to compromise in one area it leads to compromise in other areas. It does no good if you lie to your accountability partner. You MUST be vulnerable and risk being totally honest with this person. If Bob wanted, he could do damage to my ministry because he knows the struggles and problems I have had and continue to have. But I trust him and he is a man of character and integrity.

Be a man, be a woman of purity. You don't want anyone to say of you, "He/She used to be...," used to be pure, used to be committed, used to be a good example. Be a hero of the faith and not some sad statistic of someone who fell.

THINK ABOUT IT:
1. What has your spouse been trying to say to you in the area of your sexuality? Are you listening?
2. When is the last time you have been honest with someone and allowed them to hold you accountable?
3. What kind of safeguards have you established in your life to protect you in the struggle against pornography?

THOUGHTS FROM OTHERS:
It is a bad world, Donatus, an incredibly bad world. But I have discovered in the midst of it a quiet and good people who have learned the great secret of life. They have found a joy and wisdom which is a thousand times better than any of the pleasures of our sinful life. They are despised and persecuted, but they care not. They are masters of their souls. They have overcome the world. These people, Donatus, are Christians…and I am one of them." Saint Cyprian

"The question is not 'How much may I indulge in and still be saved'?" God forbid! I must rather ask, 'What about Christ's will and the example I set for my fellow Christians'?" Robert Cook

THOUGHT:
"IF YOU HAVE TO CHOOSE BETWEEN MINISTRY OR SPOUSE–PICK SPOUSE"

"A man ought to live so that everybody knows he is a Christian...and most of all, his family ought to know." D. L. Moody

Other than your relationship with Jesus Christ, there is nothing more important than your spouse. Don't give them the leftovers. Many have blown it by thinking: "after I have given to everyone else I can give to your spouse." That is so wrong. If youth ministry is coming between you and your spouse then get out of youth ministry. Make family the priority it needs to be. Here are a few ways you can do that.

1. Spend time together. The comment, "Well, we don't have a lot of time but it's quality time," is wrong. Quantity time is quality time. A strong, healthy and vibrant marriage relationship doesn't happen magically. Solid marriages are cultivated, not inherited. Just because you stood at the alter and said your vows doesn't mean you will have a good marriage. You need to work at it. I try to take my wife, Bonnie, out on a date once a week. Now, this does not always happen, but it is my goal.

People say to me, "We can't afford to do that." Go to a fast food restaurant, get a cup of water, and hang out together. The idea is not "let's spend a lot of money." It's to get away from the tyranny of the urgent - TV, phone, responsibilities, kids--and talk together. If Bonnie and I don't get out, we can feel like two strangers living in the same house. Put time with your spouse into your schedule. So, if someone wants to meet with you, you can say, "I am sorry but I already have an appointment." What about the cost of babysitting? You make a deal with another couple and say, "once a week we will baby-sit your child if once a week you will baby-sit our six children." By the way, that is a great deal for you!

Keep in mind ministry together does not equal time together. You are both in the same room but you're really not connecting on a personal level. You can spend several days a week ministering together and still feel distant from one another.

2. Love them. I already went through five ways you can love your students. Now, apply them to your spouse. Tell your spouse you love them. To be clear, actually say the words, "I love you." But keep in mind that if your actions don't back up your words, then your words become worthless. You and your spouse will have a primary love language. That means in one or two of the love languages you will feel the most loved. We tend to love others in our primary love language, but that probably isn't where they feel the most loved. So, identify your spouse's primary love languages and seek to love them in those areas. Don't ignore the others, but concentrate on the main ones. For example, my wife has two main love languages, words and service. I can bring her home a gift of a dozen flowers, which I do on occasion, and she will look at those and appreciate them. But if I get up and clean the house while she is out, "WOW," she will be so excited! What is the difference? Gifts are nice, but service is one of her love languages.

3. Satisfy each other sexually. Add this to the list of how to love one another. It is actually the sixth major love language. Sex is a wonderful way to express love to each other. Our schedules get so busy sometimes you need to plan for sex. Planned sex is better than no sex. That is a good motto to live by! It isn't what is most important, but it is very important. Talk to each other about sex. How can you effectively please one another if you aren't talking?

4. Appreciate. We put these expectations on each other. I expect...
- Meals prepared
- Garbage out
- Lawn mowed
- House vacuumed
- Clothes cleaned
- Car running
- You add to the list…

So, when our spouse meets those expectations they have done the least we expect and we never appreciate. We have become selfish and self centered. "This is what I want, what I expect, and what I demand." Get rid of your expectations and say thank you. Notice the little things they do. It keeps a spark going and prevents you from taking the other person for granted.

5. Make sure your husband/wife can get you on the phone immediately. Tell your secretary if your spouse calls to put them through without delay. Even if I was meeting with someone, I want her to be able to get to me. It is wrong for a spouse to have to get permission from a secretary to talk to you. If they are calling you on the cell phone answer it and be happy they called. Some of you answer the phone with the attitude, "you are bothering me."

6. Once a year do something to tune up your marriage. You buy a car and you put down a chunk of change. So, to protect your investment and keep it running smoothly you get periodic tune ups. Your marriage needs periodic tune ups as well. I recommend the Family Life Marriage conferences, which is a part of Campus Crusade for Christ. They do a tremendous job. It is fun and informative. It gives you a chance to get away from all the distractions and concentrate on your marriage. Bonnie and I attended one earlier in our marriage and we are now part of the speaker team.

7. Get help. For my wife and I, our first year of marriage was a little bit of hell here on earth. We finally went in and got some marriage counseling and it was very helpful. All relationships go through tough times. Be willing to get help before it boils over into a full-blown crisis. Only the strong go for help. A weak man or woman chooses to hide the problems.

"Sometimes I drive around the neighborhood a few times, so I can pray and transition, so my heart is excited to be home." Al Schuck

8. The first five minutes. The first five minutes after you get home sets the tone for the whole evening. So, on the way home strip off the work day and put on your family focus. Come home with a positive attitude and some enthusiasm. Give them all big kisses and be interested in their day and how things went. The world does not revolve around you. It has been a tough day but don't let it rob you of your family time. You can't always control your circumstances, but you can certainly control how you respond to those circumstances.

9. Look good. Treat your spouse like you were meeting the most important person in the Youth Ministry field. Show them respect. When we dated, we did the kind of things I am about to mention. Why don't we do them anymore? Maybe it's because we have started to take them for granted. Your looking good is all about being sensitive to them. You want to be saying to them, "You are the most important person in my life."

- Put on clean clothes that look nice. You don't have to greet each other in a prom dress and tux but don't greet each other in that old, gross, hole filled, smelly, but it feels so comfortable thing!

- Spray on something that smells good.

- Freshen your deodorant, make-up and breath. Brush your teeth or chew some gum. Some of you need to chew a lot of gum. Comb your hair.

- Maybe after greeting your family you need to take a quick shower to freshen up. That will help you to feel better which can improve your attitude.

- Stop passing so much gas. My wife made me write that one!

10. Surprise them. Once a month, do something fun and unexpected. Bring home flowers, go to a movie, send the kids to grandparents, show up at the door naked. Now be careful. Make sure the kids are gone and it is your spouse at the door and they don't have a friend with them. (Also, the naked person should be the one already home, not the one coming home!) Call them from the office to say you love them and you are thinking of them. Leave them a card or write a poem. Take them to the opera even though you hate the opera. Get tickets to the ball game. The only thing limiting you is your creativity. I know some of us are creative challenged so there are books to give you ideas in this area.

11. Honor them. How do you honor your spouse? Make them look good. In front of the kids, at church, out with friends, at the mall, in front of the waitress...make them look good. You do by the way you speak to them, speak about them and the way you treat them. When you make your spouse the brunt of a joke, when you slam them, when you criticize them in public, when you are sarcastic towards them, you dishonor them and make them look bad. You embarrass them and if you do it enough you crush their spirit. Be a gentleman or a gentlewoman!

12. Show affection in public. I am not talking about making out or groping each other. I mean holding hands and putting your arm around them. Do it around the teens because they need that kind of positive example. Have you considered you could be the only positive role model they have? They watch you to see and understand what a Godly husband and wife are like.

13. Forgive one another. For some of you this will mean starting over. You need to go home and say, "Honey, I was wrong, I am sorry, would you please forgive me?" It is forgiveness that draws sinners to Jesus Christ and a spouse to their partner. We have all said things to each other we have regretted. Some of you have thought time has passed and they have forgotten everything I said. You are absolutely wrong. They haven't forgotten it at all and you need to go back to them and apologize. What prevents you from humbling yourself and admitting you were wrong? Your stupid pride is preventing you from doing what you need to do.

You ask your spouse to forgive you but you also need to be willing to forgive them. If you say to me, "Greg you don't understand what they did to me and I will never forgive them." I would respond by saying, "You are right and I will never truly understand what they did to you and how it made you feel." But when you refuse to forgive you need to keep in mind these things.
- When is the last time Jesus has refused to forgive you? Never, and think about all the things you have said, done,

and thought, to hurt Him.
- ➢ When you refuse to forgive it makes you a cold hard individual on the inside. You are not a pleasant person to be around. It begins to impact all your relationships and your heart becomes hard toward your spouse, others and even God.
- ➢ When you refuse to forgive it hurts you more than it hurts them. I heard someone say, "Refusing to forgive is like trying to hurt someone by drinking poison."

You can forgive because you are greatly forgiven. Do not miss out on the joy of being free. Having a clear conscience before God and your spouse.

14. Love is a commitment. I don't always feel like I love Bonnie. There are times she ticks me off. If my love for Bonnie was based on how I feel, then I would have left her a long time ago because she does stuff that upsets me. If her love for me was based on how she felt, then she would have left me because she thinks I do stupid stuff; but she just doesn't understand! OK, I do stupid stuff too. Bonnie is from Southern California and it does not snow real often in Los Angeles. I married her and we move to Rockford, Illinois. On occasion, it does snow in Rockford. My wife came home after our first snow fall. In our driveway, the snow is less then a quarter inch deep. I came home and noticed the car was parked on the street. I pulled into the garage, walk in and ask, "Honey, how come the car is parked on the street?" She tells me, "I was afraid if I pulled it into the driveway I might get it stuck in the snow." I thought, "How cute! Honey all you have to do is back the car up, give it a little gas and you will go right through the snow."

Now, my wife came home after our first heavy snow. The wind was blowing and the snow had drifted about knee deep in our driveway. She pulled up in the car, looked at the snow drift and said to herself, "Well, Greg said all I have to do is back the car up, give it a little gas and I'll go right through the snow." So, she backed up our brand-new car, gave it a little gas, actually she gave it a lot of gas! She got the car going about 25 mph. The car hit the wall of snow, went airborne, and landed on the side of the driveway. She somehow got all four wheels off the ground. I came home that evening. As I turned the corner, I saw the car and it looks like a giant had thrown it aside. Then I saw my wife, still in her nursing outfit, digging as fast as she could trying to free the car. Now, if my love for Bonnie was based on how I felt at that moment, we would have been in trouble. Instead, I love my wife even though she does………………. creative things!

I need to tell a story on myself. I took Bonnie to the theater for a play. It was Christmas time. The theater had a big glass front was filled with women all facing out waiting for their husbands. I bought the tickets, look up and found my wife. I then proceed to walk right into the window. I thought it was a doorway, I didn't get my hands out to brace myself and I hit it HARD! Almost immediately all the women began to laugh. I am sure they were thinking, "That's the biggest bird I have ever seen." At that moment if my wife was going to love me dependent on how she felt, then I would have walked in and said, "Hi honey." She would have said, "Who is this man calling me honey? I don't know this person. Get away from me." Even though I do stupid things my wife still loves me.

Love is a commitment. It is something we do no matter how we feel. An immature person follows their feelings. A mature person does what is right. You choose to love one another. Divorce is not an option.

Go home and talk about what needs to happen next. Look at the fourteen things I have just talked about. What's the next step you need to take? Change whatever needs to be changed, adjust whatever needs to be adjusted and if you have to choose between your spouse and youth ministry...choose your spouse!

THINK ABOUT IT:
1. How often do you date your spouse?
2. Do you honor or dishonor them?
3. What kind of surprise can you bring them this week?

THOUGHTS FROM OTHERS:
"I have found it impossible to carry the heavy burden of responsibility and to discharge my duties asking as I would wish without the help and support of the woman I love." Edward VII

"There is no more lovely, friendly, and charming relationship, communion, or company than a good marriage." Martin Luther

"A man travels the world over in search of what he needs and returns home to find it." George Moore

THOUGHT:
"THE FOUR 'MUSTS' FOR YOUTH PASTORS"

"You are only what you are when no one is looking." Robert C. Edward

The buck stops with you. If you're in charge, then be in charge and take the responsibility. We are all gifted and talented in different areas but there are certain things you can do to help you to be a more effective leader. Are there any "musts" every Youth Pastor should posses? Right off the top of my head, I can think of four "musts".

1. You must love Jesus Christ and experience His love for you.
This means you are actively pursuing an intimate relationship with Him. To miss this is to miss everything. Spending time with Him, studying the Word, praying, worshiping, journaling, fasting and listening, not because you have to do it or it is expected of you, but because you love Him. But more important is the fact He loves you and He wants to spend time with you. Your desire is to be obedient because love is all about actions speaking louder than words. I serve Him with joy, follow Him with confidence and love Him with passion because I am passionately loved.

There is nothing more important to me than my relationship with Jesus Christ. I need Jesus because He is my very life and breath. It is impossible to be the husband I need to be, to love my children or to be effective in ministry without the power and wisdom of the Holy Spirit. You don't always realize this when you are young. But as you get older, you start to understand that for me to be Jesus with flesh to these students is utterly, totally and completely impossible. I must surrender myself to the control of the Holy Spirit. It is only as Jesus works through me that I can be what I need to be, do what I need to do, and say what I need to say. "Oh God, make me the kind of man you want me to be!"

"To become Christlike is the only thing in the whole world worth caring for, the thing before which every ambition of man is folly and all lower achievement vain." Henry Drummond

2. You must be a person of character and integrity.
This means choosing to do what is right, loving your spouse and seeking to live a life beyond reproach. It means your actions back up your words; you're consistent in your lifestyle. What you are like on the outside is the mirror image of who you are on the inside. You have your priorities set and you know what you will do and what you won't do. You discern the difference between what you would really like to do and what you need to do. The problem is not knowing the difference between what is good and what is bad, or what is right and what is wrong, but rather what is good and what is best.

There are a lot of good things we can do that keep us from what is best. Best is all about keeping your priorities straight. Doing what God has called you to do and not straying from your vision. Best is saying no to those things which keep me from what I need to do. Then I look to be a person of character.

Character is what you do in the dark. It's what you do when you don't think anyone is looking. D.L. Moody said, "Who you are is what you would do, if you could do anything and know you would never get caught." When you are someone of character then people can trust you. Always speak the truth in love, never lie.

You always lead by example. We would never communicate to our teenagers, "do as I say, not as I do." You live Jesus Christ in front of them. What you do in moderation, a teenager will do in excess. If you mess around a little, they will mess around a lot. It is a wonderful privilege to be a Youth Pastor but it is also an awesome responsibility. Your life is preaching to them about what it means to be a Godly man/woman, a Godly husband/wife, and a Godly father/mother.

You live out before them what it means to...

- Be angry and sin not.
- Love one another.
- Be strong and courageous.
- Show joy in the midst of trials.
- Exhibit patience.
- Be holy as God is holy.
- Flee from sexual immorality.
- Worship God.
- Forgive someone.
- Be a fun Christian.
- Follow the Lord.
- Make every effort to keep peace.
- Get up after you fall.
- Ask for forgiveness.
- Be obedient, etc., etc., etc.,

It is a huge responsibility and you should be overwhelmed by it. It needs to drive you to your knees and cause you to cry, "Jesus help me, I can't do this, and I need you!" You can't do it, I can't do it, no one can do it! A teenager learns more from their eyes then their ears. More is caught than is taught. So, get on your knees and set the example by getting out there and living it.

3. You must love teenagers.
You must want to be with them and invest your life in their lives. Leadership is about relationships. You can have the position, authority, rights and control of a leader and not have anyone follow you. To be an effective leader, you need to be a lover. You earn respect, a right to be heard and the privilege of leading by caring about individuals. Remember the old saying, "People don't care how much you know until they know how much you care."

I don't want to just share the Gospel with students but I also want to share my very life. I want to be with them to listen to them, to laugh with them and to cry with them. It is not a burden to be with teens it is a privilege. Dawson McAllistar shared this in a message, "Teens ask two questions of us constantly; do you love me and does your stuff work?" I want teens to know I love them and then for them to see the "stuff" working in my life.

4. You must be called by God into Youth Ministry.
This isn't something you do because you don't know what else to do. This isn't about you getting your needs met. If you go into youth ministry because it sounds like fun or because you have the need to be loved, affirmed, and accepted then you are headed for failure. It is a hard road and not one to be taken lightly. "Youth Ministry can be a graveyard to the unsuspecting, a landmine to the naive and a dead end to the shortsighted." That is a powerful quote by Marty Larson and very true. If you aren't called, you won't last. There are young people with some major problems and issues and they want to go into youth ministry because they were helped when they were a teenager and now they want to help others. That sounds nice but first, get healthy and then seek what the Lord wants you to do.

One church official actually said this, "You can't be a Youth Pastor unless you are administrative." When I heard that, I thought, "WHAT, that is idiotic." You don't have to be strong administratively. How do I know that? Because we can staff to a Youth Pastors' weaknesses. You can bring in an administrative secretary or have a parent volunteer who is gifted administratively, but you can't be lacking in those four "musts." Who are we to say to someone God has risen up for youth Ministry, that they aren't qualified because they aren't administrative? Wow, talk about arrogance. Understand what I am saying. It is OK for an individual church to say, "We want our youth Pastor to be an administrator." But it is wrong to say, "All Youth Pastors need to be administrators." What does this communicate to the young people, in their church, who might sense God calling them to youth ministry but they aren't real organized? If I had attended their Church I might have been discouraged about ever going into youth ministry because my giftedness does not lay in the area of administration.

Are the four "musts" a part of your life? If they are than I can see you in youth ministry. Youth ministry is not about being the "best" or "most" …best athlete, best looking, most talented, most gifted. It is all about being faithful and obedient to God's calling in your life.

THINK ABOUT IT:
1. What are you doing to passionately pursue intimacy with Jesus?
2. Who do you know that models an intimate relationship with Jesus?
3. Where do you need to grow in your character?

THOUGHTS FROM OTHERS:
"If a man hasn't discovered something he will die for, he isn't fit to live." Martin Luther

"Growth begins when we start to accept our own weakness." Jean Vanier

"No man can climb out beyond the limitations of his own character." John Morley

"Youth ministry is not for cowards." GS

"You find your greatest joy in becoming everything Jesus Christ has created you to be." GS

THOUGHT:
"BECOME A MORE EFFECTIVE LEADER"

"The secret of success is to do the common things uncommonly well." John D. Rockefeller, Jr.

If you have the four "musts" then you are qualified for youth Ministry. Now, there are other factors and characteristics we can add to the list to help you to be a more effective leader.

1. An education. College and or seminary degrees are very helpful. I highly recommend you get those degrees, but they aren't absolutely necessary to be effective in youth ministry. God is able to use the educated and uneducated. But you have to be competent to know what you are talking about and what you are doing. That is why education is good because it gives you a foundation of knowledge from which you can grow and build. However, you can still do a great job even if you don't have the diplomas because you measure the job you are doing not by comparing yourself to someone else, but against your own knowledge and experience. In other words, you are doing the best job you can do with your special gifts, talents and abilities. You will become more competent with time as you gain knowledge and experience. So, how do you know whether you should get more education or go into youth ministry? Ask God and then be obedient.

After I graduated from Bethel University, I went right to work as a caseworker for delinquent and emotionally disturbed teenagers. I also began to do some speaking and my home church invited me to come and speak for a banquet. While I was there, the Senior Pastor took me out for a Coke. They were looking for a Youth Pastor and he basically said to me, "Greg, if you are going to be hired as Youth Pastor, you need a seminary degree. If you had that, we would be interested in you." I respected him so I thought seriously about going to seminary. I prayed, but never sensed God leading me in that direction. A year later I was hired as a Youth Pastor in Rockford, Illinois. Three years later, I was invited back to my home church to do a week of meetings. During that time, the Senior Pastor approached me again, but this time asked me to join him as Youth Pastor. The bottom line is you need to do what God is calling you to do. He will take care of you, open doors of ministry and work through you. I am a living example of this with only a BA degree in sociology.

2. Be yourself. We don't need another...

- Marty Larsen
- Dan Howard
- Heather Flies
- Marvin Jacobo
- Churck Klein
- Brian Farka
- Ralph Gustafson
- Scott Anderson
- Bob MacRae
- J.T. Bean
- Randy Larson
- Brad Nelson
- Scott Pederson
- Jeff Honson
- David Boyd
- Larry Johnson
- Dave Childers
- Lisa Wiebe
- Matt Roop
- Pam Warfle
- Jeff Bell
- Karen Grant
- Scott Brown
- Scott Groff
- Giles Davis
- Brian Erickson
- Tim Lemmons
- Scott Bartelt
- Mike Maddry
- Ginny Olson
- Brett Ray
- Brandon Early
- Jamie Larson
- Don Gillaspie
- Mark Matson
- Peter Vincent
- Toni Sather
- Dann Spader
- Dan Kregel
- Brian Float
- Dawnette Scott
- Molly Sanborn
- Joe Sims
- Brett Thomas
- Al Schuck
- David Malouf
- Lisa Snodgrass
- Craig Sanborn
- Vince Purpero
- David Creek
- Kris Neider
- Sue Rooke
- Chuck Beckler
- Derek Hodge
- Bob Long
- Tiger McLuen
- Leslie Arnold

We need you! Why did I list these names? I wanted to honor these people. Here are men and women who have faithfully served the Lord in youth ministry. God has worked in and through them to make a difference in the lives of students. They are young and old, Youth Pastors, youth speakers, missionaries and musicians, from all across the US and Canada, with this in common, they love Jesus

Christ and teenagers. Do you recognize the names? Probably not, but these are some of the heroes of the faith who are faithfully serving the Lord in the area God has called them. The Lord is effectively using them to reach teenagers without seeking fame. But as effective as these men and women have been, you still need to be yourself and don't try to be like them. They all possess those "musts" and you can follow the examples they have set in those areas. But otherwise don't copy them. Don't compare yourself to anyone. You are not like anyone else. You are a unique creation of God. You are not superior or inferior to anyone. You are you and that is someone good to be. Ask Jesus what He wants you to be and do. He will mold and perfect you into His image and then he will raise you up for a unique Youth Ministry which needs your exact gifts and talents.

"Identify your highest skill and devote your time to performing it." Johann Wolfgang von Goethe

3. Be Teachable. When you stop learning and growing, then you stop living and being effective. It is exciting to learn and to grow as individuals and as a ministry. To do this, you need to listen and ask questions. When you bring in an outside speaker, do you ever ask for their opinions and evaluation? If not, then why not? This is a chance for you to learn and get some new insight. Have you ever brought someone in to evaluate the youth ministry? If you get the opportunity to be with other people in youth ministry, ask questions. Talk less and listen more. My experience in being at Youth Pastor gatherings is the person who talks the most, is the neediest. They want to tell you how important they are, how much the group has grown in just a year, all the great programs happening and all their successes. This is a person dealing with real insecurities. If anyone needs to be listening and learning it is probably them.

I am not the youth guru; I don't know everything about youth ministry. I am a youth specialist and not a youth expert. This means I specialize in teens, but it does not mean I know everything. I have been in youth Ministry for over 30 years, so I have picked up some stuff. I speak twelve to fifteen days a month, so I am doing quite a few youth events each year. How many Youth Pastors or lay staff ask my opinions, ask me to evaluate the weekend or just ask me some questions about youth ministry in a typical year? Maybe six engagements! Not six a month but six for an entire year. A couple of years ago I spoke for a high school winter retreat and the Youth Pastor had an intern drive me to the airport. He thought it would be a great opportunity for the intern. He was in seminary and wanted to be a Youth Pastor. The drive back to the airport was about 3 to 4 hours. He talked the whole time, and I mean the whole time, and he never asked me one question.

"There are no foolish questions and no man becomes a fool until he has stopped asking questions."
Charles P. Steinmetz

If we are going to make it for the long haul in Youth Ministry, then we need to be teachable and a lifelong learner. You do this by…
- Asking questions.
- Reading books. (Thanks for buying my book)
- Observing other Youth Ministries.
- Going to Youth Ministry conferences.
- Listening to internet messages, etc.

Think about this for a moment. If you have surrounded yourself with people who always agree with you and never oppose your ideas or direction, then you are missing out. Those opposing ideas will help to sharpen you. I hope you welcome correction and evaluation in the ministry. If you don't, what is this saying about you?
- You show yourself to be insecure.
- You're probably a control freak.
- You have manipulated and scared the people around you.
- You reap the counsel of mediocrity.
- You are not teachable.

I read this on the internet so you know it must be true. In a study of nine vice presidential level professionals, all who achieved their positions through excellent performance over the years, and all who became incompetent in the latter part of their careers and were terminated by their employer, had these common traits or behaviors.
- An increasing conviction of "rightness" on matters without

supporting evidence.
- An increasing internal unwillingness to be influenced by the counsel or input of others.
- A hesitancy to learn new things, which presented a challenge, and a desire to stay in their "comfort zone."
- A tendency to focus on, refer to, or function based on past successes or patterns.
- Resistance to change with a subtle attitude communicating, "it probably won't work."
- A defensiveness when challenged or disagreed with.
- Reluctance to accept criticism.
- Increasingly out of touch with the majority consensus and the overall thinking of the people they dealt with.
- Giving an aura of "I have done well, I am doing well, I now have little need for additional professional growth."
- An increasing use of power and authority over others.

I have seen youth Pastors who have been around for awhile, who have had "successful ministries" show these kinds of behaviors because they are no longer teachable, they aren't allowing others to speak into their lives.

4. Have a sense of humor. Never take yourself too seriously. You must be able to laugh with others and laugh at yourself. I was speaking at a Family Life Marriage conference. There were 800 adults packed into this ball room. I was in the middle of talking to them about sexual intimacy and I want to say, "when it comes to thinking men are compartmentalized." But all of a sudden I cannot pronounce the word compartmentalized. I stumble over it the first time and then try to correct myself by saying something like compartalmentaleezed. So, I try a third time and I still couldn't say it. How do I react to that? Do I go on and pretend like nothing happened? No, instead I started laughing at myself which allowed the whole room, which was suffering with me through each blunder, to laugh. I asked the crowd, "How do you pronounce it?" Several yelled back the correct pronunciation and I said, "That's it, thank you." We all laughed again and I went on. This actually won me favor in the eyes of the crowd. Everyone can relate and sympathize with someone struggling from the front and making mistakes. Being able to laugh with your staff and students builds unity and gives you favor. Just make sure the humor is appropriate and funny for everyone. Stay away from sexual, gender and ethnic humor.

Be careful about always slamming yourself in front of the group. It is good to be able to laugh at some of the stupid things you have done, but don't make yourself out as someone who is always doing dumb things. They need to hear about you succeeding and doing things well. It is all about keeping a balance. Don't always be the idiot and don't always be the hero. Be yourself and let them see both sides of you.

"A good laugh is sunshine in a house."
William Makepeace Thackeray

5. Be flexible. Take a rigid stand of total flexibility. You need to be able to bend and flex or you will break. You are working with teenagers who forget, lose track of time, lose things and love spontaneity.
- You are sitting down to plan snow camp and some of your students come by to go out for a coke--flex!
- You've got a game planned for winter camp, but they really want to play something else--flex.

We always take a rigid stand of total flexibility. It allows us to relax. If you are anal retentive then changes throw you and upset you. Don't get hyper about things. God is in control and it will all work out in the end. We learn to be flexible and in doing this we can also avoid ulcers. Some areas you don't flex in are the Word of God, morality, time with your family, etc.

6. Make the decision. You must be willing to make difficult decisions. Every decision involves some risk. Remember there is wisdom in the counsel of many. Listen to and seek Godly advice from people you respect. Get as much input as you can before making the decision. But bottom line, you need to make the decision and you will be held responsible and have to deal with the consequences that follow. Choose your battleground wisely. You will make decisions others will oppose. What are you willing to go to the wall for and what isn't worth the hassle at this time? I had the idea a fun outreach would be a square dance, oops. That went over with the church leadership about as well as if I would have purposed having a water balloon fight in the sanctuary. Now I could have fought this but I felt there were other things we could do as outreaches so I let it go. It just wasn't that big of a deal to the ministry.

People will always say "No" to you. Within the staff and on the board, you have what I call "dream killers." You come to them with all these great, exciting, visionary ideas and plans. They listen, smile, and then tell you why it can't work and won't happen. Do you stand firm and hold onto it or do you let it go, at least for the time being? You need to pray and ask God to give you wisdom. Refusing to fight and giving in might be the wisest choice.

"Leadership is action, not position." Donald McGannon

7. Live the passion. You are called to the most exciting, cutting edge ministry there is and that is working with teenagers. You need to have a passion, excitement and vision for what God has called you to do. Let God re-ignite that in your life. Ask Him to renew your passion for Him and for your ministry to students.

8. Anticipate problems. No matter what youth ministry you are involved in you are going to have problems. If you anticipate them then they will not catch you off guard. Everyone and every ministry have problems.

Problems are not necessarily bad. What are the benefits?
- Your own personal growth. All sunshine and no rain makes a desert. Because of the rain and problems, we can begin to grow and develop.
- Deepens your dependence upon God.
- It can be a motivation for change. Could the problems be saying
to you that something is not working?

What do you need to do?

- ➤ Face the problem head on and don't try to run from it or avoid it.
- ➤ Get wisdom and input form others. They can give you solid counsel on the next step you ought to take.
- ➤ Acknowledge you may have bias or baggage from other conflicts that could affect this one.
- ➤ Then make the changes, do what you need to do and take the steps you need to take. Too many don't take this step, why?

We are afraid. I believe God would say to you what He said to Joshua after Moses died and before he crossed into the promise land. "Be strong and courageous!"

You don't really know what the next step is you need to take. Get some input. Talk to other Godly individuals who have traveled the path you are walking now.

You know what the next step is but you don't know how to take the step. Talk to others. Spell out the problem, what needs to change and ask how you can practically make it happen.

In the midst of dealing with the problems and making the changes don't make your focus the problems. It will put you into a negative frame of mind. Bonnie and I bought our first home. The front lawn looked terrible. It was filled with weeds. So, I am out there focused on all the weeds. Meanwhile my neighbor had this beautiful, lush, green lawn. One day I am out calling curses down on my weeds when my neighbor walked over and we started talking. I told him about my frustration with all these weeds. Here is what he said to me, "Greg, just grow grass." Get your eyes off the weeds. That's what you need to do. Get your eyes off the problems and just grow the ministry. Deal with the problems but don't make them your focus. Make your life easier and remember many problems stem from either a lack of communication or poor administrative skills.

9. Choose a good attitude. You are responsible for your attitude and how you will respond in different situations. No one can make you have a good or bad attitude, that is a choice that you make. You can't control your circumstances but you can control how you respond to those circumstances. It was Henry Ford who said, "Whether you think you can or whether you think you can't, your right." Negative thinking and a poor attitude and it will bring you down.

"The greater part of our happiness depends on our disposition and not our circumstances."
Martha Washington

For 1,000 years no one had ever broken the four-minute mile. Doctors actually came out and said the body was never made to run that fast. People said that it was impossible to run faster than a four-minute mile. People believed it and so no one ever ran faster than four minutes. Then along came Roger Bannister who refused to believe it couldn't be done. He broke the four-minute mile. That was a great accomplishment, but here is the rest of the story. The next year 37 runners broke the four-minute mile and the year after that over 300 runners accomplished the impossible. What made the difference? Now they believed they could do it. You can do it! How do I know that? Because if God has called you to youth ministry, then He will sustain, strengthen and empower you to do what He has called you to do.

Don't let your feelings control you or set your attitude. You must know what is true and use that truth to control your feelings. Feelings are a terrible indicator of reality and will lead you in the wrong direction.

Feelings lead to...always...everybody...nobody.
- ➢ "I always do stupid things."
- ➢ "Everybody is against me."
- ➢ "Nobody wants to be involved."

Instead you must know God's truth will combat those feelings. Proverbs 16:3, "Commit to the Lord whatever you do, and your plans will succeed."

Jeremiah 29:11, "For I know the plans I have for you, declares the Lord, plans to prosper you and not to harm you, plans to give you hope and a future."

Philippians 4:13, "I can do everything through Him who gives me strength."

Those are God's promises to you, they will help you combat negative feelings and a stinking attitude. For you who have a bad attitude, here is an exercise I would like you to do. Feel free to use this with any of your teenagers whose attitudes are pathetic. Drive down to the supermarket and buy yourself some limburger cheese. Have you ever smelled it? It is kind of a cross between skunk and vomit. Unwrap the cheese and you will notice there is a thin skin. Stick your finger through the skin and you'll find the cheese soft and gooey on the inside. Pull out a big glob on your finger and spread it under your nose. Then pick up a rose and smell it and the rose is going to stink. Now smell your favorite cologne or perfume and it will stink. Then smell your favorite food and guess what? It is going to stink! Why? Because you have limburger cheese under your nose. Get rid of the cheese and stuff smells good again. When you have a bad attitude then everything stinks. Get rid of the attitude and life will look brighter.

How do you do that?
- Focus on Jesus and not the problem.
- Take responsibility. Do what you need to do and change what you need to change.
- Stop blaming others for your bad attitude.
- Be thankful.
- Choose to have a good attitude.

This is very important because your attitude will impact your students and staff for good or for bad. Someone once asked D.L. Moody, "What people give you the most trouble?" He answered, "I've had more trouble with D.L. Moody than any man alive." Failure or success begins inside of you. What will you choose?

Congratulations, you are the Youth Pastor and this means the buck stops with you so start leading. Are the four "Musts" in place? Then you are ready to go. Step out in faith and accept the responsibility for the youth ministry. You are the leader - so lead!

THINK ABOUT IT:
1. Who are you learning from? Are you asking questions?
2. What are some of the problems you can anticipate and how will you deal with them?
3. What has your attitude been like?

THOUGHTS FROM OTHERS:
"If a man is called to be a streetsweeper, he should sweep streets even as Michelangelo painted, or Beethoven composed music or Shakespeare wrote poetry. He should sweep streets so well that all the hosts of heaven and earth will pause to say, here lived a great streetsweeper who did his job well." Martin Luther King, Jr.

"The will of God will not take you where the grace of God cannot keep you." Anon.

"What God expects us to attempt, He also enables us to achieve." Stephen Olford

THOUGHT:
"YOU CAN'T BE A LONE RANGER"

"It takes a great man to give sound advice tactfully, but a greater to accept it graciously." J. C. Macaulay

The days of being a Lone Ranger and doing it all yourself are over. As you multiply yourself, the ministry can grow and you are able to effectively reach more teens. It is true, bigger is not better but neither is smaller better. Thank God for good volunteer staff. They will be such a source of blessing and encouragement for you and the teens. Pray the Lord would raise up Godly men and women of all ages who will make an impact on the lives of the teens.

The recruitment of lay staff. What characteristics will be important to you in the people you entrust these teenagers with? This is not to be taken lightly. This is an awesome responsibility. These are the individuals you invest, and multiply yourself in, so teenagers are impacted for the cause of Christ. These are people you will stand with you on the front line. These are the people you are going into battle with. Your lay staff needs to be made up of all ages, shapes and sizes. Because different teens will relate to different staff. If all you have are college age and those in their twenties then you are out of balance. You will be missing out on the maturity, wisdom and stability age brings. That is why it is so good to have parents on your team.

Another huge reservoir for youth staff are senior citizens. They make tremendous accountability partners because they have time. They are amazing prayer warriors and a number of your teens will be drawn to the Grandfather-Grandmother figure. Your biggest challenge will be to convince them the teens want to be with them and they can be effective.

Have all potential staff fill out an application and run a background check. You do not want a convicted child molester as a part of your youth staff. As they observe the program you can observe them. You team them with another staff so they can learn, ask questions, meet

the teens and not feel left out or awkward. It is the whole concept of...
- ➢ I will do it and you watch.
- ➢ I will do it and you assist me.
- ➢ You will do it and I will assist you.
- ➢ You will do it and I will watch.
- ➢ Then you do it!

I was amazed at who God would raise up to work with the teens. People I might never have picked on my own. Some who came across a little weird but they loved teenagers and the students were drawn to them.

So, what characteristics are you looking for in your staff?

1. A deep love Jesus Christ. They must be maintaining a close, personal walk with God. A leader is not necessarily the best looking, most talented or greatest athlete. A Christian leader is someone empowered by the Holy Spirit, available to be used, and faithful to the calling of Christ. I want to know my lay staff is studying the Word of God and spending time in prayer on a regular basis.

2. A love for and a desire to be with teenagers. This is a given. It doesn't make much sense if you are involved in Youth Ministry but don't love teenagers.

"More than just loving teenagers they must love people, all people. I have worked with leaders who are great with teens but don't get along well with their adult peers. You want leaders with a good reputation among everybody, young and old." J.T. Bean

3. They must be a person of integrity. It must be someone you can trust. A person who speaks the truth and chooses to do what is right. You want a staff that believes in and refuses to compromise on the truths of scripture.

4. You want your staff to be emotionally stable. You can't have staff

Who are up and down emotionally like a yo-yo. I understand people have issues, problems, and needs, but I say to them, get healthy and then join us. Emotional instability will be a huge distraction to the teenager and limit the staff person's effectiveness. Be careful of people who want to be staff to meet needs in their own lives.

5. They need be teachable. We all need to be life-long learners. You want staff who are open to new ideas, staff who want to be on the cutting edge of youth ministry and are willing to make changes.

Here is a word to you who are lay staff and reading this part.
First of all, thanks for buying my book! Then, secondly, you need to follow your leader. A new Youth Pastor will make changes and do things differently than your previous Youth Pastor. Because something is different doesn't mean it is wrong. You resist the change because it isn't what you are used to or you don't think it is the best. But if God has called this person to the position then you need to support them. Sometimes a Youth Pastor fails because their lay staff rebels. It's not that he or she is doing anything wrong; it's just the volunteer staff doesn't like it. A word of warning: don't do this to your Youth Pastor. When you rebel against the person God has placed in that position, you have rebelled against God. That is something God takes very seriously. Don't ever put yourself in opposition to the Lord and what He is trying to do. You need to be submissive and supportive.
"Everyone must submit himself to the governing authorities, for there is no authority except that which God has established. The authorities that exist have been established by God. Consequently, he who rebels against the authority is rebelling against what God has instituted and those who do so will bring judgment on themselves." (Romans 13:1-2).

"Obey your leaders and submit to their authority. They keep watch over you as men must give an account. Obey them so their work will be a joy, not a burden, for that would be of no advantage to you." (Hebrews 13:17).

There are exceptions to submitting and obeying. You would disobey them if they contradicted God's Word, got involved in sin or put lives in jeopardy. But other than that, you must be supportive, submissive and obedient. If you can't, for some reason, then you need to get out of the youth ministry and don't try to drive the Youth Pastor out.

6. They must be gifted in the area they want to serve. I have talked about three areas staff can serve in; relational, task, and vision. Because a volunteer wants to serve in a certain area doesn't necessarily mean they are gifted in that area. Make it very clear what gifts are needed to serve in the different areas. Observe your volunteer staff and if they are not gifted for what they want to do then move them for the good of the teens and ministry. In the long run they will be happier, more effective and last longer if you get them into their area of giftedness. Meet with your lay staff, if possible one to one, and ask them some questions that will help you to better understand and evaluate them.
- Ask questions about them as a person; Family, work, background, interests, etc.
- What has been their role in the Youth Ministry?
- Tell me what you see are your strengths?
- What do you see are your weaknesses?
- What has been your biggest frustration with this youth ministry?

As you talk with them and observe them over the next several weeks, you'll need to make some decisions. Your staff will fall into one of four areas.
- They are doing a great job. They are in the right place, doing what they are gifted to do and doing it with excellence.
- They are doing a good job but need some help, more training and development. They are in the right position and with encouragement they can be do a great job.
- They are in the wrong position but can be effective in youth ministry if we get them in the right position. Make the change.
- They need to go. Their gifts do not lend itself to youth ministry and you need to encourage them to get plugged into a different ministry in the church. You need to be

firm but you do this with love, out of a desire for what is best for them.

7. They need to be a team player. You want everyone to be on the same page, working for the same goals, fulfilling the vision and mission for the church and youth ministry. You need to keep them informed and they must be gaining feedback from you about the job they are doing. Anytime your staff does anything you can respond to them in one of three ways.
- Compliment them. You are noticing what they are doing and you are reinforcing those things. By building their self esteem, they are feeling better about themselves and the Youth Ministry as a whole.
- Constructive Criticism. This can be very encouraging and helpful. You give your staff the freedom to fail and help them to learn from their mistakes. You are saying, "Here is what you did wrong and this is what you need to do next time." But if all you do is criticize without complimenting them you will end up discouraging them.
- Silence. This is the worst thing you can do and I should know because I have fallen into this trap over and over again with my staff and students.

Here is what happens with me. I am a confronter, so I am quick to approach someone when they make a mistake or I will praise someone who does something outstanding. But what do I say to someone who consistently does well? Nothing? That is not much motivation for that person to continue to do well. Plus, how do they feel when I compliment other people but not them? I am expecting them to be self-motivated and to not need my feedback. No, I am setting a bad example and I risk discouraging people and causing them to give up. I want to give them feedback, mostly complimentary, so they want to continue doing well. I go back to the need to catch them being good. When I see them do something good, I compliment them immediately. Unlike criticism I do not need to pull them aside, I can compliment them in front of others. The more immediate it is the more powerful it becomes because I am reinforcing the behavior in the moment. I want to be very specific so they know exactly what they are doing right. That way they can continue.

If I say, "Good job Mary." It's nice but it's so general that it can apply to anything. Instead I say, "Good job Mary, thank you for setting up those chairs." I have caught Mary doing something well and I have complimented her specifically and immediately.

In the past have I have not said much to the person making progress but isn't where he needs to be? Why? Because I am waiting for him to get there before I say anything. I need to look at it from his perspective. He is trying to do better. I noticed when he did poorly and now he wants to know if I will notice when he improves. If I don't, he gets discouraged and will stop trying. I must remind myself to compliment even if it is just a slight improvement, because it is an improvement. Don't just look at how far they must go but look at how far they have come. They won't do everything right, but they can get better and I need to notice when they take even just one positive step.

As part of the team I must empower them to make decisions within their areas of responsibility. Giving them opportunities to evaluate and give feed back. On occasion have brainstorming sessions and encourage them to think outside the box. Here are some questions.
- ➢ What's the next step we need to take as a youth ministry?
- ➢ If you were youth Pastor what would you do?
- ➢ When it comes to our programs, what do we do well, where can we improve, should we add anything?

You'll get some responses where you will smile, say "Thank you" and think, "That was so stupid." But you will also get some great ideas you can begin to incorporate.

8. They must make a commitment. You need people who are going to be involved and stay involved. You don't want someone who is hit and miss. You've got to have people who you can count on to be where they need to be and do what they need to do. Clearly explain to them what you need. Show them a job description. Every position should have a job description with responsibilities, expectations, and hours per week needed to fulfill those responsibilities. Make sure you have them fill out an application.

Then I say to them, "You see the expectations and responsibilities so tell me what you can do, commit to it and then be faithful to your commitment."

9. They must have a sense of humor. If you're going to work with teenagers you have to be able to laugh. I have so many experiences with teens where I laughed until I cried. Laughing together creates unity. It wins hearts and draws you to one another.

"Humor is to life what shock absorbers are to automobiles." Jonathan Swift

I am not a good golfer. Once, a long time ago, I broke 100. So, I was out with three teenage guys, playing a par 3, over water. The first guy stepped up and hit it into the water. The next guy took more time, concentrated and put it right in the middle of the.... pond. Now it was my turn to hit, I swung, head down, nice follow through...hole in one! O.K. just kidding, I also put it right into the water. The fourth guy had been smack talking us and now he is going to teach us how to hit a golf ball. He addressed the ball, beautiful swing and the ball arched over the water and onto the green! Very impressive, except his club slipped out of his hand and went right into the middle of the pond. The three of us were on the ground, we were laughing so hard.

I took my students to the boundary waters to go canoeing for a week. One of my guys was helping with breakfast. He had a big pan of biscuits in one hand and a pan of bacon in the other. There was a pan of eggs sitting on a rock. He went to step over the eggs, slipped, threw both the biscuits and bacon over his head and sat down on the eggs. It is wonderful to be able to laugh together with students and staff. These kinds of shared experiences will draw you closer as staff and students.

You can never have enough solid volunteer staff. Ask God to raise up a team so together you can see the Lord work through you to change the lives of teenagers!

THINK ABOUT IT:
1. Do you have enough volunteer staff?
2. What can you do to recruit more?
3. What qualities are important to you in your volunteer staff?

THOUGHTS FROM OTHERS:
 "Very few men are wise by their own counsel, or learn by their own teaching. For he that was only taught by himself had a fool for his master." Ben Johnson

"A good example is the best sermon." Anon.

"Example is not the main thing in influencing others. It is the only thing." Albert Schweitzer

"A sense of humor can help you overlook the unattractive, tolerate the unpleasant, cope with the unexpected, and smile through the unbearable." Moshe Waldoks

THOUGHT:
"BUILD YOUR VOLUNTEER STAFF"

"To teach is to learn twice." Joseph Joubert

We need to be developing a volunteer staff so together you can minister to the students. To build your staff means you invest your life in theirs. Be faithful, develop a team and let God grow your ministry. Here are some tips on developing both adult and student leaders.

1. It will take time. You must commit to meeting together regularly. Time together is critical because it builds unity. You need to be of one mind as a staff and to have the same vision, direction and purpose. Your staff needs to feel like they know where the ministry is going and they are adequately prepared and trained to do what God has called, and you have asked, them to do. There will be a number of ingredients that go into the meeting. Here are some possibilities.
- Worship together. One person on a guitar is all you need.
- Pray together for individual students, the ministry and each other.
- Testimony. What is God doing through the ministry and in the lives of the teenagers and themselves? Sometimes, as we grow, we don't really hear everything that is going on. Listening to what God is doing builds excitement, enthusiasm and is a huge encouragement.
- Teach. Giving them some of your pearls of wisdom and insight into teenagers and ministering to them.
- Inform. Give them all the information they need. Keep the vision and purpose always before them. Never assume they know. What happens when you assume? Things fall through the cracks, people get frustrated, stuff doesn't get done and you get frustrated.

2. Don't be threatened. Do not be threatened by people who are very capable. You are teammates, not competitors. I am sure you <u>used</u> to be a really good athlete. Aren't all youth Pastors great athletes in their own minds? When your teammate did something really well did you get upset? No, you were excited because you are a team all working toward the same goal - winning! So, in youth ministry you are excited when teens feel closer to one of your staff than they do to you. You rejoice when one of them hits a home run speaking. Because you all have the same goal - to see teens become fully devoted followers of Christ.

You need to trust your staff. If you can't trust them then they should not be part of the team. If you trust them then you will be open and vulnerable with them. You will treat them with respect. Always assume the best about your staff unless they prove otherwise. Surround yourself with lay staff who are Godly, talented, gifted and capable. Then set them loose to do what God is calling them to do, what they are gifted at, and the responsibilities you have given them. If you are threatened by these types of people then MAYBE you don't belong in Youth Ministry.

3. Build them up. One of the biggest motivators is encouragement. You can't compliment your staff too much. Talk to them one-on-one and express your thankfulness to God for their lives and the impact they are having on the ministry. Build them up in front of the students. Give them favor in the eyes of the teens. When you do this, you are honoring them. Your staff and the teenagers will do better, feel better and live better when you encourage them and build them up. Your staff and students will reflect the belief, trust and confidence that you show them. They will also reflect the lack of belief, trust and confidence.

4. Delegate. Delegate and allow your staff to take responsibility, make decisions and complete the ministry to which they have been called. If you don't delegate then either you or your staff are incompetent. Or maybe you are a micro manager who is very bad in youth ministry. Let your staff make decisions appropriate to their level of responsibility. You want them to know you trust them. If you don't trust them then either you have them assigned to the wrong responsibility or they shouldn't be working with teens at all.

5. Empower. You are drawing out of them their God given gifts, talents and abilities. Then you set them free to become everything

Jesus Christ has created them to be by using those gifts to serve the Lord in the ministry.

6. Let them lead from their strengths. Don't put your lay staff or student leaders in a place of responsibility where their weaknesses will prevail over their strengths. In other words, don't try to pound a square peg into a round hole. Don't put someone in a position where you set them up to fail. I don't care how desperate you are to fill the spot. That borders on abuse, to put someone in a position they are either not gifted for or not adequately trained to do. Keep in mind you get energy from doing what you are gifted to do but you can get drained when you aren't in your area of giftedness.

7. Give them the freedom to fail. You will fail, they will fail, I fail, everyone fails. Let them know they have the freedom. But you want to make sure they learn from those failures. Be sure you correct your staff in private, never in front of other staff or students. If you confront them in front of others then you will embarrass and humiliate them. You also run the risk of embittering them.

When you are talking to them in private make sure you are very specific about how they failed and then be just as specific about what they need to do next time. Be sure you are seeing the things they are doing well too. Look for opportunities to build them up and compliment them.

**"When I lovingly confront a staff I ask, 'What was your thinking process to move you to the decision you made? Help me understand how you came to this decision'."
Marvin Jacobo**

When you lovingly confront them stay away from "why" questions. This goes for the students as well. If you ask "why" questions what are you asking for? Excuses!

- ➢ You ask, "Why didn't you get that done on time?
  - "Because I thought you would remind me."
  - "Because I didn't think it was important."

- "Because I had so much come up last minute."
- "Because my dog died."
- "Because aliens tried to kidnap me!"

Excuses are stupid and irritating. It doesn't really help to get us anywhere. That usually either leads to a lame response from us like, "Sorry and I hope aliens stop bothering you," or because of frustration you get mad which can lead to an ugly conflict.

Instead, try asking "how" and "what" questions. "What could you do next time to make sure this gets done?" or "How can you make sure this is done on time?" What if they make excuses even when you are asking a "how" or "what" questions? That is what they have always done and it's their natural response when they have blown it. You just keep going back to those "how" and "what" questions. For example:
- You: "I see you didn't get the multi-media done. How can you make sure it gets done next time?"
- Them: "I had all this stuff come up last minute and I didn't have time."
- You: "I understand but what can you do so this doesn't happen again?"
- Them: "The film clip, you wanted, wasn't where I thought it was,"
- You: "Sorry to hear that but how can you get the multi-media done on time?"
- Them: "Aliens! There were aliens everywhere!!"
- You: "That must have been...have been...anyway, what can you do this week so that the multi-media is done by Sunday?"
- Them: "I need to start on Monday rather than Sunday."
- You: "That is a great idea."

When you ask those "What" and "How" questions you are letting your staff and students be part of the problem solving. When they come up with a good idea be sure you compliment them and encourage them. This way you are teaching them to take responsibility rather than make excuses. A word of warning, this will take practice. Chances are you are in the rut of asking "why" questions. Here is a bonus, this works really well with your own children too.

8. Communicate effectively. Spell out their responsibilities and expectations. Make sure everyone is on the same page. Many problems occur because of a lack of, or break down in, communication. So over communicate. I cannot stress how important this is for everyone around you. Parents, teens, staff, everyone needs to know what is going on. If they don't feel like they are in the loop then they will become frustrated and begin to lash out at you. This will then make you frustrated.

Be sensitive to different styles of communication happening within your staff and in the youth group. You will find two basic types of communicators.
- Cognitive communicators - They want to deal with the facts. They want to know the bottom line. "What's the point; I don't want a story, just get to the facts. If you need something fixed emotionally, spiritually or physically then come to me. If you need a shoulder to cry on then go someplace else".
- Emotional communicators - They want to deal with feelings. "How do you feel; how do I feel and how do we feel?" These will be great people to open up with and cry on their shoulders but they aren't good at coming up with lists.

This will help you soooo much in communicating effectively. Always respond to emotion with emotion and fact with fact. For example, you are at camp and one of your staff says to you, "I am so frustrated because the teens wouldn't settle down in the cabin. I am hurt and I feel like giving up." How do you respond? "Trust in the Lord with all your heart...!"

Or a teen comes up to you and says, "I had the worst morning. I couldn't do the high ropes course. I was so afraid and Jennifer laughed at me and I feel like a total failure." How do we respond, "Well, don't do the high ropes course anymore."

In both situations, we have responded to emotion with fact. The first thing they will think is, 'You don't really understand me." If you do it enough they will eventually say, "You don't really care about me." That's not true but it is how you come across.

You respond to their emotion with emotion by saying something like, "I would be frustrated too if the students had treated me that way, I am so sorry." or "The high ropes can be really scary and that must have hurt when Jennifer laughed." When you respond to emotion with emotion you say you understand and you open them to the truth.

In the same way if someone comes up and says, "I can't come to staff meeting on Tuesday because my work is sending me on a trip." Don't respond by saying, "You don't care." It has nothing to do with the emotion of caring. The fact is their work is sending them on a trip. Responding to emotion with emotion and fact with fact will help you to connect with others and they will feel understood and cared for.

Effective communication is all about listening as well as talking. James 1:19 says, "My dear Brothers, take note of this: Everyone should be quick to listen, slow to speak and slow to become angry." You will never truly understand your staff or students if you aren't taking the time to listen to them.

Every communicated message has three parts:
- 7% are the words
- 38% is your voice inflection, volume, how you say it.
- 55% is nonverbal. Facial expression, body posture, what they are doing with their hands, etc.

You must listen to what people are saying to you beyond words. If you don't, then you will miss out on significant communication. For example, James was going to do his testimony on Wednesday night but you have so much going on you decide to postpone him till later in the month.
- You: "James, we have so much going on this Wednesday I am wondering if I can move you back a few weeks?"
- James: He lets out a sigh, puts his hands in his pockets,

> shrugs his shoulders, wrinkles his brow and says, "Yea, sure, that's fine."
> You: "Wow, praise the Lord, thanks James."

If that was your response then you haven't listened to him at all. Seven percent of the message said, "That's fine," but ninety-three percent said, "I am really disappointed and discouraged."

You walk up to Sara and ask, "How are you doing?" She doesn't make eye contact, folds her arms in front of her, rocks back and forth nervously and replies, "Great!" Chances are Sara isn't great and there is something going on. But if you aren't really listening you're going to miss the message.

What else can enhance your communication so you can better understand and be understood?
> Trust. If people don't trust you then they aren't going to open up. What builds trust? Time and consistent behavior over a period of time. What can take you months to build can be destroyed in a moment. How? By betraying a confidence and living opposite of what you are professing. Students want to open up to someone who sincerely cares about them but they will first look to see if they can trust you.

> Time. It takes time for students and staff to open up. Before I have a strong relationship developed with a person I usually discover the first thing a person brings up may not be what they really want to talk about. They just want to see how I am going to react. If I act shocked or come off insensitive then they are going to shut up and not go any further with me. I need to give them confidence so they want to open up to me. I do this by making eye contact, giving them focused attention, seeking to understand and being patient. If I'm not patient and willing to take the time then I might miss out on what they really want to talk about. I remind myself if I am too busy to spend time with students then I am way too busy and have my priorities mixed up.

I was speaking at a youth conference and was heading back to my room to relax a little right before dinner. I wanted to read over my notes before speaking later in the evening. All afternoon I have been hanging out with students. A girl walks up to me and asked if she could talk with me. I am really tempted to say, "I would love to but I am tired and I need to get ready to speak and could we talk later?" But something, I know now it was the Lord, told me to take the time with her. I said sure and we stepped off to the side. I asked her, "What did you want to talk about? This sweet girl, a sophomore in high school looks at me and says, "I want to become a Christian." Wow, how great is that? Now I believe God is in control and He was calling this girl to Himself, so if I had put her off He would have led her to someone else. But that's the point, it would have been someone else and I would have missed out on the privilege and joy of seeing her step from darkness into light!

> Being vulnerable. If we are going to get beyond the surface then we need to be vulnerable. That starts with you being open and honest. It's you risking and sharing some of your struggles and failures. As you are open with staff and students they will be open with you. You want to show wisdom and discernment about what you share and with whom. A good rule of thumb is to share more in generalities and don't go into all the details. You might say, "I struggled with my relationships with the opposite sex at times. There were some things I did I regret now." Don't talk specifically about the things you regret. It will be easier for others to open up to you if you help them to feel comfortable. How can you do that? One way is to get them talking.

When a person first sits down to talk to me, especially students, I try to put them at ease by asking them questions that are non-threatening. I do this especially if I don't really have a relationship with this person. Things like...
> Where do you live?
> Do you have any brothers or sisters?
> Any pets? What are their names?
> Are you into sports, music, drama, computer, etc.?
> What did you want to talk about?

By asking them some questions and getting them talking I can see them relax and start to become more comfortable.
- ➢ Give focused attention. You need to make eye contact with them and not be looking around. Giving focused attention says they are someone special, significant and what they are saying is important to you. At that moment, they are the most important person and you are not going to let others distract you from them.

9. Be relational. This means you are a people person. You care about the students and staff and want to make sure they are doing well emotionally, spiritually and physically. You have time for others and you are a good listener. I told staff and students my door was always open and they could come by me anytime.

If a task is most important then you will have the tendency to overlook, neglect and use people to accomplish the task. You will not maintain staff over the long haul and you will discover a lot of turnover happening. People will feel abused, like they are something rather than somebody.

How can you become more relational?
- ➢ Learn their names and call them by their name.
- ➢ Force yourself to stop and talk with those on your staff. Remember everyone's favorite subject is themselves. So, ask them questions.
- ➢ Compliment people and build them up. That will win you favor and people will be drawn toward you.
- ➢ Every once in a while, text, e-mail or call.
- ➢ During a meeting make it a point to walk up to everyone of your staff to greet them if possible. If your lay staff has grown to over 100 that might be impossible.

Take the time to build a team. Together God will use you to impact the students. You will be able to touch and reach more students than you could ever do on your own. God would like to grow your ministry but I don't believe He will do it until you start multiplying yourself in other adults. It is a balancing act between time with students and time with volunteer staff but it will pay off as more students are cared for and nurtured.

THINK ABOUT IT:
1. Do you spend enough time with your volunteer staff?
2. Are you delegating and allowing your staff to lead from their strengths?
3. Does your staff have the freedom to fail?

THOUGHT:
"YOU CAN BE BETTER ORGANIZED"

"Many Youth Pastors act without a plan. Then they complain about a lack of support from others. It is so much easier to find support if you are crossing all your T's" Scott Groff

This may not be a strength for you and you may not like this part of the ministry. You're not task oriented or very good with detail. You are relational and would rather be hanging with people. I understand because I am the same way. But I improved in this area and you can improve too.

You can be disorganized and still do well with the students because you're relational and fun to hang with. But remember, the students didn't hire you and they won't be the ones who fire you. Every job has its pros and cons. There are some things you won't like doing but you must do it well. Here are some simple things you can begin to do which will help you to be more organized.

1. Write things down. You think you will remember but you won't.

2. Return phone calls immediately. People are important and they get frustrated when you don't call them back. You are communicating to them, "I don't care." That is not the kind of message you want to be sending to the very people, or peoples children, you are trying to impact. This also applies to E-mails.

You can leave a message on your phone telling people where you are and what you are up to each day. People will be patient if they know you are out of town or at an all-day staff meeting.

3. At the beginning of the day list all the things you need to get done. Put them in order of priority. Now work through the list and finish each item before you move on. When you don't complete things then everything starts to pile up. We get frustrated when we have too many balls in the air. Everything is half done, more stuff is screaming for your attention and your stress level is through the roof. Whatever you don't get done move over to the next day.

4. Delegate whenever you can. Remember, you get energy by doing what you are gifted to do and you get drained from doing what you are not gifted to do. What can you pass on to someone else? If you can delegate it than do it but make sure it gets done. That means you must follow up with the person. Don't give it to them and assume it will happen. That leads to distress and frustration on your part when it isn't done. Remember, you must inspect what you expect.

5. Show up five minutes early for all your appointments. When you arrive early you are showing people respect. Don't make anyone wait for you. I hate being late. One of my pet peeves is when a person shows up late for an appointment with me. They are saying what they are doing is more important than meeting with me. OK, that may be, but then at least call me and tell me you are going to be late. Having said this, let me now apologize to Bob MacRae, my accountability partner, who I have stood up too many times.

6. Ask for help and learn from those who are administrative. Borrow ideas from their systems that will help you. Talk to others who are doing well in this area. Seek to get better in this area by being willing to learn.

7. Keep your office relatively clean. I know, a clean desk is a sign of a sick mind, but when your office is becoming a pile upon a pile upon another pile then it leads to lost stuff and disorganization. If you have parents who come to visit you in the office, they are not going to be impressed with your mess. Throw things away like mail, advertisements, broken ping pong paddles and anything else you can part with. Some of you are pack rats and never throw anything away. In a relatively short amount of time your office will be out of control and look like a disaster area. Try cleaning up your office at the end of each day. Put stuff away and if you do it daily it becomes manageable.

"The difference between ordinary and extraordinary is that little extra effort." Homer

8. Turn things in on time. When you have a dead line then get it in when it is supposed to be done. People will be gracious the first time you get something in late but if it becomes a habit you will alienate others.

9. If your Senior Pastor asks you to do something make it your top priority. Do it right away and then report back when it is done. I don't care how much stuff I had to do and how important things were if my Senior Pastor asked me to do something it became my top priority.

I had just been hired as the Youth Pastor at Temple Baptist Church and Gordan Hanstad is my Senior Pastor. We are having out first staff meeting and all the Pastors are gathered in his office. He is giving out some assignments and I have pen and paper ready to write down whatever he wants me to do. He gets to me and says, "Greg if the rapture occurs I want you to handle the preaching." I start to write it down and then I think…what? I look up and the whole room busts out laughing. I would do whatever the Pastor wanted me to do and I would do it immediately, but I am not preaching after the rapture!

10. Hire an administrative secretary/assistant. Now I understand many of you are laughing right now because you do not have that kind of authority, you are in a small Church and there is no money. So here is what you do. Get down on your hands and knees and say, "PLEASE, I need help administratively even if it is part time. Then I will be freed up to do all the relational things which will help this ministry to continue to grow."

There might be a parent who would help you out in this area. What can they do for you?
- ➢ Organize your work load.
- ➢ Answer simple, standard questions from parents and students.
- ➢ Screen phone calls.
- ➢ Remind you of calls, appointments and promises.
- ➢ Protect you. When you meet with members of the opposite

> sex they can check in with you every so often. They can keep you accountable.
> A good sounding board for you to bounce ideas off of.
> Take care of a variety of administrative tasks.
> Pray for you.

If you get this person, drop to your knees and thank the Lord like I did. Then keep in mind you want to make their job a joy and not a burden so they will want to stick around. If you are going to keep this wonderful administrative secretary what do you need to do for them?

> Get them things ahead of time. Do not be last minute.
> Communicate with them regularly and often. For you who are a part of a team and have a full time administrative assistant it is very important for you to communicate with them on a regular basis. We would meet as a youth ministry team every Monday from 9:00am to 1:00pm which would include lunch. Four hours is a lot of time but it is part of team building and the youth secretary/administrator was part of all of it.
> Verbally affirm them and let them know when they are doing a good job. That should be easy because they are saving your neck on a daily basis. Thank you, Sandra Rodgers and Kendra Johnson, you are the best! You saved me on many occasions and made me look good because of your administrative skills. You were competent, highly skilled and best of all a friend. I can not thank you enough!
> Let them know where you are going and when you will be back. That way they can speak knowledgably when people ask them questions. Otherwise you make them look uninformed and stupid.

11. Work ahead. I would take the full-time staff away for a weekend each year and we would plan the upcoming year. It is great to know things are set for a year down the road. It takes a lot of weight off your shoulders. You can always flex and do things differently but at least you have a foundation and direction for what you are going to do.

"What counts is not the number of hours you put in, but how much you put in the hours." Henry Ford

12. Learn as you go. After an event write down everything that needed to happen for it to run smoothly, hindsight is 20-20. There will be problems and things you wish would and wouldn't have happened. Learn from the mistakes, make a list of what needs to happen next time. Now you are set for next year or next week, you've got the details nailed and you know what needs to happen. You will discover things will start improving and getting better as time goes by. People will like that! You will like that!

Just putting these twelve things into effect will help a lot with organization. Are there other things you can do? Sure, but this gives you a place to start. As you do these things you will build trust and confidence in those around you. That allows everyone to relax and people begin to become more and more positive. Now you are becoming more organized and people feel like they can depend upon you. You are doing what you said you would do, being where you said you would be on time, returning your phone calls and keeping your promises.

If I can do it, then you can do it, because I do not have the gift of administration. This is something I have worked on for years. It is an area I have improved in but I still don't do it great. One of the reasons is because I don't like doing it, I would rather be out with students talking and hanging out. But just because I don't like it doesn't mean I can't do it or shouldn't do it. We all have things about our jobs we like and don't like. So, do what you need to do even if you don't like doing it.

"Come on, I am pulling for you. We're all in this together." Red Green

THINK ABOUT IT:
1. What is the next step you can take to get more organized?
2. Who could you ask for help in this area?
3. What do you need to delegate?

THOUGHTS FROM OTHERS:
"Great things are not done by impulse, but by a series of small things brought together." Vincent van Gogh

"Victory is won not in miles, but in inches. Win a little now, hold your ground, and later win a little more." Louis L'Amour

"Nobody makes a greater mistake than he who did nothing because he could only do a little." Edmund Burke

THOUGHT:
"AVOID SOME OF THE ROOKIE MISTAKES"

"Learn by experience-preferably other people's." F.B. Meyer

We all make rookie mistakes when we start out in youth ministry. Here are some common pit falls that can get you in some hot water with parents and others. Even though I will try to point these out, chances are you will still have to learn some of them the hard way. Why do we have to go through the rookie mistakes and why can't we just learn it now? Because nothing teaches like experience. It leaves a mark you never forget. As you read this it may sounds like I am saying some of the same stuff over again. That is because I am! What I am trying to say to you is, "THIS IS IMPORTANT." That is why I repeat it! So here are some rookie mistakes you should try to avoid.

1. Lack of communication. You can't communicate too much to parents about what is happening. Parents will get upset if they feel they are in the dark about what is going on or if they are always hearing of stuff last minute.

Here is what I would do to try to communicate with parents:
- Have regular parents' meetings where we would talk about where we have been and where we are going. This also gives parents a chance to ask me questions.
- Announcements in the bulletin on Sunday Morning. There was a small section for youth ministry announcements.
- Set up a web site with information, release forms and details.
- A quarterly parents' newsletter including a three-month calendar with what was coming up, tips for parents, spot light on lay staff, etc.
- A hotline voicemail box you can update weekly with program details.

2. Disorganization. I have already talked about this in some detail. But let me remind you again people like parents, your youth ministry team, Pastors and even the students will get very frustrated with you if you are continually disorganized. It means you are flying by the seat of your pants, not communicating well, planning stuff last minute, forgetting appointments, losing stuff and driving everyone around you crazy.

When I started in Youth Ministry disorganized was my middle name. So here is one more idea to improve in this area. Marry a wonderful spouse who is very organized. Thanks Bonnie!

3. Not following through. You tell people you are going to do something but it never happens. Your word needs to mean something. Never make idol threats or empty promises. If you say you are going to do it then...DO IT! A frustration is when you say you are going to be back at the church at a certain time, after an event, and you are always late. Pretty soon people don't believe you. When you give a time, people add an hour to it before they show up. Then you're frustrated because you are stuck waiting at the church with these students. Set up a phone tree or a hot line where people can be updated on times of arrivals. If you say you are going to call someone, call them. If you say you are going to change something, change it. Do what you have promised you're going to do. Your word is your bond.

4. Showing a movie or clip you have not previewed. I cannot even begin to tell you how many youth Pastors have gotten in trouble by doing this. I don't care who recommends it or how good they say it is or how they just recently watched it and it was fine. If they are not in youth ministry they are not watching it with the same concerns you would have. Either you or a trusted staff needs to preview something before you show it. Don't even trust your memory. A disaster waiting to happen is when you say, "I saw the movie six months ago and I THINK it will be fine."

I made this rookie mistake. I showed a movie on a bus, on the way to snow camp that I hadn't previewed but was assured it would be fine. There in the middle of the movie, they said the mother of all swear words, they dropped the F-bomb. The bus went dead quiet and everyone was looking at me. Don't repeat my blunder. It can be funny to sit around as Youth Pastors and tell stories of DVD blunders we showed in youth group and how we've lived to deeply regret it! But at the time it isn't funny at all.

5. Off color humor. It is not worth it if you are going to offend. I find this usually happens informally, when we are just hanging out rather than being a part of a teaching time. Everyone is laughing and you keep going and eventually you step over the line. Then they go home and tell their parents and then you are in trouble.

6. How you handle injuries. Anytime you are anywhere and a student gets hurt, beyond the normal scrapes and bruises, you need to call the parents and inform them. If I have to take a student to the emergency room, even if it turns out there is no break or serious problem, I call the parents. When it comes to injuries, it is always better to err on the side of caution. I would rather take a student to the emergency room and have them tell me their ankle is fine than to send a student home from camp with a cracked ankle. I don't make any decision about an emergency room visit based on the teen's opinion. What will they always say to me? "I'm fine, I'm OK, really, I don't need to go to the emergency room." Their arm could be almost severed off and they say everything is OK. Then you have the other extreme, with the student who is always getting hurt and makes everything a crisis.

Garrett, one of my sons, went to a summer camp years ago. He received a rather serious cut on his face which needed stitches. The camp nurse decided not to take him to the emergency room. She decided to put a butterfly Band-Aid on it instead. It left Garrett with a permanent scar on his face. Bonnie and I were not happy. I called the camp and let them know I wasn't happy. Better to be safe than sorry. When it comes to injuries try to think like a Mom.

7. Not keeping your Pastor informed. You never want your Senior Pastor caught off guard by something that happened in Youth Ministry which he didn't already know about. If it is serious, if there are problems, if parents are apt to complain about something let him know. He can be your biggest supporter but it is hard for him to do if he is caught off guard.

When I served with Pastor John Crocker I asked, "How much do you want to be involved or informed about youth ministry?" He said to me, "Not at all. Greg, I trust you." Wow, John was a great Senior Pastor to serve with. I had tremendous freedom. I didn't have to keep John informed but I choose to keep him up to date. He was one of my biggest supporters. Keeping your Senior Pastor informed with the Youth Ministry is to your benefit.

8. Not being under authority. You need to keep yourself under authority to the Senior Pastor, Assistant Pastor, commission, board, etc. When you get out from under authority you are moving way out on the limb and you are a heart beat away from a major fall. Why wouldn't you want the benefits of being under authority? Here are some big pluses for being under authority.
- Godly individuals who you can go to for insight and wisdom.
- Developing friendships with these people.
- Having a group that will stand with you. Someone to support you when things get hard or people are upset with you.
- These people want you to succeed.

9. Not teaching the Word of God. Humor and stories are great but the Word of God is life changing. Don't ever compromise or water down God's word. The Bible needs to be the meat of your message and stories the dessert. Get those mixed up and you become sick spiritually. I want my children to sit under the ministry of a Youth Pastor who teaches the Word of God!

10. Trashing the past. Don't ever slam the previous Youth Pastor because there are individuals in the group who are still loyal to them and you end up alienating them. Do not put down past programs from previous ministries because there will be people who were impacted by those programs and loved them no matter how pathetic they seem to be. You can make the changes without attacking or putting down the past people or programs.

11. Hearing only one side. When a student comes to you and tells you something remember you are only getting one side of the story. Do not take any rash action until you have checked everything out and heard all sides. "He who answers before listening, that is his folly and his shame," Proverbs 18:13. There are many teens who struggle with lying. You can end up looking very bad and getting yourself in trouble if you act before listening to all sides.

"I won't believe everything your child says about you without checking and don't believe everything your child says about me or this ministry without checking."
Dan Howard.

12. Sins that disqualify you from ministry. There are sins that can disqualify us from ministry. The sin that kills you is the one you know is wrong, the Holy Spirit warns you not to go there and then you do it anyway. Psalm 19:13a says, "Keep your servant from willful sins, may they not rule over me..." These are not just mistakes but this is a choice on your part to do what is wrong and to put yourself, the ministry and God's reputation in jeopardy. These sins include...
- Opposite sex.
  - Isolating yourself with them. Being in a vehicle or room alone together
  - Flirting with them.
  - Touching them in a romantic way.
  - Being sexually involved

- Addiction to pornography.
  - Most of us have struggled in this area, myself included but we can't give into it. Once you begin to drink deeply of pornography you become spiritually and emotionally poisoned. It impacts your thought life and how you view your spouse and students in your youth ministry. Your relationship with Jesus Christ suffers. It negatively impacts your self worth. You give Satan a foothold in your life.

- Lying.
  - God hates a lying tongue.
  - You speak Satan's native tongue.
  - People can no longer trust you.
  - You show yourself to be a person who lacks character.

"I would rather be the man who bought the Brooklyn Bridge than the man who sold it." Will Rogers

- Embezzlement.
  - Taking money from the church and using it personally, even though you have good intentions on paying it back. Don't take camp or event money, have one of your staff or your secretary handle the cash and remove the temptation.

- Drunkenness.
  - It is a very poor example to the students. What we do, even in moderation a teen will do in excess.

- Breaking the law.
  - Using illegal drugs.
  - Committing a crime other than a traffic violation, unless the traffic violation involves the church van or bus loaded with teenagers and you put their lives in jeopardy.

Sin is a terrible thing. For the wages of sin it death. Death to the youth ministry, death to you spiritually and death to the students emotionally when they find out what you did. It's not worth it. Don't go there. Don't do it!

Cut back on the rookie mistakes and you'll feel a lot better but at the same time give yourself the freedom to fail. Some of you are way too hard on yourself. No one is tougher on you than you are. It is not healthy and I know from first hand experience. When I made a mistake, I would feel bad for days. I took criticism way too personally and would beat myself up with it. A guilty Youth Pastor is not an effective Youth Pastor. You thankfully receive Christ's forgiveness, forgive yourself and apologize to whoever you need to and keep going. Life is not about perfection, it is about process.

How do we learn? We learn from education, experience and exposure to more experienced leaders. Sometimes we just need to learn the hard way. We all make mistakes and show poor judgment at times. Learn from those mistakes and stop beating yourself up. It doesn't do you, the teens or God any good to keep punishing yourself.

THINK ABOUT IT:
1. Are you making any rookie mistakes now?
2. Do you keep your Pastor informed?
3. Are you staying under accountability?

THOUGHTS FROM OTHERS:
"From the errors of others, a wise man corrects his own." Pubilius Syrus

"A prudent person profits from personal experience, a wise one from the experience of others." Dr. Joseph Collins

"To make no mistake is not in the power of man; but from their errors and mistakes the wise and good learn wisdom for the future." Plutarch

"Do not blame anybody for your mistakes and failures." Bernard M. Baruch

"Any man can make mistakes, but only an idiot persists in his error." Cicero

THOUGHT:
"DISCIPLINE IS NOT A DIRTY WORD"

"Cast your cares on God; that anchor holds." Alfred Lord Tennyson

Discipline is important. If you love the students and you want to see them do well you must be willing to discipline them. We love our students enough to risk our relationship with them. To say to them, "I love you so much I am going to confront those rough edges even if you get mad at me." Some of us are afraid if we discipline a student they won't like is. Just the opposite is true. When you don't discipline you lose their respect which in turn will cost you their friendship. It is hard to be friends with someone you don't respect. So first you gain their respect and then that leads to friendship and loyalty.

Before I suggest what to do let me suggest 5 approaches NOT to take.

- **OK corral Method.** You are a stickler for law and order. You can almost see your badge and six shooter. If any student gets out of line you stride toward them. It's high noon at the OK corral and you are Wyatt Earp. You draw and shoot someone with intimidation and fear. Bull's-eye! They settle down while the rest of the room silently cheers for the underdog.

- **Ostrich Method.** Stick your head in the sand and hope it goes away. Ignore what is going on around you and keep talking as fast as you can. Ignoring the problem doesn't solve the problem; you aren't gaining their respect by pretending everything is fine. All the other teens can see everything isn't fine. Problems never go away on their own just like a car doesn't fix itself.

- **Pile it on Method.** Always keep them busy. Try to do fun stuff so they stay entertained. Go rapid fire through all kinds of activities so they don't have time to cause trouble.

But, as you will soon discover, there are certain students who always have time to cause problems. There's no way you can keep them entertained all the time. Again, you aren't dealing with the problems. Plus, you are heading for an emotional break down. Trying to keep a bunch of teens entertained is exhausting.

> **The Military Method.** If one person acts out you punish the whole class. Granted you do gain control but at the same time you create an atmosphere of hostility. People are mad at the teens messing around but they are also mad at you. There is the risk of crushing some individuals.

> **Ticking time bomb Method.** You slowly get madder and madder. The fuse is burning down. You get louder and louder and then you explode. What you end up doing is scaring everyone and giving yourself a heart attack. This can easily lead to abuse. You can end up in a physical or verbal confrontation. Then you end up saying or doing something you regret.

When I was in grade school, back when the earth's crust was cooling, things were very different. In the 6th grade I had a male teacher I loved, he was a great teacher. He wore a big ring with a large round stone. He would walk around the room and if you weren't doing what you were supposed to be doing he would smack you in the back of the head with his ring...ouch! In the 7th grade I had a male English teacher who would throw an eraser at you if you were messing around while he was teaching. That all stopped when he threw at a guy in the front, the guy ducked, and it nailed the girl behind him right in the face. Could you imagine teachers doing that now? No way, they would be fired. You too can lose your job if you touch a student in anger.

Physical abuse is touching someone in anger. What is the difference between abuse and discipline? It is the difference between emotion and intellect. When your emotions are in control it can lead to verbal and physical abuse. Abuse says I want to get even. You hurt me and now I am going to hurt you. You made me mad so I am getting revenge. Abuse, at best, only teaches them to behave when you are around.

When your intellect is in control it will lead to discipline. You are then saying, "I want what is best for you." As we discipline we are developing character and helping them to make good choices even when no one is around. Through discipline we are seeking to train, teach and develop them. We are saying "What you are doing is not appropriate and if you keep it up it will cause you problems in your future. Because I love you I want to help you to change." We discipline them and allow them to suffer some emotional pain now to save them, potentially, from greater pain down the road.

Some people say it is better to stand back and let teenagers go whenever they want to go, and do whatever they want to do, without any guidance or direction. I disagree. A teen will usually choose to do what feels good to them. But not everything that feels good is good for them. Some of the things that feel the very best to a teen can hurt them in the long run. Given the freedom many teens will...
- Stay up late,
- Sleep in late,
- Procrastinate,
- Skipping school,
- Not do homework,
- Eating poorly
- Choose destructive behaviors, etc.

Teens today need direction. They will feel secure when there is an atmosphere of love framed with discipline. They need, and most of them want boundaries. They want adults who will love them with a tough love. When we discipline in love we are following the Word of God and doing what the Lord has called us to do.

Hebrews 13:5b says, "My son, do not make light of the Lord's discipline, and do not lose heart when He rebukes you, because the Lord disciplines those He loves and He punishes everyone He accepts as a son." Also check out Proverbs 13:24. If you love your students then you will discipline them.

"You can judge the quality of their faith from the way they behave." Tertullian

Proverbs 19:18 says, "Discipline your son, for in that there is hope, do not be willing party to his death." With discipline comes hope because it holds the possibility of a changed life. To not discipline is to condemn the teenager to repeat it which can lead to spiritual, emotional and even physical death.

Proverbs 29:15 says, "The rod of correction imparts wisdom but a child left to himself disgraces his mother." Physical discipline is up to the parents not you. When you discipline in love the teenager gains wisdom. To not discipline will lead to disaster. They will make bad choices and disgrace their parents. They can also end up disgracing the youth ministry. When I first became youth Pastor I took over a group that hadn't experienced much discipline. At our first camp, along with other things too numerous to mention, a number of my guys threw knives at the brand-new wood paneling in their cabin. One knife went all the way through the panel. So, they ripped the paneling off the wall to get back their knife. The camp was not happy and they brought disgrace on our youth ministry and the church as a whole.

Proverbs 29:17 says, "Discipline your son and he will give you peace, he will bring delight to your soul." Through discipline you will bring peace to your youth ministry. When this happens, it will bring delight to your soul.

Hebrews 12:11 says, "No discipline seems pleasant at the time, but painful. Later on, however, it produces a harvest of righteousness and peace for those who have been trained by it."

Ephesians 6:4 says, "Fathers, do not exasperate your children, instead bring them up in the training and instruction of the Lord."

Do not exasperate or provoke the teens in your youth ministry. What could you do that exasperates them? Here are seven things I would like you to avoid that will provoke and exasperate them:
- ➢ Physically abusing them.

- Being rude. Telling them to shut up, not showing them respect and talking down to them.
- Too many rules and regulations. It can discourage them and we end up nagging and being excessively critical. This is youth group and not a marine corps boot camp.
- Falsely accuse. It is good to discipline as long as you are disciplining the correct person. It is very upsetting for anyone to be disciplined for something they didn't do.
- Compare in a negative way. Never say to a teen, "Why can't you be more like him or her?" Because they aren't him or her, they are someone unique. Never transfer one child's bad reputation to their younger brother or sister.
- Make fun of them, prank them, having them the brunt of a joke or pointing out their weaknesses. Never make fun of a teen's weakness, their weight, eye sight, acne, and other areas they are struggling with.
- Embarrass. Never correct them in front of their peers, unless they are causing a major disturbance in front of the whole group.

Our house has been the hang out for Monday night football and the SuperBowl. I came home from a speaking trip, one SuperBowl Sunday, and I couldn't even get into my driveway or get a seat in the family room because of all the teens gathered. That's a good thing. Our house is also a hang out for Monday Night Football. Bonnie and I will supply soft drinks and snacks; we enjoy the teens hanging out for the game. There have been some Monday nights, when the game is bad, I decide to go to bed early. I ask my beloved child to keep things down as I hit the rack. I'm laying in bed and it sounds like a riot downstairs. Students are screaming, yelling, laughing and just being teenagers. So, I have to get up and get fully dressed because I don't want to cause emotional scaring. Then what do I do? Well, I could walk back into the family room and begin to yell at the teens about being quiet, showing respect and being kind, just like I'm not doing. But I would embarrass my children horribly and which would end any of them coming back to the house for football. Or I can walk back into the family room and motion for my child to come talk to me. Then we step into the hall and I ask them, "Do you want me to get them quiet or will you quiet them down?" They always say, "I'll do it Dad and thanks for getting fully dressed so you didn't cause emotional scarring!" Don't embarrass your teens or it will alienate and embitter them towards you.

What should you do? I know it isn't easy and some of us find it the hardest thing to do. As you think through discipline I encourage you to take these three steps.

1. Clearly define expectations and policies. Students need to know what is acceptable and what isn't. Spell it out for them. I worked for Reign Ministries. During the summers, I lead teams for Royal Servants, a missions program for teenagers. Right from the start we tell the students what the policies and expectations are. Among other things we tell them they are expected...
- To be on time for everything,
- take responsibility,
- show initiative,
- stay organized,
- don't get involved romantically,
- stay away from cliques,
- show respect and don't talk when someone else is talking,
- yield your rights,
- don't let your emotions control you,
- and don't even think about talking after you go to bed.

Don't look to set policy and expectations on your own but seek input from several sources. Talk to the Pastoral staff, boards, parents and even allow the students to have some input. This is their youth ministry and they need to own it.

2. Enforcement of these policies through an agreed upon process. The process is then agreed upon by the church leadership, your volunteer staff, parents and you. It is explained to the teens so they understand. Here is what we are going to do and how we are going to do it. Now you have set up the perimeter and let them know what is going to happen if they cross those lines. The process needs to include Matthew 18:15-17
- Verse 15: "If your brother sins against you, go and show him his fault, just between the two of you. If he listens to

you, you have won your brother over.
- ➢ Verse 16: "But if he will not listen, take one or two others along, so every matter may be established by the testimony of two or three witnesses."
- ➢ Verse 17a: "If he refuses to listen to them, tell it to the church..."
- ➢ Verse 17b: "...and if he refuses to listen even to the church, treat him as you would a pagan or a tax collector."

3. Be consistent and follow through. Teens need to know your word means something. As soon as you have set the policy one or more teens will test it. They want to know who is in charge. Are you in charge or am I in charge? At this point you better be consistent and follow through. If you don't, then your word means nothing, the policy is worthless and they will try to take charge. I have learned as a Youth Pastor and mission's leader you must be tough at the beginning and then later you can loosen up.

At the same time, you express to them they have the freedom to fail. We all fail but you want them to learn and grow from those failures so they don't have to repeat them. They need to know you discipline them because you love them. If you didn't love them you wouldn't care what they do. Take them into the Word and show them what God says about discipline.
- ➢ Proverbs 6:23: "For these commands are a lamp, this teaching is a light and the corrections of discipline are the way to life." (Proverbs 10:17)
- ➢ Proverbs 12:1: "Whoever loves discipline loves knowledge, but he who hates correction is stupid." I love this verse.
- ➢ Proverbs 13:18: "He who ignores discipline comes to poverty and shame but whoever heeds correction is honored."
- ➢ Proverbs 15:5: "A fool spurns his father's discipline, but whoever heeds correction shows prudence."
- ➢ Proverbs 15:10: "Stern discipline awaits him who leaves the path, he who hates correction will die."
- ➢ Proverbs 15:12: "A mocker resents correction, he will not consult the wise."
- ➢ Proverbs 15:32:" He who ignores discipline despises

himself, but whoever heeds correction gains understanding."

Make sure the consequences fit their actions. You don't want to overreact because you are tired or frustrated. After the consequences have occurred be sure you go back to them and break the ice. Let them know you love them and forgive them. When you choose to forgive them, you are no longer holding this offense over their heads. You let it go by no longer bringing it up. Down through the years there have been those who have gotten in trouble during a Royal Servant summer or in youth group when I was their youth Pastor. They suffered the consequences but then we move on and I don't even remember it anymore. I'll see a student several years later and they ask, "Remember when I did that? Wow, I still feel bad about that." I can honestly say, "I don't remember it at all." I don't remember, partly because I have chosen to forget and partly because I am old. Set students free from the past.

All your volunteer staff must be in agreement with the rules and the enforcement of those rules. This is a team effort and it is all about loving and helping the students. Answer any of their questions and respond to concerns and objections, but in the end, they must all agree to be a part of the discipline process. You don't want some staff addressing the problems and some staff refusing to take those steps. This will lead to frustration and division on your youth staff.

When students act out look for root causes. They are obnoxious on the outside which usually has to do with the pain, insecurities, fears and problems on the inside. Let them cool down and then talk to them. Be a listener and try to see things from their perspective. You don't have to agree with everything they say but you are seeking to understand them.

Remember your intellect needs to be in control. If your emotions are in control you will end up saying and doing things that will get you in trouble. How do you get your intellect in control of your emotions?

When I was little I would get in trouble. Wow, what a surprise! My father would call me, "Gregory!" Now, if he called, "Greg," I knew everything was OK. But if he called "Gregory" I knew I was in big trouble. He would ask me, "Gregory, did you do this?" I always wanted to say, "No, it was my brother or my sister, they did it." But I was an only child and I knew it would never work. So, I would either say yes or try to blame mom. Then he would say, "You go to your room and I will be down to talk with you in a little while." "Ohhhh," that was like a death sentence. I would wait, anywhere from 30 to 40 minutes. Then I would hear the "footsteps of doom" coming down the hall. My door would swing open, my eyes would get very big and in would walk my father. Sometimes we would have a serious man to Speck talk, but other times, even now I am breaking into a cold sweat, he would begin to take off his belt. I would hope and think, "Are you a little full Dad?" Then he would utter the famous parental phrase, "Gregory, this is going to hurt me a lot more than it's going to hurt you." I used to think, "Well then let me hit you and save you from all the pain." But I never said it out loud.

When I got older I asked my Dad one day, "Remember when I was little and you would make me wait in my room for 30 minutes? What were you doing, torturing me?" He said, "No, I'm sorry, I should have explained. I would do two things." I have taken these two things, added a third, and applied them to disciplining my own children and teenagers in general.

> - First step: **"Calm down emotionally."** If I am upset at a student I need to walk away and calm down emotionally. I specifically name what I am feeling: anger, hurt, frustration, sorrow or combinations of several emotions. This will force my mind to kick in and then I gain control over my emotions. When I feel myself calming down then I can start to think clearly. I do not want to confront a teen if I am upset emotionally because it can lead to me saying and doing things I will regret.

> - Second step: **"I pray for wisdom."** I ask the Holy Spirit to fill and control me. I surrender to Him and my desire is to do what is best for the student. When it comes to discipline, prayer is the most important step to take. Skip this step and I can almost guarantee you will end up doing or saying

something you will feel bad about later. I ask the Lord to give me direction and insight. I don't know when to be tough and when to be gentle, but God knows so I cry out, "God help me." When I do what He wants me to do, everything turns out fine in the end.

- Third step: **"I ask myself three questions."**
  - **"What did the student do wrong?"** I want to be able to come in and express to the student exactly what they did wrong, so there is no confusion.
  - **"What do they need to do next time?"** I want the student to learn from this experience. I want what is best for the student and what will help them in the long run. I say, "If you are ever in this situation again this is what you need to do." Students need this kind of information. For them to understand there are alternatives to their behavior and they can do things differently, so they don't fall in this area again. Otherwise, they continue to do the same stuff over and over again.
  - **"What is the best way to teach them?"** I want to walk in with a plan.
    Do there need to be consequences? What are those consequences? I can be calm because I am prepared and know exactly what I want to accomplish. When I walk in, the first thing I do is pray with the student. I want the teen to know this time is surrendered to God. I also want the student to know, even though I do not approve of what they have done, and they may have to face some consequences, I still love them.

We discipline our teens in love. Today no one wants to discipline teenagers. The school doesn't and parents have given up. For some, there only hope for direction is you and the Body of Christ. It will be hard, but God will use it to change their lives, maybe save their lives. One day they will thank you for it.

THINK ABOUT IT:
1. Is there a need for more discipline in the youth group? Of the five approaches mentioned in this chapter, which one would you naturally be inclined to do?
2. When you discipline are your emotions or intellect in control?
3. Do you have clearly defined expectations and policies?

THOUGHT: "YOU CAN BE A BETTER COMMUNICATOR"

"It is not sufficient to know what one ought to say, but one must also know how to say it." Aristotle

I have been traveling and speaking to teenagers for a loooong time. Other than Jesus Christ and my family, this is my passion. To be able to travel around the world speaking to and meeting with teens is the best. God has laid it on my heart that I need to be reproducing myself in others. Each year I pick a young (everyone compared to me is young), man to help develop as a youth communicator! They travel with me for 9 months, two engagements per month. I want to help them to be an effective youth communicator. What is the one thing they all shared in common? They improved over those 9 months. You may not get the chance to speak before thousands of teens but you can definitely improve in your communication skills.

So, what will make you a better youth speaker?

1. Dependence upon Jesus Christ. There is nothing more important than your relationship with Christ. How many times have I already said this? A lot and I will keep on saying it because this is what will make the difference in your life, keep you in youth ministry for the long haul and make you a better communicator. Study the Word of God every day, not because you have to but because you want to spend time with Him. Study the Word, not for message preparation, but for personal application. Choose to be surrendered, controlled, and empowered by the Holy Spirit. The Holy Spirit will give you understanding and wisdom as you prepare the message. He will give you clarity of thought as you present it. He will personally and powerfully apply the message to each individual student. Just spending time with Jesus and being filled with the Holy Spirit will be a huge boost to your ability to communicate effectively.

Then add prayer. Remember what I said before. Get on your knees and pray for your preparation time, for the Holy Spirit to speak through you, for receptive hearts and for changed lives. Go into the youth room and pray over it before the morning or evening event. Put your hands on the chairs and pray for those who will be sitting in them. Pray for individual students as God brings them to mind. Pray for your visitors. Warfare pray over the room. Try it and see if the students aren't better behaved, more attentive and more open to the truths that God is communicating through you. Your priority over EVERYTHING is spending time with God.

- When you are really busy - pray.
- When you are stressed out - pray.
- As you start your day - pray.
- Before you meet with someone - pray.
- As you prepare your message - pray.
- When you have plenty of time - pray.
- When you have no time - pray.
- As you go to bed - pray.
- Do you feel like praying - pray.
- Don't feel like it - pray.

Matthew 6:33 reminds us to "Seek first the kingdom of God and His righteousness and everything else will be added to us." The quality of your life, your relationship with your family and the ministry as a whole would all improve if you would spend quality and quantity time praying. God has promised if you seek Him first and foremost He will take care of the details. This doesn't mean life will be problem free or without suffering. It does mean an abundant and fulfilling life.

2. Work ahead. Some of us feel like we have the gift of procrastination. Our talks will be lacking if we are preparing them the night before. You will be much more effective and at peace if you work ahead. I realize at first it will be tough but once you get it down it will be a lot easier.

Three months ahead: You're planning a series. Each quarter you are going to head in a direction and cover certain issues. It can be a book in the Bible or it can be topical. At this point you know the topic and scripture to go with it.

Four weeks ahead: Complete an outline. You have the major points and the scripture that goes with each point. Now you have a general idea of what you want to stress with the students. Come up with the three major points you want to make. You are also looking for illustrations to fit with the general points.

Three weeks ahead: You are going to put the meat on the bones. You will fill in your outline. This is specifically what you want to communicate to your students. You are also putting together ideas and delegating for multi-media, drama, worship band and other things this will help students to understand and be impacted by the message.

Two weeks out write your introduction, conclusion and add your illustrations.

One week out you are practicing it several times and making any subtle changes.

The day before, start all over because you have lost the message. Just kidding!

Some of you are saying to me, "Are you crazy? I have to speak three times each week and this is totally impractical." OK, then what step can you take to work ahead? How about planning a series three months ahead of time? That will give you some direction and focus for your talks.
As you work ahead this will give you credibility because you have taken the time and you know the material you are presenting. You'll also be able to say it with confidence and conviction. It gives you the opportunity to own the message. This is what you believe and not what someone else believes. You haven't had to pull it, last minute, from a book of messages.

Take the time to put it together, listen to the Holy Spirit and what He wants to say through you. This will have a much greater impact on students. As you prepare remember "less is more." Meaning it is better for you to end and have students say, "I wish they would have gone longer," rather than finally stopping and for students to say, "I thought they would never end." One builds anticipation and excitement for future talks while the other builds dread.

3. Copy the master. Jesus was the master communicator and it would seem wise to examine some of the Lord's methods and then follow in His footsteps.

- ➤ Lecture - This old method was a powerful way of teaching. People would sit and be amazed as He spoke to them. The Sermon on the Mount, Matthew 5:1-12.

- ➤ Object Lesson - The use of visuals to illustrate points and make them more understandable. A child, Mark 9:33-37 and a coin, Luke 20:20-26.

- ➤ Storytelling - Jesus was incredible at telling stories. As I read them I can see young and old alike, sitting spell bound and hanging on every word. He told a lot of stories and we call them parables, Luke 8:5-8.

"Communication is depositing a part of yourself in another person." Anonymous

- ➤ Teaching through questions - He asked people questions that forced them to think, make application and make a choice. Asking penetrating questions is a great teaching tool, Matthew 16:13-20, "Who do you say I am?" And Luke 6:46, "Why call me Lord, Lord?"

- ➤ Experiential - Jesus knew the value in learning by doing, Luke 10:1-24, the sending out of the seventy-two.

- ➤ Example - One of the best teaching tools is to live Jesus in front of them. What would Jesus do? Let the teens see what it means to be a fully devoted follower of Jesus Christ by watching you. It is a great privilege to be a Christian but it is also an awesome responsibility so we live lives our teens can follow, John 13:1-17, the washing of the disciples' feet.

4. Be aware of what teens like and dislike. When you talk to teens about what they like about a speaker or dislike you will hear some of the same things coming up over and over again.
- ➢ **Dislike**
    - Not funny. There was no humor or they tried to be funny but it just didn't happen.
    - Huh? I couldn't really understand them. The talk was way over my head. It was hard to follow. Didn't apply to my life.
    - Bad opening. Your opening sets the tone for the whole time. If you get off on the wrong foot it is hard to recover.
    - Too preachy. They feel like you are talking down to them.
    - Boring. It is a sin to bore students with the Word of God. It shows a lack of time, thought and preparation into your message.
    - Went too long. Remember, less is more. You can have a great message but kill it because you have gone way too long.

- ➢ **Like**
    - They were into it. The person was excited and enthusiastic. They said it with conviction.
    - Got it. It was easy to understand and it applied to my life.
    - Didn't go too long. Or it didn't seem like it went too long. One person can speak 20 minutes and they went too long while another person speaks 40 minutes and it doesn't seem like it went long at all.
    - Funny. Teens love to laugh. Everyone loves to laugh except the one old guy in Church. You know who I mean. Every Church has this guy.
    - Honest and didn't beat around the bush. You said it like it was and didn't pull any punches. You spoke the truth with love.
    - They spoke right to me. It was like you really

understood me and what I was going through. Much of it has to do with you being surrendered to the Holy Spirit and praying.
- They took time with me. The time you spend with students off the platform gives you favor with them when you are on the platform.

5. Problem areas. There are certain things you want to be aware of and careful about when it comes to communication. These things can be very distracting and people will miss what you are saying.

➢ Rate. The amount of words you speak per minute. Stay away from the extremes. Don't talk like an auctioneer or a person slipping into a coma. Too fast or too slow are both bad.

➢ Pitch. You need to have voice inflection, to go high and to go low. Speaking in a flat, monotone voice is a crowd killer.

➢ Volume. Do not scream at your students. That is emotional manipulation, lacks integrity and usually means you don't have much to say. When a person doesn't have good content, they make up for it by jumping around and shouting. On the other hand, your students need to be able to hear you. It doesn't really matter what you say if they can't hear it. Volume needs to fluctuate as well which helps keep the message interesting. Speak to the people in the last row. Project to them and if they can hear you then everyone can hear you.

➢ Articulation. Do not slur your words or run them together. Enunciate them so people can clearly understand you.

➢ Movement. Do not pace back and forth. So many fall into this trap. You walk back and forth like a caged lion. It becomes distracting for your audience. It is good to move. After you have moved then stop. Talk to them from that spot for at least 15 seconds and then you can move to a different spot. Do not favor one side of the room over the other.

➢ Favorite word. OK, you have a favorite word, OK, you use

over and over and over again. It becomes kind of a filler word, OK, while you decide what you want to say next, OK? The word for a number of people is...OK. "OK, tonight we're going to talk about fear. OK, now, OK when we fear we stop trusting. OK, it's like, OK when you take your eyes off Jesus, OK." Once students pick up on your favorite word it becomes, either incredibly annoying, OK, or hysterically funny. Either way it is distracting, OK, from what you are trying to communicate, OK?......................OK! Other favorite words are; um, uh, so, kayak and Istanbul.

➢ Temperature. If the room is too cold or too hot it becomes distracting.

➢ Bad sound system. Once at a public-school assembly they put me on the equivalent of a "Mr. Microphone." Here I am in a gym speaking for 2,500 students and it sounds like I am in a closet with my mouth taped shut. It was a disaster! You need a sound system adequate for the room and the crowd.

➢ Seating.
- It is bad when chairs are too close to each other: It adds to the messing around factor.
- When teens are too far away from you: It will be hard to hold students' attention if they are so far away you can't see their faces, unless they have you projected on big screens.
- You do not want students facing you with a big window behind you: There are way too many things to distract them as they look out the window.
- Don't have students facing the exits: They will see everyone who enters and leaves.
- Having them sit on a hard floor: This causes their backsides to go numb after a few minutes, which is bad. Their brain can only absorb as much as their rear can withstand.

➢ Individual students. Teens who are there but they don't want to be there. Students can be apathetic, angry, hurting and preoccupied with what is going on in their lives. Students can be distracted by the people sitting around them. You can have negative or positive peer pressure going on. Positive means things are under control and negative means students are being squirrelly.

- ➢ Spiritual warfare. When you work with teens you are on the front lines. You better be warfare praying before you speak. The enemy would love to disrupt and cause all kinds of distractions.

- ➢ Wrong message. Not really knowing your target audience can get you into trouble. Is it senior high or middle school, public, private or Christian school, outreach or growth, inner city, suburb or rural, Hispanic or African American? This all has a bearing on your message preparation. You don't want to come into an engagement clueless and realize it is the wrong message.

- ➢ Know your limitations. It is OK to say no to someone who wants you to speak. For example, I don't speak for first through fifth graders. They are great but I don't relate to them and I am not an effective communicator with that group. So, I am speaking at a Christian school and they ask me if I can help out by speaking to their 4th or 5th graders? I politely say no because I know my limitations.

- ➢ Retroactive inhibition. This just means the more points you make the less they will retain. Have I mentioned, "less is more?"

6. Putting together the message. I am going to tell you what I do. This isn't the only way or the best way, it is just what I do. It is pretty simple, preach the Word, make it practical and illustrate it. I do those three things for every point I make.
- ➢ The Word of God is my foundation. God's Word is life giving and life changing. I was speaking for a large youth convention. They flew me in to speak the last message on Sunday morning. When I finished the talk, I came off the

platform to greet people as they left. A number of individuals came up to me and said, "Thank you, you're the only speaker who used the Bible." That is terrible! It scares me, if we don't use God's Word. What are we really telling them? If it is merely my opinion then it can be interesting, humorous, informative and even inspirational but it won't be life changing. If you build on anything but the Word you are building on sifting sand. You never make the Bible fit your points but your points are the natural flow from the Bible.

➢ Make it practical. Now they have heard the Word of God but how does it relate to their lives? Making it practical means you take it to their level and where they live. How can they begin to apply this and what does the Lord want them to start doing or stop doing? Teens need to see it is practical so they can begin to live it out. Otherwise it is wonderful Biblical truth which doesn't seem to apply to them at all.

➢ Then I illustrate it. The Bible is the foundation. Making it practical is the house they live in, which allows the teens to apply the message. The illustrations are the windows that let the light in and gives understand the Biblical principles. When it comes to illustrations keep these things in mind:
- Speak accurately. Let them know whether it is true or not. Be sure of the facts and let them know if you are borrowing. I was speaking at a winter retreat made up of 15 different youth groups. A youth Pastor came to me to apologize because he had preached one of my talks in its entirety and did not mention to the students it came from me. We all borrow from each other. I don't mind if someone borrows one of my illustrations but don't pretend it's yours if it isn't.
- Don't waste time. Don't tell students you are going to tell them a story. Just tell them the story.
- Be creative by using objects, acting it out and using sound effects. Make it interesting so there is a greater chance they will remember it and when they remember it they can relate it to the Biblical truth.
- Be excited. If it is worth telling then it is worth getting into.

- There are six types of illustrations. I believe the effectiveness grows as you move down the list.
    - ✓ You make it up. Making up an illustration is totally fine as long as everyone knows you have made it up.
    - ✓ Historical. There are so many wonderful stories from history.
      Be sure you tell students about heroes of the faith, Godly men and women who have gone before them and set the example.
    - ✓ A living person. This is usually someone famous, so chances are
      they know who this person is and may be able to identify with
      what is going on.
    - ✓ A friend or acquaintance. Something someone told you and
      you actually know this person.
    - ✓ You saw it. You were right there and you know it is true
      because you saw it happen right before your eyes.
    - ✓ It happened to you. Sharing personal stories of what happened
      to you is the best. You are being open and vulnerable. You are allowing the students to peek into your life.
- Humor is good. Some of us are naturally funny and some of us aren't. But we can still use humor. I am not a joke teller but my humor comes from my telling stories. Humor wins you favor and opens teens to the truth. When I speak most of my illustrations are funny but they don't have to be. Be careful you do not offend with your humor, it just isn't worth it. Stay away from sexual, gross bathroom, sexist, ethnic and confrontational sarcastic humor. I have seen a speaker try to be funny by confronting some kid in the audience and making fun of them but it totally blew up in his face. You don't want to insult your audience. Some comedians get away with it in a comedy clubs but don't you go there.

- Here is a word of warning. If you are going to tell stories about your spouse and kids, be sure you get their permission ahead of time. Then make them look good. If you want to embarrass someone embarrass yourself.
- Start collecting illustrations. This will be the hardest thing to come up with week after week. Put them in a file on your computer. You get them from the newspaper, magazines, books, movies, things you see and stuff you do. You think you'll remember them but in time you forget a lot so store them away.

➢ Introduction. Now I have the body of my message down how do I want to introduce it? I keep in mind this will be their first impression so I want to build interest and anticipation. I might kick it off with a story or video clip or maybe I will just tell them what I am going to talk about. For example, if I start by saying, "I am going to talk about demons and how they are impacting you" or "Let me tell you why sex is so great." At this point I have their attention.

➢ Conclusion. Here is what I want to leave them with. If you don't remember anything I have said up to this point then just remember this. It may be the main point of my message or one point I want them to start putting into practice now. I might end with a story to ask them a question to get them thinking. I could give them an assignment or challenge for the week.

7. Be a storyteller. Draw pictures with your words. So much for teens is visual. I believe to be an effective youth communicator you need to be one who can tell stories.

8. Doing the same talk. For you to use the same talk several times for different groups is fine. It doesn't matter whether you are doing the talk for the first time or the five hundredth time. What is important is you are surrendered, controlled and empowered by the Holy Spirit. D.L. Moody preached the same series of messages across the British Isles and God brought revival. Keep reworking the message so you keep it current and relevant.

"Your first few minutes of a message are crucial and you have to grab them with humor or intensity. You blow those first few minutes and you spend the rest of the talk trying to get their attention." Dan Howard

9. Public school assemblies. This is the hardest thing I do. Students are becoming ruder and ruder. Teachers are having less control. Plus, in public schools I can't mention anything about God, Jesus Christ, Christianity, The Bible, etc. This means, I am telling them what they need to do without any power to do it. I realize once I am introduced I have about 3 minutes to capture them. If I haven't, then I can pretty much kiss the assembly good-bye. So, for 3 minutes they are wondering, who is this guy, should I listen to him, why should I listen to him? I can grab them in those first few minutes by doing one of two things. First, I can say something to touch their hearts and make them think, "He really understands me." or I can get them to laugh. It is just easier for me to get them to laugh. Once they begin to laugh they start to settle down and begin to think, "Maybe this guy will be OK."

10. Privilege and responsibility. It is a wonderful privilege to be able to speak to teenagers; but it is also an awesome responsibility. Communicating God's word should never be taken lightly. Do not blunder theologically, don't mislead students, don't be careless in your preparation. Do not communicate to teens the Bible is anything less then the inerrant Word of God, because you will be judged. Also keep in mind your biggest attacks from the enemy will follow your greatest victories.

11. You're attractive. When you are up front you become very attractive to the opposite sex. Some will "fall in love" with you. Be careful you don't fall into sin with them, instead, you point them toward the person of Jesus Christ.

12. Get help. There are excellent seminars you can go to that will help you be a better communicator. When you speak video yourself and watch it. I know it can be painful but it will help you improve. Ask someone who is an effective youth communicator to critique you live or by watching a video tape. Be patient and make the changes you need to make and you can be a better communicator!

13. Get plenty of sleep. You will do better as a communicator if you aren't slipping into a coma because of little or no sleep.

14. Appearance. Dress comfortable and appropriate for the setting. If you are a guest speaker it is better to be a little over dressed than under dressed.

THINK ABOUT IT:
1. What is the next step you can take to be a better communicator?
2. Are you planning far enough in advance?
3. How well have you balanced Bible principle, application and illustration?

THOUGHTS FROM OTHERS:
 "Once a word has been allowed to escape, it can never be recalled." Horace

"If you haven't struck oil in your first three minutes, stop boring!" George Jessel

"Men of few words are the best men." Shakespeare

"My father gave me these hints on speech-making: 'Be sincere…be brief…be seated'." James Roosevelt

"Originality does not consist in saying what no one has ever said before, but in saying exactly what you think yourself." James Stephens

"Less is more." G S

THOUGHT:
"LET THEM HEAR SOMEONE BESIDES YOU"

"Stand upright, speak thy thoughts, declare the truth thou hast, that all may share; Be bold, proclaim it everywhere. They only live who dare." Lewis Morris

Variety is good and it is good for your students to hear different speakers. Consider exposing your students to different Speakers. As a Youth Pastor, I was always looking for significant others to invest in the lives of my teens, even for just a weekend. You and I both know youth speakers are not the nitty-gritty of the ministry. The Youth Pastor is the one on the front line and in the trenches day in and day out but they do play a part. We all play different parts within the Body of Christ.

1. Why should I consider bringing in an outside speaker?
- It allows you to take the whole weekend and concentrate on relationships. You are able to hang out with your students and staff. I loved being able to just be with my students and not having to worry about speaking.

- You have to opportunity to sit under someone else's ministry. You give God the chance to speak to you and you don't have to be "on". To can sit back listen, learn and relax.

- It's good for your teens to have a change of pace.

- A youth speaker can be uniquely gifted by God to effectively communicate with teenagers. Take advantage of those gifts. Let God use them to speak to the hearts of your teens.

- They can say the same thing you have been saying for the last year but because they are someone different, all of a sudden it will sink in for your students. Rejoice and don't be jealous God spoke through someone besides yourself to touch your teens.

2. What should you expect from a speaker?

- They will be prepared. This is something they have been working on and thinking through. It is wrong for a speaker to come in and shoot from the hip. You can ask for an outline, discussion questions and major direction for each message ahead of time.

- They will follow your direction and theme. You should feel free to tell them what you would like them to share and what you would like them to stay away from. Do this right away and if they don't think they can speak effectively to the theme than you can find another speaker. Feel free to say, "We do not want you to speak on sex." Or you can ask them to speak on character. It is up to you. My philosophy has always been, "You know your students better than I do so tell me what you would like me to do."

- They will stay within time parameters. But you need to make it clear. I spoke for a group that told me I was to speak 30ish minutes. I took that to mean they were flexible and it didn't really matter. However, they expected me to be done in thirty minutes. Saturday night the Youth Pastor was mad at me because I had gone over. I apologized to him but he needed to be a lot clearer. If you want a speaker to be done in a certain amount of time then make your parameters known.

- They will use the Word of God. Any speaker who spoke for my group was expected to have a Bible on the platform and use it.

- They will communicate with excellence. They will share with excitement and total commitment what God has called them to do. They will give you 110% whether there are 4,000 or 40 students.

"Excellence is never cheap. It is costly. Constant care, serious preparation, and continual application are required. Excellence involves desire plus discipline plus determination." George Sweeting

> They will spend time with your students. You do not want a speaker who will show up to speak and then you never see them until the next speaking time. I believe you validate everything you said from the front by spending time with students during the day. I love spending time with students. How can I stay current if I do not listen to them? You should expect your speaker to be hanging out with your students during free time. The speaker may need to rest a little in the afternoon but you want a speaker with an attitude that wants to spend time. They need to be aggressive toward the students. If I want students to come up to me to talk than I better be going up to them.

> They will have a positive attitude and seek to be a servant. The speaker should be excited to be a part of the week or weekend. They are there to serve and not be served. As speakers, we need to take a rigid stand of total flexibility. They need to be open to doing what you want them to do and going where you want them to go. Now it is important you do not abuse your speaker. But they should be open to change. A speaker leads by example. If their actions do not back up their words then the words are empty.

> They will have reasonable travel costs. They should be booking airline tickets at least two weeks in advance. Does a speaker really need to fly first class? Only if there are medical concerns but otherwise they should be willing to fly coach. They do not need to rent a car but should be open to doing it if it will help you out. They should have receipts for everything and you should not feel bad about questioning any of the receipts.

When I fly somewhere I am turning in a airline receipt and a bus receipt. A number of Youth Pastors have said to me, "What is the bus ticket for?" There is a direct bus from

Rockford, Illinois to O'Hare airport. It doesn't bother me they question the receipt, I would do the same thing.

➤ They will be open to discuss their honorarium. When you contact a speaker, ask if they have an honorarium. If they do than they will tell you. At this point you can say, "Great we will take you." Or you can say, "We can't afford that but would you be willing to come for this amount?" Now they have the option of accepting it or not. If they don't than please do not judge them. If they are traveling full time this is their source of income to support their families.

➤ They will be willing to supply you with a brochure, web site, CD or DVD so you can hear them speak. They should also be open to giving you the names of some Youth Pastors who have heard them speak RECENTLY and you can contact them as resources.

3. What should a speaker expect from you?
➤ You will clearly communicate expectations. What do you want us to speak on, how long and how many times will we speak? Do you want us to lead a communion time? Will you want us to extend an invitation to the teens and if so how do you want us to do it by raising hands, coming forward, filling out cards, looking up, etc.? What airport do you want us to fly into and when should we arrive by? When are they free to leave? You also need to provide directions for a speaker who is driving to your church or camp.

➤ You will have a private place for them to stay. Do not put a speaker in a cabin with teens unless they want to be with the students. Staying in a person's house is not always a good idea. There may not be enough privacy. If I am asked to stay in a house I request there are no small children. Small children are great but they cause a lot of noise, are demanding of time and I find it hard to relax in that kind of setting. If I am in a house I run the risk of ending up in the house at the same time, alone, with females. This is not a good situation. I find the best situation is having my own

cabin at a camp and a hotel room when I am speaking for a church.
- You will not abuse your speaker. This means the number of times you are asking them to speak and the hours you want them available. I usually say I am willing to start early in the morning or go late into the evening but not both. If you are asking a speaker to come for less than their usual honorarium than you need to be willing to make adjustments in their schedule.

In some cases, I am booked years in advance. So, if I get sick I can't say, "I am not feeling well, can we rebook for three years down the road?" I just suck it up and go. I was scheduled to fly to Denver to speak at a weekend retreat for high school. At 4am, Friday morning, I come down with the flu. I am sicker than a dog. I spent the whole flight in the bathroom. I even feel asleep sitting up in the bathroom. Two staff guys pick me up at the airport. It is about a three-hour drive into the mountains to get to the camp. Twenty minutes from camp they decide they are hungry and want to pick up some fast food. I say to them, "I am sorry but the smell of food will make me throw up." What do they do? They stop for dinner and leave me sitting in the car. That is abuse of a speaker. They needed to get me to camp and than drive back for their dinner. Treat a speaker like you would want to be treated.

- You will be on time to pick up the speaker at the airport. I know stuff happens and you get behind. But sometimes you don't leave soon enough and just leave the speaker waiting in the airport. I can't tell you how many times I have gotten my bags and than looked for a place to sit down because no one is there to pick me up. That is just common kindness. Also, you should send the same sex to pick up the speaker or if it isn't the same sex send two or three.

- You will have the honorarium check with you. It isn't right for a person to minister and than for you to say, "We will mail you the check". In the past I have had to wait for weeks for a check to arrive. I have even had to call a church to remind them; that is wrong! I have had groups say to me, "We couldn't write you a check until you filled out these forms." It isn't my fault you didn't get me the forms ahead of time. You need to pay your speaker when they are with you and not make them wait. I can understand if you need to send the expense check.

- It is nice if you promote the materials the speaker has to sell. I always appreciate if the Youth Pastor will promote my materials from the front. That way I don't have to sell my stuff from the front and I can spend time with students instead of at a table.

Bringing in a speaker can be a great encouragement to your group. Work together with the speaker so it becomes a positive experience for everyone involved.

THINK ABOUT IT:
1. Have you considered bringing in outside speakers?
2. Do you clearly express to them your expectations?
3. What do you want you speaker to do more of next time?

THOUGHTS FROM OTHERS:
"A speech is a solemn responsibility. The man who makes a bad thirty-minute speech to two hundred people wastes only a half hour of his own time. But he wastes one hundred hours of the audience's time-more than four days-which should be a hanging offense."
Jenkin Lloyd Jones

"Speech is the mirror of the soul; as a man speaks so he is."
Publilius Syrus

"Talkativeness is one thing, speaking well another." Sophocles

"The finest eloquence is that which gets things done." David Lloyd George

THOUGHT:
"KNOW THE ISSUES HURTING OUR STUDENTS"

"Vision is the world's most desperate need. There are no hopeless situations, only people who think hopelessly." Winifred Newman

What is happening in the lives of our teens? What are the issues they are facing? Some things come and go depending on the generation. There are other issues that span the generations. You need to know what the issues are so you can prepare teens to face them. These are not listed in order of importance. But I have also included some scripture that you can use to address the issues.

1. Conflict resolution. Students do not know how to work through problems with others. So, they resort to violence. (2 Timothy 2:22-24, Galatians 5:14-15, Proverbs 20:3)

2. Anger. Teens are angry for a variety of reasons. Many have learned to try to suppress or ignore it but it only leads to explosions. (Proverbs 15:1, Proverbs 16:32, Proverbs 17:27, Proverbs 19:19, Ephesians 4:26-27)

3. Occult. Wicca groups are very popular and the occult draws a lot of teenagers with the promise of acceptance, adventure and power. As the days get darker the enemy will become bolder and we will see more and more teens demonized. (Leviticus 19:26B, Leviticus 19:31, Deuteronomy 18:10-13)

4. Pre-marital sex. Everywhere a teen turns they are exposed to sex: TV, internet, movies, videos, music, magazines, billboards, mall advertising, etc. They need to hear a clear, straightforward presentation on sex from a Biblical, Christian, perspective. This includes topics like, what is sex, how does the opposite sex respond, what should my standards be, what does God say, solid reasons to wait, what about S.T.D's, is oral sex really sex, what about masturbation, etc? We need to be preaching abstinence and regaining purity. Regaining purity says, "I have already had intercourse but starting now I will honor God with my body, respect myself and respect members of the opposite sex." They need to know it is not too late and there is hope. I have written a book that addresses these sexual issues and a lot more. It is published by Moody Press and is called, *Sex, It's Worth Waiting For*. (That was a shameless plug!) (1 Corinthians 6:13b and 18-20, Ephesians 5:3 and 5)

5. Substance Abuse. Alcohol is still the drug of choice but you may have teens involved in a whole variety of drugs, from marijuana to black tar heroine. Look at the statistics of how many teenagers are alcoholics. Look at how many teens die in car crashes where drinking is involved. (1 Corinthians 6:19-20, Galatians 5:19-21, Ephesians 5:18)

6. Sexual Abuse. There are a significant number of teenage girls and guys who will experience sexual abuse or harassment as teenagers. Date rape continues to be a big problem. Our men need to be educated on what it means to be gentlemen. Our women need to know what to do if they are faced with abuse or harassment. A rape or incest survivor also needs to know they are still a virgin because no one can take your virginity from you, it is something you freely give. The shame is not on the one who has been abused but on the abuser. (Genesis 34:1-2, 5, 7, Leviticus18:6-17, 24, 29, Deuteronomy 22:25-26)

7. Disintegration of the family. Divorce is leaving deep emotional scares. Same sex marriages cause confusion. Teens have bad examples and poor modeling. They experience physical and verbal abuse from parents who were also abused when they were kids. Single parents are on over load. They try to be both Mom and Dad and end up burning out. (Malachi 2:13-16a, Matthew 19:1-9, Ephesians 6:1-3)

8. Food issues. These impact female and male alike. You have young people who are anorexic, bulimic and perpetually dieting. Teens are very body centered and struggle with their self worth. (1 Corinthians 6:19-20, 1 Corinthians 10:31)

9. Cutting. More and more teens are cutting themselves. The emotional pain becomes so intense that hurting themselves physically becomes a relief. I think the enemy has a big hand in all of this. Satan delights in mutilating, distorting and destroying what God has created. (Leviticus 19:28, Romans 6:13, Romans 12:1)

"The glory is not in never failing, but in rising every time you fall." Anon

10. Bullying. Teens find themselves either getting picked on or being the ones who bully others. This leads to serious ramifications, with one result being violence. You can only take so much abuse and then you hit back. These verses are directed toward those who are being picked on. For the bullies, I would take them to scriptures talking about loving one another. (Romans 5:3-5, Romans 8:18, Romans 12:12)

11. Suicide. This continues to be one of the leading killers of our teenagers. For a variety of reasons students have gotten to a point in their lives where they have said, "Death has got to be better than the emotional pain I am experiencing. Life is no longer worth living" (Jeremiah 29:11, Ecclesiastes 7:16-18, 1 Corinthians 6:19-20)

12. Stress. Our students are over committed and under tremendous pressure from parents, school, sports, work and sometimes even church. They feel the pressure to perform. (Luke 12:22-31, John 14:27, 1 Peter 5:6-7)

13. Pornography. It is so accessible today it is hard to find a teen who hasn't been exposed to some degree. This can become addictive just like drugs. Many of our students are caught in the vicious cycle of pornography, lust and masturbation.
(Matthew 5:27-28, Ephesians 4:19, 1 Thessalonians 4:3-7)

14. Lying and cheating. I am amazed at the number of students who lie and cheat and see nothing wrong with it. (Proverbs 6:16-17a, Ephesians 4:15, Colossians 3:9-10)

15. Depression. "I first feel sad and I don't really know why." I heard this from a teenage girl recently. A depressed person has an overall feeling of gloom and hopelessness. There are many teens under the cloud of depression today. This is becoming a bigger and bigger problem. We are seeing a dramatic increase in the numbers of teens struggling with depression. (1 Kings 19:5-18)

16. Fear. Afraid of the dark, afraid to be alone, afraid of silence, afraid of the future, afraid of..., you fill in the blank. Panic attacks are on the increase. Fear will paralyze our teens. (Psalm 34:4, Proverbs 3:24, 1 John 4:4, 18a, 16b)

17. Apathy. "I just don't care." You hear this all the time. "I am not doing well, I am struggling in a number of areas, I am spiritually dry and I just don't care." When a teen has a heart of stone it leads to apathy. They need a heart transplant. God is ready to take their heart of stone and give them a heart of flesh so they can care again. It's only a prayer away. I have another book by Moody Press called *Living for Jesus after the party's over.* It talks about how to live for Jesus once you get home from the retreat, missions trip and come off the spiritual high. (Two shameless plugs in the same chapter). (Ezekiel 11:19, Zechariah 7:11-12, 1 Thessalonians 5:16-18)

18. Self hate. Not liking who they are and wishing they looked differently. Teens see themselves as worthless and unlovable because they compare themselves to the world. They choose to mirror themselves in the eyes of the world. (Psalm 119:73, Psalm 139:13-16, Romans 1:6)

19. Stealing. The pressure to fit in, belong and look right leads them to shoplift. They can't afford it but desperately want it, so they steal it. Or they steal money from their parents to buy the things they want. (Exodus 20:15, Isaiah 61:8, Ephesians 4:2)

THINK ABOUT IT:
1. What issues are you seeing in the teens around you?
2. What other issues, not mentioned here, do you think students are facing today?
3. What do you do to stay current in this are?

THOUGHT:
"WE NEED TO HELP OUR STUDENTS DEAL WITH THE ISSUES IN THEIR LIVES"

"An infinite God can give all of Himself to each of His children…to each one He gives all of Himself as fully as if there were no others." A.W. Tozer

What do we do when a young person talks to us about issues in their life?

- ➤ **Pray and ask God for wisdom.** He is the one who can give you understanding, insight and the right words to say. I have met with students and God has given me knowledge about their life, problems and needs that I could never have known on my own. I walk away amazed at how God worked through me even though I didn't know the teen at all.

- ➤ **Take them to the Word of God.** You want to make them independently – dependent. Independent of you and dependent upon God and His Word. The Bible is a practical book for today that speaks to the issues teenagers are facing. In the Thought entitled, "Know the Issues that are hurting our students", I have included scripture you can use in helping them face the issues in their lives.

"The Bible is God's chart for you to steer by, to keep you from the bottom of the sea, and to show you where the harbor is, and how to reach it without running on rocks or bars." Henry Ward Beecher

> For example, if a student comes to you struggling with depression take them into the Word to give them insight into this area and practical steps they can take. Here are four steps from scripture to help teens deal with depression.
>
> Elijah has just defeated the prophets of Baal on Mount

Carmel. The whole experience has taken hours, he has just finished running several miles and he is physically and emotionally exhausted. Then Jazebel hears what has happened to her prophets and threatens Elijah's life, 1 Kings 19:2. Now add to the exhaustion, fear as he begins to run for his life. He finally gets to the place where he is ready to give up. He just wants to die, 1 Kings 19:3c. How does God deal with his depression? Exactly the same way we ought to deal with teens who are depressed. God takes him through these four steps.

- **Step 1:** 1 Kings 19:5-8a, make sure they are getting enough sleep and eating properly. One of the major causes of depression for teenagers and college students is sleep deprivation and a poor diet.
- **Step 2:** 1 Kings 19:9b-10 and 13b-14, be a listener and let them dump on you. They need to get all the things bothering them out in the open. Don't try to fix it. At this time, a teen needs a listener and not a lecturer.

- **Step 3:** 1 Kings 19:11-13a, every teen needs to be reminded of the personal presence of God in their life. To know He is there and cares no matter how they feel. You begin to speak truth to them. Encourage them to look for God in the little things.

- **Step 4:** 1 Kings 19:15-18, now it is time to get out and do what you are supposed to do no matter how you feel. A depressed person will do the very things that cause depression. If they don't feel like anyone likes them will they venture out to see if this is true? No, they will go into their rooms, withdraw, listen to the blues and cause themselves more depression. Therefore, we need to help them to get out and discover the truth. Elijah felt like he was all alone and he was absolutely wrong. So, after resting, eating correctly, sharing their feelings and seeking God we encourage them to step out in faith and get back to doing what God has called them to do.

There can be physical and deeper psychological reasons for depression that would call for professional help. If the depression is on going then get them in for a complete physical and make an appointment for counseling. Treat depression seriously and get them the help they need. Depression can lead to something as serious as suicide.

- **Seek to encourage and give them hope.** You may be shocked by what they tell you but don't let them see it. If you do, chances are, they will stop talking and may never come to you again. Let them know God is ready, willing and able to forgive them. Two things you can do that are of great worth to a teenager, love and listen to them. Just doing those two things will greatly encourage them.

- **Help them take the next step.** Give them some practical direction. This will also give them hope as they start to move in the right direction. Know your limitations. If you aren't a professional counselor, there are some issues that are way beyond your ability to help them and they may need professional help. Sometimes we can do more damage than good if we try to go deeper into an issue we don't have the training or skill to effectively help. Be willing to refer them so they can get the help they need. If the issue is serious then the parents have to know as long as it doesn't put the teen's emotional and physical well being at risk. I usually give students three alternatives when it comes to talking to their parents.

1. We will go together and tell one or both. I am fine if they want to tell one parent but not the other. I will leave it up to the one parent to communicate with their spouse.

2. You can tell them by yourself, but I will call them tomorrow to make sure you did this. They will ask me, "Don't you trust me?" I will respond this has nothing to do with trust. This is about me keeping you accountable and staying involved so I can continue to help you and your

parents.

3. I will go by myself and get the process started.

How do you respond when a student says, "If I tell you something do you promise you won't tell anyone else?" I say, "No, that limits my effectiveness in helping you but I do promise I will never go behind your back." I have NEVER had a student say, "Well, then I'm not going to tell you." It is important you keep what they say confidential, except for those who need to know. But never go behind their backs because word of that will travel fast and students will stop trusting you.

You must love the students enough to risk your relationship with them. We get them help and talk to whoever we need to even if they get mad at us. If a young person says, "I am thinking about killing myself but please don't tell my parents," I am going to tell their parents even though they may hate me for awhile.

I was speaking at a Christian school for spiritual emphasis week. A girl wrote me a note saying she was anorexic and bulimic. She shared how depressed and desperate she was and didn't know what to do. I found her and asked if I could talk to her parents or Youth Pastor and she said, "No." I said pick one or the other and she said, "No." So I told her I would be calling her Youth Pastor and she started yelling at me about how she was trusting me and how I was betraying her trust. I called the Youth Pastor who came to the school immediately and we met with the girl again. She broke down and told everything but after she had gotten it all out she told me to leave and that she hated me. The Youth Pastor contacted the parents and they began to get her help. Would I do it again? Yes, and without hesitation. Youth Ministry is not a popularity contest. It is all about loving Jesus and teenagers and loving the teens enough to risk your relationship with them.

Some other thoughts, do not tell your spouse if they are a gossip. Some of you are married to gossips and for the sake of the young person and the youth ministry don't tell them. Remember not to do on going counseling with the opposite sex. Finally, there are some issues your state requires you to report like child abuse. It is the law and to ignore it is to risk jail time.

- **Move them toward a close, personal relationship with Jesus Christ.** I am more convinced than ever that the ultimate answer to the issues and needs of teenagers is Jesus. We are not their savior, Jesus is the Savior and we point our students to Him. I find the closer a teen draws to Jesus the healthier they become emotionally and physically. No one loves our students the way Jesus loves our students. Teach them to depend upon Him.

THINK ABOUT IT:
1. Do you pray before giving students counsel and advice?
2. When you meet with students do you give them your opinion or take them into the Word of God?
3. Should you really be telling your spouse what individual students tell you in confidence?

THOUGHTS FROM OTHERS:
"O Divine Master, grant that I may not so much seek to be consoled as to console;
To be understood as to understand; To be loved as to love; For it is in giving that we receive; It is in pardoning that we are pardoned; and it is in dying that we are born to eternal life." Saint Francis of Assisi

"Care is a state in which something does matter; it is the source of human tenderness." Rollo May

THOUGHT:
"WATCH OUT FOR BURNOUT"

"The best bridge between hope and despair is often a good night's sleep." Heraclitus

Burnout is very real and very serious. In this fast-paced world, where expectations go through the roof, we are seeing more and more Youth Pastors hit the wall emotionally. We have become "MEGA," mega Church, mega responsibilities, mega hours, mega stress, mega expectations and mega temptations. One day it all catches up with us and we shut down.

I first learned about the tanks in our life from Bill Hybles when I heard him speak at Willow Creek. He identified four tanks, physical, spiritual, relational and emotional. Those tanks need to stay filled. If they hit empty, then, like a car, you can end up coming to a screeching halt. When your physical tank hits empty you can become lethargic, you lose energy, stamina and you wear down quicker. You can fill the tank up fast as you exercise, sleep and eat better. Your spiritual tank hits empty and can rapidly be filled as you spend time with God and develop your relationship with him. Our relational tank gets drained because we surround ourselves with very needy people. We need to spend time with adults that will love, listen and invest in our life. As we do this then our relational tank fills up pretty fast. However, the emotional tank is different. If you hit empty it does not refill rapidly. When your emotional tank is on empty, you are headed toward burn out.

What are the danger signs or red flags you may be moving toward or are already in the midst of burn out? What are some things we can do to begin the recovery process? Before we look at the specific areas I want to build for you seven pillars that will protect you from burnout. These seven will support you through the problems and pressures youth ministry brings.

Pillar #1 - Your personal relationship with Jesus Christ.
Everything pales in comparison to your love for Jesus Christ. To love the Lord <u>YOUR</u> God with all your heart, soul, mind and strength. If you read your Bible every day and pray all the time for the next 6 months, will God love you more, at the end of the 6 months, than He loves you now? NO! If you never pray or read your Bible for the next 6 months, will God love you less? NO! So, individuals ask me, "Then why should I read my Bible and pray?" Here is what I say, "I do not read my Bible or pray so God will love me. I know he already loves me unconditionally. I read the Word and pray because I love God and I want to experience how much He loves me." Make time for Jesus.

Pillar #2 - Who you are on the inside. Be a person of character and integrity. Refuse to compromise and refuse to settle for anything less then God's very best. Than you make choices which flow from that kind of commitment to Christ.

Pillar #3 - Your family. Teens grow up and graduate, ministries change but your family lasts a lifetime. This is your only opportunity in all of eternity to have children. Do not miss out, don't miss the joy of growing older and deeper in love with your spouse. Don't miss the special times with your children. I can come home from a speaking trip as a total and complete failure. I can tell my family I bombed big time and people thought I was the worst speaker they had ever heard! Bonnie will say to me, "Honey, I love you" and my children will say, "We think you're the best Dad," and that is a pillar in my life. With Bonnie, I have a best friend until death do we part. How great is that?

What if your spouse gets burnt out? You may need to step down for awhile to take care of them. At the very least you want to get them some counsel and encouragement. Protect your spouse and do whatever you need to do for them to heal emotionally.

Pillar #4 - Fulfilling God's calling. It means you are willing to go where He wants you to go and do what He wants you to do. You discover joy, peace that passes all understanding and abundance when you are in the center of God's will, doing what He has called you to do. To live your life to glorify Him so when you get to the end of your life you can look back with no regrets. A poor substitute is money, big house, elegant car, nice stuff and fame. These things will, at best, bring you temporary happiness. Don't ever settle for second best. Fulfilling God's calling is about you being obedient.

"The future is as bright as the promises of God." William Carey

Pillar #5 - Needing others. It is good to need others. No one had a closer or more intimate relationship with God than Adam did. The Bible says God and Adam would hang out together, Adam would ask God any question and they would walk together in the garden. Then God says something truly amazing, "It is not good for man to be alone." To need others is good and right. "As iron sharpens iron, so one man sharpens another." This comes from an accountability partner or group you can meet with on a regular basis, I would suggest every week. For you to really share yourself you must share your feelings. You may not like it or be comfortable doing it - do it anyway. You are going to allow others to love and care for you. We forget one of the attributes of a servant is to allow others to serve us. We get so busy giving to others we don't really allow others to give and minister to us. This is someone you will allow to speak truth into your life even though you don't want to hear it. Be honest and admit you might need some professional counseling. God has gifted individuals with the ability to look into our lives and give us practical tools to help us deal with what is happening emotionally. Seeing your need and being willing to get help is a tremendous strength, not a weakness.

Pillar #6 - Time. You serve an eternal God who has all the time in the world. So, you need to be patient with yourself and take the time to work through what is going on in your life. Take time off! Get away for a day, weekend, week, month, or longer. If you are in the midst of burn out you need to take time off. Go to whoever you need to go to, Senior Pastor, Board and say, "I am hurting and I need some time off." If your church refuses to give you time off then quit. This is about you majoring on the majors not majoring on the minors. Right now, your emotional wellbeing, relationship with your spouse and relationship with your children are the majors and the ministry at the church is the minor. God is sovereign and in control. He will take care of you when you step away to do what is right. Get away to rest in the arms of Jesus.

Pillar #7 - Hope. With Jesus Christ, the best is always yet to come. You will get through this and God will use it to shape and mold you more into His image. Learn from the burn out so you can make the changes which will protect you from falling into this trap again, this isn't the end. You may have experienced burn out in your church but you haven't burned out from youth ministry. Learn the lessons you need to learn. You will be wiser and better equipped to serve.

"Don't be afraid of pressure. Remember that pressure is what turns a lump of coal into a diamond" Mark Twain

Here are some of the danger signs and red flags that may say we are moving toward or are in the middle of burnout and some steps you can take to avoid it.

1. "I am so stinking busy. I am working way too many hours but still don't feel like I am getting anywhere. I am exhausted all the time and I even wake up tired. I find it really hard to even get out of bed."

- You need to refocus. There are thousands of things screaming for your attention, but what are the few that really need to get done if the youth ministry is going to remain healthy and move ahead? Learn to say no and be OK with the decision. Some of us say no but then feel guilty about it.

- Make a list of priorities. This way you can start working on what is really important.

- Delegate as much as you can. What do you need to do that no one else can do? These are the things you need to concentrate on.

- Being busy is not the same as being productive. I fly a lot.

Sometimes the plane taxies away from the gate and stops to check something. All of a sudden the engine power increases, the plane starts to shake, the sound is deafening, flaps start moving up and down. It is all very impressive but we aren't moving. You can be very busy, doing a lot of stuff, looking impressive, working long hours but you aren't getting anywhere. Don't work longer but work smarter. Be productive by doing what is most important to the youth ministry.

2. "I am not getting time alone with my spouse. I am experiencing an increase in conflict with my family and I am lashing out at them for small stuff that wouldn't have bothered you in the past. I have no patience at all and everything seems to bother me"

- You need time alone and time with your family. Start talking about what you are feeling. Get away for a weekend, just you and your spouse. Chances are you have been neglecting your family.

- Ask for forgiveness and grant forgiveness. You have hurt each other and there needs to be restitution. You have said and done things you regret. You try to forget about it and move on but I guarantee your spouse hasn't forgotten about it.

- What needs to change so you don't go through this again? What are the hot buttons leading to the conflict? What do we need to stop doing and what do we need to start doing?

3. "I am doing stuff outside of youth ministry and I am not gifted in the area. I hate it and I feel trapped"

- Review your job description. This way you are sure of your responsibilities.

- Sit down and talk with your Senior Pastor. Let them know exactly how you feel. Tell him about your frustrations, concerns and desires.

- It's OK to say, "NO." To say, "I can no longer be effective in the area you have called me to minister, if I have to do these other things." Ask them, "If you want me to do these extra things, then what do you want me to let go of in the youth ministry?" Now I know emergencies come up and you need to be a team player and help out. But the extra responsibilities they give you need to be short term.

- If it continues you may need to consider looking for another position.

4. "I dread coming into work. There is no more joy for me. I use to be so excited and I couldn't wait to get to work."

- Identify exactly what it is you dread.

- Is the problem something that can change?

- What would have to happen in the youth ministry to cause you to be excited again?

- Talk to someone in charge about this.

5. "I am avoiding students. I lock myself into the office, stop going to their events and don't set up appointments. Then I become really hard on myself for not getting out with the teens. What is wrong with me?"

- Chances are you lack the emotional energy to minister and meet their needs.

- Get away and relax.

- Do you just need a break or could God be moving you in another direction?

- Youth Ministry can be a lifetime calling but maybe it isn't God's calling for your life.

6. "I feel so alone. I don't sense much support and I don't feel like people really understand what is happening to me. They don't know what it takes to keep a youth ministry going or that I need help. I am caring for all these teens but no one is caring for me."

- Reach out to those around you. You may feel like no one cares, but your feelings may, and probably are, totally wrong. Maybe you have given off an impression you don't need other people. Make it a priority to establish friendships with your peers.

- Develop a team within your youth ministry.

- Express your feelings. Hold them in and they will only grow bigger.

7. "I've lost my creative edge and I am bored. I'm stuck in a rut and it just seems like same old-same old. I'm not into it like I used to be."

- Maybe you need a new challenge. Can this happen within your present youth ministry?

- Talk with your Senior Pastor about what you are passionate about now.

- Put together a plan which would allow you to move in that direction. Present it to those in charge.

- Is God preparing you for a move?

- Read some good books to challenge yourself and get you back on the cutting edge.

8. "Wow, lately it seems like I have made some very poor choices and bad decisions. I am lacking in common sense. I've started to question my own judgment."

- Who is in control of your life, you or the Holy Spirit?

- If you lack wisdom ask God. Wisdom is seeing life from God's point of view.

- There is wisdom in the counsel of others. Seek out Godly advice.

- Be sure you are getting enough sleep and eating correctly.

9. "Tough decisions need to be made but I can't make them. I know what needs to be done but I just don't have the energy or courage to make it. I wish someone else would do it."

- When we are tired we become cowards. But the stuff won't go away and waiting may make it worse.

- Talk to others about how to approach it.

- Then set up specific steps you are going to take.

- Ask God for the strength to do what you need to do.

- Then just do it! (Sounds like a commercial)

10. "Emotionally I am on the edge. There is a ton of stress on my shoulders. I am afraid, angry, depressed and sad. Sometimes I feel all these emotions in the same day. I am overly sensitive to what other people say and how they act. I can feel I am on the verge of tears."

- Stress can be a good thing because it motivates us to get things done. But too much stress begins to overwhelm and crush us. How we respond to stress can be harmful. To escape stress, we sometimes choose at risk behaviors.

- Fear is a weapon of the enemy. It can grip your life. You become afraid of failure, success, being found out, putting your life in God's hands, stepping out in faith, taking a risk, being rejected, returning phone calls, meeting with people, etc. Truth is what tears down the lies of the enemy. Greater is Jesus Christ in you. Perfect love casts out fear and perfect love is our Lord. Draw near to God and He will draw near to you. Then stand firm and resist the enemy.

- Anger and depression can go hand in hand. Anger can be a sign of depression. They can feel like a cloud of doom hanging over your head. So, you seek to escape it, to experience some relief by sleeping, eating, watching TV, etc. Sometimes it gets so bad you think death would be an option. You need to get some help. If you don't, the anger will turn into rage. Then the depression will deepen. Often depression is anger turned inward.

- Feeling sad and wanting to cry is OK. A good, long, hard cry with someone you trust can be a very good thing.

- Take time off and humble yourself by getting some help. Professional counseling is a very good idea. I recommend a Christian counselor but keep this in mind, it is better to have a competent non-Christian then an incompetent Christian counselor.

- Get organized, being disorganized will add to your stress.

11. "Things aren't turning out right. I came in with all these great plans and dreams but it just isn't happening. Reality is not meeting my expectations."

- Pray. Maybe the problem is it's your plan and your dreams and not God's. You may need to go back to square one and start over by doing what God wants you to do.

- Maybe the goals are God's goals but your approach has been wrong. There are many different ways you can approach a goal.

- You might just need to be patient. Things are not happening as fast as you would like them to happen but it doesn't mean they won't happen.

12. "I am caught up in sin."

- Confess and turn from the sin. "The wages of sin is death." That is death to you as a person and sometimes death to the ministry. You can not effectively lead a youth ministry when you have the weight of sin hanging around your neck.

- Be accountable to a group or individual.

- Be proactive rather than reactive. Plan what you can do to avoid and refrain from the sin.

13. "I am gripped by pornography and lust of the flesh." Satan's plan is two-fold. First he wants to invite and entice: "Look at how pleasing this is to your eyes. How good it feels and how sweet it tastes. Enjoy, you deserve these hidden delights. This is hurting no one." Then secondly he wants to accuse and degrade: "You are so sick and disgusting. What kind of a pervert would look at what you just looked at? God will not forgive this; you have lost your chance. You might as well just give up." Do you ever think to yourself, "as long as I am not acting on my fantasies or lusting after girls in my youth ministry then it's OK?" It is not OK!

- Confess and turn from it. God is ready, willing and able to forgive you and give you a new beginning.

- Get under accountability. You need others in your life who will hold you to purity. You need help in this area. Don't fool yourself. You think, "I can handle this," and you do for awhile but then you are back into it. It is a cycle which is slowly killing you spiritually and emotionally.

- Put safe guards on your computer. Move your computer to a high traffic area. Get it out of the basement.

- Get rid of whatever you need to get rid of: videos, pictures, magazines, books, TV, internet, etc. Remove from your house everything that is feeding your lust.

- Feed on the Word of God. David said, "Your Word have I hid in my heart that I might not sin against you."

14. "I am under attack. There is this person or people who don't like what I am doing. I have become defensive and insecure. I find myself snapping at people. I'm experiencing road rage. I'm losing my sensitivity toward others. No longer am I aware of needs like I use to be. I don't care anymore. I don't care about the people or the ministry. I am sick of everything going on."

- Tell the leadership and get their support. You feel all alone and you need others standing with you at this moment.

- You need to meet with individuals one at a time but don't meet with an entire group of people who don't like what you are doing. To meet with an entire group is to set yourself up to getting hurt emotionally. Listen to what they say. If their concerns are legitimate then what changes do you need to make? But they have no right to be cruel, rude, insulting or emotionally abusive. If they are you end the meeting and go to your board. They need to step in and confront these people.

- If you meet with them and they are out of touch or just plain wrong what do you need to do? All you can do is speak the truth to them in love. Sometimes you have to agree to disagree.

- What happens if they are wrong and still continue to be a problem? You take the steps in Matthew 18.

- Be a God pleaser. Sometimes you just need to do what God calls you to do even though some people oppose you. If you want everyone to love you all the time and this is what drives you than you will be frustrated.

15." I'm having personal and family problems. I don't make enough money, there has been some poor money management, the in-laws are driving me crazy, the car broke down and the San Francisco 49ers aren't winning." (Oops, I was kind of projecting my own personal problem).

- Identify what the problems are, make a list.

- Sit down with your spouse, friend, counselor or advisor and begin to make a plan. What are practical steps you can begin to take to solve these problems. Like putting together a budget, cutting up credit cards and starting a savings account. Spending less or more time with the in-laws, or maybe the 49ers should keep their good players, stop messing around, get back to excellence, stop frustrating their fans and then...OK, I need to calm down and take a deep breath.

- Implement the plan and begin to take the steps.

16. "It's not my fault. If they hadn't done this I wouldn't have done that."

- If you are the leader then the buck stops with you. You are ultimately responsible for what happens in the youth ministry. You can like or dislike it but it is reality.

- If you can't stand the heat then get out of the kitchen.

17. "I just feel spiritually dead. It feels like I'm in a spiritual wilderness." I was speaking at a Christian school for what Tony Campolo calls, "A be nice to God week." I was spiritually dead and worse and I really didn't even care. We were about half way though the week and I was back in my room when the phone rang. It was

one of the administrators who wanted to invite me to dinner the next evening. I didn't really want to go but I wanted to be polite and said, "That would be fine." I just wanted to get off the phone with this guy. "Everyone just leave me alone, I want to be by myself and I don't care anymore." The conversation was winding down and it goes something like this:
- Me: "OK, thanks for calling, I need to get going."
- Him: "My family is excited to be with you."
- Me: "Great! Well, I need to go."
- Him: "See you tomorrow."
- Me: "Bye."
- Him: "Wait a minute."
- Me: "What?"
- Him: "God wants me to tell you something."
- Me: "Huh?"
- Him: "God wants me to tell you something."
- Me: "Uh...OK...What is it?"
- Him: "God wants me to tell you what a blessing you are to Him."
- Me: I just stood there with the phone to my ear and I began to sob. I was totally broken with the realization that when I was at my lowest God was right there loving me. When I was at my worst God was at His best.

  - God is right there with you, right now. Reach out to Him because He is reaching out to you.

  - Take a spiritual retreat. Get away for a few days to pray, fast, journal, study the Word, seek after God and get some sleep.

Here is a word of warning. When we are emotionally on empty we have a tendency to think it is a spiritual problem. That is not true. Now the spiritual may play a factor. But what we do is pour into the spiritual tank while the emotional tank remains empty. Don't ignore burn out. Face it and allow others to support you.

THINK ABOUT IT:
1. Is your emotional tank on empty?
2. What steps do you need to take now?
.3. Would it be good if you got some counseling?

THOUGHTS FROM OTHERS:
"There Remain times when one can only endure. One lives on, one doesn't die, and the only thing one can do, is to fill one's mind and time as far as possible with the concerns of other people. It doesn't bring immediate peace, but it brings the dawn nearer.: Arthur Christopher Benson

"The healthy and strong individual is the one who asks for help when he needs it. Whether he's got an abscess on his knee, or in his soul." Rona Barrett

"We not only need to be willing to give, but also to be open to receiving from others." On Hope

THOUGHT: "GET ONTO YOUR PUBLIC HIGH SCHOOL AND MIDDLE SCHOOL CAMPUSES"

"To love what you do and feel that it matters-how could anything be more fun?" Katherine Graham

Today the public-school campus is a battle ground in the physical sense with students hurting each other and spiritual sense with the battle between light and darkness. There is a whole segment of Christians who would propose deserting the public school. I do not agree with this. There are certain teens who would not be able to stand strong in the public school and would be drawn toward compromise and sin. For them, it would be the wrong choice. But for many other students the public school is an opportunity to be salt and light, the chance to take a stand for the person of Jesus Christ and to see their peers and teachers impacted for all eternity.

The public schools get a lot of bad press. But there are great things happening. You will find some wonderful Godly teachers who are faithfully serving and making a difference and teenagers who are committed to Christ and living for Him. Organizations like Student Venture, Young Life and Youth for Christ are bringing the good news to public schools. Some of your strongest Christian leaders in youth group may come from the public school. What would happen if the Christian teachers, students and organizations pulled out of the public schools? I shudder to think. The answer for every student is not Christian school or home school. Sometimes Christian schools breed apathy and carnality. In the Christian school, you can find the Pharisees alive and well, which makes it very difficult for teens to live for Jesus. They are mocked and ridiculed for their faith by their peers. It can actually be easier for teens to live for Jesus on the public-school campus because students respect them for the fact they live what they believe. Plus, all the sin you find on a public-school campus you find at a Christian school. If you don't believe that then you are out of touch.

Here is what I am saying, Public school, Christian school or home school, one is not any better than another. It is being obedient to the Lord and going where He is leading you. It is arrogant and wrong to try to say all teens should be home schooled or go the Christian school. Parents determine what is right for their child, not for all children.

We want to see students from the public school coming to the youth group. If we want teens to come onto our turf then we need to reach out to them on their turf. Get onto the public-school campuses. Youth ministry is about you reaching out to teens and not teens reaching out to you. It is about you entering their world. Schools are very open to anyone that will bring a positive influence and help. So, what do you need to do and consider so you can get onto the public-school campus?

1. Pray. Get your parents and students praying! Ask God to open the door and to give you favor. You will find things will go smoother if you have bathed everything in prayer.

"The possibilities of prayer are found in its allying itself with the purposes of God, for God's purposes and man's praying are the combination of all potent and omnipotent forces." E.M. Bounds

2. Make an appointment with the principal. Do not just walk in and ask to see them. By calling and setting up an appointment you are showing him or her respect. Dress up a little. Introduce yourself; express your appreciation for them and the positive impact they are having on teens. Ask for their permission to come on campus to visit your students. Assure them this isn't about you telling other students about Jesus. If they say "no" don't argue with them. Just say, "I understand, thank you very much" and leave. Then inform your parents and have them start calling. Parents hold a lot of power. In most cases the principal will change their mind and let you on campus. If they don't then pray God would either change their mind or move them out. If they say "yes" express your appreciation and let them know you are happy to help any way you can. At the end of the year make another appointment to thank them and ask their permission to come back the following year. Do not assume that because you were on campus this year you will be on campus next year. Unless they say you are welcome every year. Then follow up with a letter of appreciation.

3. Always check in at the office. Don't start taking things for granted and getting lazy by skipping some steps. Learn the secretaries' names and call them by name. Be friendly and reach out to them. You win their hearts and the school is wide open because they will help you, speak highly of you and give you favor in the eyes of the administration.

4. You are not being kind to people so you can get something. You are called to love God and others. Not just teens but principals, teachers, secretaries, janitors, etc. You have been called to youth ministry but before that you were called to be a lover. The school staff will be able to tell whether you really care about them or if you are just using them to get something you want.

5. Always respect the rules. To not do that is to wreck things for yourself and for others as well, see this as pre-evangelism. You are laying the ground work and winning a hearing so you can tell them about Jesus when they come to youth group. The principal is putting his or her neck on the line to let you come on campus. You want to make their job a joy not a burden.

A principal opened the door for me to come and do an all school assembly. I arrived and he said to me, "There are some moms who have shown up with their lawyer. They said if the speaker mentions anything about Christianity they will sue the school." You could see he was pretty nervous and concerned. I told him not to worry about anything and after the assembly I would like to meet the moms and the lawyer. The assembly went great and he came up to me with a big smile on his face, thanked me and then told me the moms were embarrassed and didn't want to stick around. If a principal goes out on a limb to make it possible for you to be on campus, don't do anything to make them look bad. You will discover most principals will be delighted to have you on campus. I remember one principal, after our first meeting in his office, took me down to the library to get my picture taken so I could get a pass that got me into all school activities free.

6. Lunch time is a good time to meet students. Come on campus and meet with your students. As you do, ask your students to introduce you to their friends. Every once in a while, bring a pizza or two with you to share with the students. You will instantly become very popular. Your goal is to make contact and build relationships. You want to establish some face recognition so when a teen comes to the youth group they will recognize you. They are more open to coming to your church if you have come to their school. But you are not there to do evangelism. You are asking God to draw students to you and give you favor so later you can point them to Jesus Christ after school.

7. After school is a good time to see students. Go to practice to watch teens in sports, cheerleading, and band. Get to a rehearsal for the play or musical. Even if you are only there for 15 minutes. Let the students see you and spend just a moment encouraging them. After school, you will see students just sitting around campus hanging out. Stop and talk with them. Every opportunity is a point of contact in which to build a relationship.

8. Speak in the classrooms. If you have a relationship with any teachers volunteer to come in and talk to their classes. Talk about whatever they want to talk about. Do not mention God, Jesus Christ, the Bible, Christianity, etc. Be a storyteller, use humor and give them something practical to apply to their lives. If you go over well and I am sure you will, then that will open the door for you to speak for other classes. If you don't know any teachers then have your students talk to their teachers about having you come in and speak.

Get to know the health teacher because they are looking for speakers to address topics like self-esteem, making good choices, peer pressure, drugs, drinking, sex, etc. Let them know you are available and willing and if you are lucky you will be compensated with a delicious school lunch!

9. Volunteer. You need to balance your time so some of this will be impossible for you to do. You may have a number of schools feeding into your youth ministry; I had students from over 15 high schools coming to the youth group, so your time is limited. Here are some possible things you can do.

- Assistant coach:

Baseball	Water polo
Softball	Cheerleading
Track	Volleyball
Hockey	Cross Country
Soccer	Basketball
Wrestling	Swimming/Diving
Lacrosse	Ping Pong
Football	Rugby

  If I forgot your favorite sport I am sorry.

- Help at sporting events:

Run the clock	Do play by play
Record stats	Take tickets
Work concessions	Sell programs
Help on the field	Give the inspirational talk
Be the team Chaplin	

- Work with the drama or musical:

Help direct	Coordinate meals
Do choreography	Work stage crew
Help the make-up artist	Conduct the band
Organize costumes	Set up and tear down
Build sets or design them	Pass out programs
Take tickets	Sell flowers

- Be a lunch monitor.
- Help with traffic flow.
- Chaperone a dance.
- Go on a field trip.
- Help with the yearbook.
- Work with the school newspaper.
- Serve on numerous committees.
- Chaperone a field trip.

> After they get to know you come in and speak at a faculty meeting. Give them some practical tips on working with teenagers and then be sure you express your appreciation for everything they do.

10. Attend their events. These are so important. Students have worked and practiced hard. Some won't even have their parents showing up. The fact you came will mean so much to them. After the event, be sure you go up and congratulate or console! This is also a great opportunity to see and talk with parents. They will appreciate you took the time to come to the event.

11. Get to know the teachers. If parents are having problems with their teens they will target two groups to blame, teachers and youth pastors. We are in the same boat and we need to support each other. Learn the teacher's names. Ask how they are doing and then be willing to stop and listen. Try bringing a couple of pizzas into the faculty lounge. You will win big points. If they are in the middle of a job stop and give them a hand. Organize an appreciation day for teachers where parents from the church bring in treats and write letters. The better administration and teachers know you, the more comfortable they will feel around you. The more comfortable they are, the more they will trust you. The more they trust you, the more freedom you will gain.

12. Go to where your students work. If they are in sales buy something from them. Do they wait tables? Then request their table and be sure you leave them a good tip. Put in a nice word to the manager or their supervisor if they did well.

Bonnie and I where eating at a steak house where we were friends with the manager. He came over to the table and told me he needed more employees. So next youth group meeting I announced the restaurant was hiring and if you applied to mention my name and the church. Three of my students went in and got jobs. A few weeks passed and we went back at the steak house. He immediately came up to the table and asked me if I knew any other students who needed a job.
> I ask, "Is there a problem?" Aren't they cutting it?"

> He says, "Are you kidding me? They are great and I want to hire more of them!"
> I said, "Do you know why they do such a good job? Because they are Christians!"

He told me, if there was a student I would recommend, to have them come and talk to him personally, mention my name and he would hire them. I was able to tell the students working there what great witnesses they had been. It was a great lesson for the entire youth group to learn. To paraphrase St. Francis of Assisi, "Always share Jesus Christ, if necessary with words." You also get a chance to meet the people they are working with so they have a connection with you.

13. Bring in resources. There are excellent Christian speakers and programs that would have a positive impact on the public school. Set up some assemblies with the school. As these people hit home runs (we pray), the school's appreciation for you will grow. Then invite students to come in the evening to hear them again at your church. Then they can present the gospel. The assembly is pre-evangelism and the evening is evangelistic. Make sure the individual or group doesn't cross the line when speaking.

I have heard some speakers say, "Most of these students will not come back out in the evening so this is my only chance to present them with the gospel." That is probably true. But it is not God's only chance, it is not the church's only chance and there are more speakers than just you. A speaker can destroy in 40 minutes what a youth ministry has tried to build for many years.

For a speaker to step over the line without permission is arrogant, self-centered and sin. You are not trusting in the sovereignty of God and you do not believe other speakers will come after you and be used by the Lord. You do not believe there is effective ministry in the area to follow-up. Do not let a speaker say to you, "God told me to do it." God would not tell you to put the principal's job in jeopardy, alienate the faculty, offend students, embarrass the youth ministry and church, close doors and blemish the reputation of Jesus Christ. Someone did tell you to do it, but it wasn't God. If a speaker wants to talk about God in an assembly then they need to have the guts to go through the proper channels and get permission. They need to sit down with the principal and ask if they can talk about Jesus Christ. If this is what God wants then He will change the heart of the principal and make it possible. If the principal says "No," then that is God saying, "Keep your mouth shut, be obedient and trust me." There have been a number of times when I have spoken for schools that have been closed to assemblies for a number of years because some speaker came in and was offensive. I am there to see if we can bring some healing, establish trust and build a bridge between the ministry and the school. It should never have happened in the first place. If you are providing an assembly for the school be sure you spell out, very clearly, what the expectations are and what they can and can't say to the speaker. Do not assume just because they have done many assemblies they won't do something dumb.

Get onto your public-school campuses. This is one of your primary mission fields. The harvest is ready but the workers are few. God will open the doors as you step out in faith and honor Him.

THINK ABOUT IT:
1. Are you getting on the public-school campus? If not, then why not?
2. What is the next step you can take to impact the campus?
3. Are you getting to know the administration and faculty? Do you know their names? Have you been showing appreciation? Are you psyched for a school lunch?

THOUGHT:
"IT'S GOOD TO GET ALONG WITH YOUR SENIOR PASTOR"

"You can always tell a real friend: when you've made a fool of yourself he doesn't feel you've done a permanent job." Laurence J. Peter

As Youth Pastors, we all have to work with a Senior Pastor so it only makes sense we should have a good relationship with them. I was blessed with two great Senior Pastors, Gordon Hanstead and John Crocker. I am also aware there are Senior Pastors with a variety of problems. Working for them is not a joy but a burden. If you are going to get along with your Senior Pastor then like any relationship, it is going to take work on your part.

Let's talk about what you can do to get along with and strengthen your relationship with the Senior Pastor.

1. Honor them. How can you do this? By making them look good. Make them look good in front of the teens, parents and other Pastors. Make them look good when you're at the restaurant or on Sunday morning. Honor them when you are with them and when you aren't. Show them the respect due according to their high calling.

2. No surprises. You don't want them surprised by anything. If a parent is upset at you - let them know. If a young person gets hurt in a serious way - let them know. If people are going to complain because of an event - let them know. You do not want them to be blind sided. It makes them look stupid and they will not be thrilled with you.

3. Reach out. Do not wait for them to come to you. Some youth pastors have complained to me because their Senior Pastor doesn't spend time with them. Look, their plate is full and they may assume if you need anything you will come to them. Take the responsibility for the relationship and reach out to them. Invite them out to lunch once a month. Be sure you ask them far enough ahead so they can get it on their calendar. If you need something, go to them and don't wait for them to come to you. I knew I could go to my Senior Pastors anytime and they would put down whatever they were doing to spend time with me.

I understand if you are in a mega church your contact with the Senior Pastor can be limited but it doesn't have to be non-existent. When I was the youth specialist at Moody Bible Institute we had a change in Presidents. George Sweeting stepped down and Joe Stowell took over. I called and made an appointment with Dr. Stowell so I could introduce myself. We had a great time. Now if I had waited for him to call me we might never have gotten together. Not because he doesn't want to spend time with me, but because he's busy! So, give them the benefit of the doubt and reach out.

4. Do what they ask immediately. My Senior Pastors did not ask me to do a lot of stuff, but whenever they did I would do it right away. If they were asking then it was important to them, even though it may not be crucial to the youth ministry. Because you respect and honor them you make it your top priority. Obviously, don't do what they ask if it involves sinning or compromising your character. If they ask you to change your whole philosophy of youth ministry then maybe it is an indication your time is up.

5. Invite them to speak. Once a year ask them to speak for a retreat or evening meeting. If they connect well, then maybe next time you ask them to do a series of talks. It gives the teens a chance to hear them up close and personal. After the talk, they can even hang out with their Senior Pastor. If they do not connect well with teenagers then one evening a year is fine.

6. Ask for advice. There is wisdom in the counsel of many. On occasion make one of those many your Senior Pastor. When you do this you communicate to them you value their opinion. It always feels good to be needed.

7. Show them appreciation. If they preach a message God uses to touch your heart then let them know. Send them an e-mail, drop them a note or tell them face to face. We get into this mind set, "They know they're doing a good job." When we think this, then we stop appreciating. Get rid of that mind set and look for chances to build and appreciate them.

"A trouble-making woman once told John Wesley, 'God has given me the talent of speaking my mind'. Mr. Wesley snapped back, 'God wouldn't mind if you buried that talent'." George Sweeting

8. Support in public and disagree in private. Your Senior Pastor will make mistakes and show poor judgment at times. Never gossip to others. If they make a mistake talk to them in private. As much as possible support them in public as long as you are not compromising what Jesus Christ would have you do. Do not listen to people gossip about your Senior Pastor. If they start, just say, "Have you talked to the Senior Pastor about this concern? Let's go right now and find them so you can express this to them personally." If they don't want to go, let them know you will inform the Senior Pastor of their concerns. You only need to do this once and people will stop gossiping to you. Never get in the middle, between your Senior Pastor and someone else. If a group or individual is having issues with the Senior Pastor then they go to him and not to you.

9. You are part of a team. Support and share the vision of the church as a whole. You are part of the Body of Christ. Don't become a severed limb doing your own thing in youth ministry and not connected with the church as a whole. At times, you will be asked to make sacrifices for the good of the whole body. This might mean cutting back your budget or doing without in some areas. You do it because you are a part of a team. God has called you to youth ministry but He has also called you to minister to the Body of Christ as a whole.

10. Keep short accounts. The enemy will try to divide you from your Senior Pastor. Don't let it happen. Maintain a clear conscious with them. If something has offended or bothered you then go to them immediately. Do not let anything build or simmer inside of you. The enemy will use this as a wedge between the two of you. Be willing to ask for and grant forgiveness quickly. They will have struggles just like you do. If you are sharp enough to discern weakness then be mature enough to forgive them.

11. Never excuse willful sin. If your Senior Pastor is involved in sin then you need to follow the steps in Matthew 18. If the sin is one that jeopardizes the ministry then you need to inform someone else. An example would be having an affair. You confront them and then you let them know you are going to the chairman of the Board. Do not let them talk you out of it through promises, tears, pleading, intimidation, etc.

12. Be sensitive to their children. It is not easy being the children of the Senior Pastor just like it isn't easy being children of the Youth Pastor. What can you do to encourage them and the family as a whole? They may be in the midst of rebellion. If the enemy can't get to the Senior Pastor he will target the children, so perhaps God can use you to be a significant other in their life. Pastors live in a fish bowl and it is easy for others to cast stones and judge. After years of this, children can become bitter. Do not hold them to a higher standard than the rest of the group. Be a listener and lover. For you to invest your life in the lives of the Senior Pastor's children can be one of the greatest blessings you can give your Pastor.

13. What is your Senior Pastor's love language? Identify it and then look to love them in that area. As you do this, God will use it to win their heart and draw them toward you. That is not why you love them but it is definitely a benefit.

14. Offer information. Let them know what is happening in youth ministry. Ask them how often do they want an update on the ministry, once a week, month, quarter? How do they want to be informed, staff meeting, e-mail, voice mail, one to one, etc.?

15. Get together as couples. On occasion set up times to get together as couples just to have fun, to talk, laugh and play together. Have dinner and then go play miniature golf, bowl, go-carting or maybe just play some board games. If there is anyone who knows how to have fun it is a Youth Pastor. Help them to loosen up and to be a little crazy. There is nothing like hitting each other with paint balls to build love and unity!

16. Pray for them regularly. As you do this God will move your heart toward them. You are certainly aware of some of the issues, pressures and problems they are facing. Go to them and ask if they have anything specific you can pray about. Then be sure you go back and ask how God answered the prayer. This communicates to them you have been serious about praying for them.

THINK ABOUT IT:
1. What can I do to deepen the relationship with my Senior Pastor?
2. When was the last time I appreciated and complimented them?
3. Is there anything coming between the two of us? What do you need to do about it?

THOUGHT:
"WHEN YOU CANDIDATE–YOU BETTER CHECK OUT THE SENIOR PASTOR"

"One of the most tactful men I ever knew, says a California manufacturer, was the man who fired me from my first job. He called me in and said, 'Son, I don't know how we're ever going to get along without you but starting Monday we're going to try'."
James M. Braude

It is a fact there are some Senior Pastors out there who are having emotional and spiritual problems. You do not want to be on staff with them. Some are ministering in small churches and some lead mega churches. Just because a church is large doesn't mean it's healthy. Ask permission to talk to some former Youth Pastors who have served with this Senior Pastor. If the church refuses to give you the information, without a legitimate reason, then they are hiding something and I would highly recommend you not go to that church.

Ask the previous Youth Pastors these questions.

1. What did you like about working with the Senior Pastor?

2. What did you dislike?

3. Did you experience any verbal abuse or emotional intimidation? If they do this they are being disrespectful to you. Abuse is wrong and it is wrong in every situation. To verbally assault you before the other Pastors, teens, parents, congregation or in private is abuse and you should not tolerate that at all. For them to yell at you or use sarcasm to embarrass you are forms of intimidation and ways they try to gain control over you. You do not want to work with an individual who would treat you like that.

4. Are they micro managers? This is a control freak. They want to have their hands on everything. This type of Senior Pastor will drive you insane. They will tell you what to do, when to do it, where to do it and how to do it! You want a Senior Pastor to set you free to do what God has called you to do and not hold you back. A micro manager is saying, "I don't trust you, I think I can do a better job and I want to control you." They are probably insecure and fear you will do a good job and not need them.

5. Are they theologically sound? I had a church contact me about being their youth pastor. After some talking they confessed they didn't believe in the inerrancy of the Scripture but they didn't mind if I taught it. That would be crazy to serve with someone off theologically. It would only lead to conflict and disharmony.

6. Do they speak the truth in love? Truth without love is cruel and love without truth is deception. I spoke for a camp in the west. The youth Pastor was great and the students he was producing were tremendous. I spent a weekend with this group and was totally impressed. During the weekend he confessed the church was going to let him go. They were saying he wasn't really equipped or gifted to be a youth pastor. They were sending him for vocational tests and counseling in the midst of having him step down. But later I discover it isn't the church wanting him to step down, it's the Senior Pastor. It was the Senior Pastor saying he really wasn't gifted to be a Youth Pastor. This was such baloney! He and his wife still felt called to youth ministry, the teenagers loved him, he was producing Godly young men and women and a member of the church board, who is part of the youth staff, thought he was doing a tremendous job.

This Senior Pastor was a very successful Youth Pastor and of all the people in the country he could choose, he chose this guy to be his Youth Pastor. Why? Because he is gifted, talented and effective in youth ministry. But now, for a variety of reasons, he doesn't want him to be Youth Pastor anymore. So instead of having the courage to just let him go and dealing with the consequences from the decision, he, instead, came up with the notion he is not gifted to be a youth Pastor. He did this so he doesn't have to deal with teens and parents who are going to be upset if they just canned him. That is so wrong. It is fine if the Senior Pastor does not want him as a youth Pastor but it is wrong to put doubts in this young man's mind. This Senior Pastor was a coward and didn't have the character to speak the truth in love.

7. Does the Senior Pastor support and back you when you're under attack? There are some Senior Pastors who will love and support you when things are going well but if things get hard they disappear. You want someone who will stand with and support you during the good times and hard times.

8. Are they weird? A young man said he was the candidate at a church and the Senior Pastor wanted him to sign a paper that said he would commit to being the Youth Pastor until the rapture. I said, "I think that is very weird!" What else is this guy going to ask you to do if you become the youth Pastor? If he is weird before you come do you think he will get better after you have been there for awhile?

"You can't drive straight on a twisting lane" Russian Proverb

9. How do they respond to your success? Are they excited for you or do they become jealous and insecure? Both Senior Pastors I served with were supportive. They would give me opportunities to preach and would be excited and complimentary from the front when I would do well. But there are some who become threatened because of their insecurities.

10. How does the Senior Pastor and their spouse treat your spouse? You do not want to put your spouse in a situation where they are being treated poorly or looked down on by the Senior Pastor or their spouse.

THINK ABOUT IT:
1. Have you asked all the questions you need to about the Senior Pastor?
2. Have you talked to any past Youth Pastors from the church you are looking at?
3. Make a list of any concerns you have about the Senior Pastor and seek some Godly advice.

THOUGHT:
"BEING IN YOUTH MINISTRY FOR THE LONG HAUL IS A GOOD THING"

"Any man can work when every stoke of his hands brings down the fruit rattling from the tree...but to labor in season and out of season, under every discouragement...that requires a heroism which is transcendent." Henry Ward Beecher

Like I mentioned before, Youth Ministry is not a stepping stone to something better...it is the best! It can be a lifetime calling. It is for me. Why should you consider staying in Youth Ministry for the long haul?

1. Because this is what God has called you to do. You are never happier, more at peace or experiencing greater fulfillment than when you are in the center of God's will. You always want to do what He has gifted you to do. You may shift to *para* church, itinerate speaking, camp, missions, etc., but your focus is still teenagers! If God has called you to youth ministry, why would you want to do anything else?

2. You are better equipped as the years go by to minister to teens. As you get older, you become smarter and wiser, I hope! You are better equipped to develop, help and pour into teenagers. Getting older is a terrible, lame, and pathetic excuse for getting out of youth ministry. You are concerned because you are changing and you aren't able to do some of the things you use to do. Like...

- Skiing all day and staying up all night
- Schooling them in basketball. Your mind knows what to do but you body won't cooperate.
- Looking forward to all-night lock-ins
- Taking on three of them in wrestling at one time
- Being-up-to date with all the music groups
- Playing tackle football on Saturday and then being able to get out of bed on Sunday

So, because you can't do what you use to do you're thinking it is time to move on. Wrong. It is nice to be able to play with the students but this is not what they really need. They need someone who will lead and model for them, and only gets better with age. You become a better listener, more understanding and you know how to love unconditionally.

3. The Joy of seeing God work in students lives after they graduate. When you stay around you get to see what God does in their lives through college and beyond.

There was a young man who was a pain through High School. He gave me a lot of problems. He graduated and went off to college and when he returned home he came into my office and he was a changed man. The first thing he did was apologize for all the problems he had caused. Then he thanked me for all my love and patience. Finally, he told me how God was working in and through his life. All of a sudden, he had a vision of what the Lord would like to do with his future. Wow! Tears came to my eyes as I listened to this young man share his excitement. It did two things for me.
- ➢ I realized it was all worth while. All the tears, sweat, and problems were worth it.
- ➢ It gave me a hope for all my problem teens in the group now. I needed to have a vision God would work in their lives beyond the Youth Ministry. My responsibility was to love them, challenge them, and never give up hope.

You get the privilege of performing weddings and dedicating the children of your students. How great is that? As they grow up, get married, have children and settle down, they become great supporters. They can even become part of your youth staff.

4. The joy of ministering to generations. One day you will have teenagers coming up to you and saying, "When my mom/dad was in middle/High school you were their Youth Pastor!" At that point you can think, "Should I hug or hit them?" I am so humbled and thankful I get to minister to a whole new generation. That's just one of the bonuses of sticking with youth ministry for the long haul. Parents who heard me speak when they were teenagers now bring their teens to hear me speak.

Here is a funny result from ministering to generations. I graduated from Bethel University in St. Paul, Minnesota. Now all four of my children have gone to Bethel and have had other students come up to them and say, "My mom used to date your dad." That is scary! My wife looks at me and I try to explain I never went out with many women.

To be used to impact generations is a blessing more than words can express. But watch out how you act on dates because you could be ministering to their children in the future.

"Success in Youth Ministry equals longevity." Dan Howard

5. Your credibility goes up. No longer are you the young pup who has a lot of energy but doesn't really know what is going on. Now you become the old dog. You have the experience and knowledge in working with teenagers. People grow in their respect and there is less questioning. People trust you because you have stood the test of time and have remained true to your calling.

6. Parents become your peers. You have children who are teenagers and parents feel like you can really understand what they are going through because you are going through the same thing. As your children graduate from high school and move on you will still have their confidence because you have already walked the path they are walking now. It is easier for them to follow your leadership because you have been there. I remember speaking to a group of parents about working with teenagers. At the end, a mother raised her hand and asked, "How old are your children?" My oldest was almost ten years old. She said, "I thought so. Just wait till you have teenagers." She was really saying, "You don't know what you are talking about because you haven't walked that path yet." I don't agree with her, but I understand where she is coming from. Today I say the same thing but because I have children who are beyond the teenage years I don't get this kind of response. Parents think differently, respond differently, and see you differently when you become one of their peers. It is like, "OK, now you're one of us."

7. Teens keep you young. I never think of myself as old. Working with teenagers gives me an excuse to be wild and crazy. I have a mug that was given to me which says, "You can only be young once, but you can be immature for the rest of your life." Working with teens keeps you thinking young and age really is a state of mind. I was sitting with a teen at camp having a coke. He says to me, "I wish I could talk to my dad like I talk to you. He is so old." I asked him, "How old is he?" He tells me, "Forty-one." I almost spit out my coke. I can't even remember when I was forty-one. It is all about a mind set. He didn't think of me as old as his dad. Working with teenagers keeps you thinking, feeling, and acting young. OK, maybe not feeling young. I love the quote by Satchel Page, "how old would you be if you didn't know how old you were?"

8. It gives you an appreciation for the process. God is all about building, developing, and changing lives. When we first start out in Youth Ministry, we want everything to be instant. We live in an instant society, instant cash, instant replay, fast food, microwave, instant pudding, etc. There is no surprise we want instant Youth Ministry, instant changed lives, instant growth, instant numbers, we want it all and we want it all right now! We think success is an event, but it's not. Success is a process and journey. That is why you can't come in with the idea that I will be successful in two years. Success does not happen instantly. Youth Ministry is not instant. A teen can step from darkness into light in a moment and meet Jesus Christ as Savior. But to become a disciple of Christ takes time. We give up the instant gratification of trying to be the biggest, fastest, flashiest youth group, to gain a deeper satisfaction of seeing individual students change and grow in their faith. They came in as immature freshman, and leave, hopefully, prayerfully, as spiritually mature seniors. Those Youth Pastors who are in and out of the ministry in two years never gain an appreciation or understanding for the process.

9. You become more of a parent or grandparent figure. You start as this young, hot, good looking youth Pastor. (Ok, at least I was young.) Then the years roll by and you develop furniture disease. This is when your chest falls into your drawers. No longer are you the attractive, young youth worker you once were. Instead of them falling in love with you because you are a potential boy/girl friend. Now they fall in love with you because you are the parent/grandparent example. Now we do not have to worry, as much, about romantic feelings from the teens. We are able to love, direct, nurture, and challenge them the way a parent does. The shocker comes when you discover one day the parent looks more attractive than the teen. Then you realize, "I am getting old."

10. The opportunity to impact future youth workers. Staying in youth ministry for the long haul gives you the chance to reach out to the next generation of youth workers. You will have the privilege of teaching, leading, and encouraging those just starting out. To be able to invest your life in theirs, helping them work through all the problems and pit falls and then being able to rejoice with them as God moves.

There are many great reasons to stay in youth ministry for the long haul. The best reason of all is because I am being obedient to God and doing what He has called me to do.

THINK ABOUT IT:
1. Can you see yourself in Youth Ministry for the long haul?
2. To make it for the long haul what would you need to start doing?
3. What would you need to stop doing?

THOUGHT:
"BE AWARE OF THE BASIC NEEDS OF TEENAGERS"

"Pay attention to the young, and make them just as good as possible." Socrates

We battle against a lot of outside influences which pull the students away from us. We need to be aware of what calls to our teens and impacts their lives in significant ways.

- **Time.** They are way too committed. Hundreds of things scream at them for attention. Youth Ministry is just one of a long list of things with demands on their time.

- **Stress.** One thing piles onto another and the teen feels like they are going to explode. Pressure for good grades, making money, loving relationships, excellence in sports, lead in musical, captain in cheerleading, latest styles, first chair in orchestra and on and on it goes.

- **Technological literacy.** It is very hard to impress them. The world can do a much better job at flash, pop, and wow than we can ever do. While it is important we continue to progress beyond the flannel board and overhead projector. This is not where we put our hope. Doug Fields says, "Whatever you seek to get them there with you have to use to keep them. Are you using 'bells and whistles' or 'love and acceptance?' Which one is more effective in keeping students and really helping them to grow?"

- **Media Directed.** No longer are teens merely influenced by the media. Today executives spend millions of dollars to influence the thinking and spending of teenagers. The media today targets teens with the purpose of shaping, directing, and exploiting them.

> **The demise of absolutes.** Today teens ask the question "why" and really mean it. Why not lie, why not have sex, why not cheat, WHY? They want to know if Christianity is really relevant for today. To them it seems out dated and out of touch.

> **Sexual attack.** Every time they look at TV, internet, video, movies, magazine advertisement, billboards, music videos, etc, they are being smacked in the face with sex. Free sex, safe sex, oral sex, sex with multiple partners, same sex partners, sex without consequences, and sex NOW!

> **Isolation.** TV, iPhones, Video Games, texts, technology, computer games, divorce, emotionally withdrawn parents, abuse, and busy parents. These have all contributed to teens drawing more and more into isolation.

Our teenagers have basic needs which cause them to act and react the way they do. They'll do almost anything to get those needs met. Are we aware of the needs and do we seek to meet them? Students want to go where their needs are being met. No matter what you are doing, a teen asks themselves, "What am I going to get out of this?" You plan something but they don't come because they don't see it as important or of value to them. It is not meeting needs in their lives. So, what will combat everything screaming for their attention and get them involved in Youth Ministry? The Holy Spirit using you and the ministry to meet their needs. Let me suggest five needs every teenager has.

1. Need to be loved. A teenager will go wherever they experience love. If it's a party, they will go to a party, but if it's at Church, then they will go to church.
So many of our students only experience conditional love. This says I will love you if...
> Parents-I will love you if you keep your room clean
> Date- I will love you if you take off your clothes
> Teacher-I will love you if you get good grades
> Coaches- I will love you if you perform for me
> Boss- I will love you if you make me money

Any wonder teens feel used and feel like they are something rather than somebody?

They will come to your youth ministry if they experience genuine, unconditional, agape love. We treat the teenagers the way Jesus Christ treats us. We can love them unconditionally because we are unconditionally loved. We can forgive them because we are greatly forgiven. We are patient with them because He is patient with us. We understand because we are understood. We discipline out of love because He disciplines those He loves. Teens mirror themselves in the eyes of those who they see are important to them. What do they see when they look in your eyes?

2. Need to belong and be accepted. This is why peer pressure is so strong. A student wants to fit into a group. Even those who would claim to be individuals, who are dressing and acting radical, are fitting into a group of other individuals dressing and acting just like they are. Some students will do anything to fit in and be loved. So, what can we do in youth ministry to help them belong?
- Give them ownership in the youth ministry. We are going to talk about this more when we talk about the third need.
- Individual attention. Someone knowing their name, who is taking the time to listen and getting to know them. This isn't necessarily you, but they need to be connecting with some youth staff person and one or more students.
- Small groups. Assign every young person to a small group and allow them to plug in at one of these four levels.
  - Level 4 - I don't want to know what small group I am in, but they can pray for me. So, the youth pastor or small group coordinator is passing on prayer requests to their small group leader.
  - Level 3 - I want to know who my small group leader is and I want the freedom to contact them, but I don't want them to contact me. You are still passing on prayer requests but they may also be contacting the small group leader for prayer.
  - Level 2 - The small group leader can contact me. You make sure the leader is calling and coming up to them

on a regular basis.
- Level 1- I want to be in the small group.

The young person can move from level four to level one immediately. We want every teen connecting and at the very least being prayed for on a regular basis. When a teenager says, "I hate youth group and I don't want to go." They are usually saying, "I don't feel like I have any friends. I am not connecting and I don't feel like I belong."

3. The need to achieve. They want to do something and they want to do it well. Teenagers today want to do something significant and feel like they are making a difference. What can you do to open the door so they have the opportunity to achieve? What aren't you doing that you could start doing?
- Expand Multi-Media - You have teens who can think way outside the box.
- Dance team - As part of your worship.
- Ministry to deaf - Those who can sign.
- Environmental group - Clean up, plant, and protect the environment.
- Animal care group - Volunteer at humane society, work with vets.
- Prayer Team - Plan concerts of prayer.
- Sports ministry - Coach younger teams, hold clinics for neighborhood kids. Compete with other groups.
- Car repair Team - A lot of students are really into working on cars.
- Now you think outside the box. What about senior citizens, Cancer and AIDS patients, families whose loved one is in intensive care, military overseas, skaters, movie lovers, poets, etc, etc, etc?

"The common idea that success spoils people by making them vain, egotistic, and self-complacent is erroneous; on the contrary, it makes them, for the most part, humble, tolerant, and kind. Failure makes people cruel and bitter."
W. Somerset Maugham

4. The need to be recognized for their achievements. When you recognize what they are doing as significant, then you validate the ministry and the individual. If they can't achieve in a positive way in your eyes then they will seek to achieve in the eyes of their peers and this can lead to negative and destructive behavior. Things like partying, drinking, drugs, and sex. These things will give them a lot of recognition from those who are also doing the same things. So, encourage them and look for opportunities to build them up. To say, "Great, wonderful, awesome, I noticed, good job," is life giving. You are saying to them they are someone of worth and value.

They need to know it is not too late for them. God will forgive them and give them a brand-new start. You are helping them see God does have a special plan for their life. Starting now, they can begin to become everything Jesus Christ created them to be. You need to develop a mind set among your youth staff that you are going to look for opportunities to build up and encourage the students in your group.

5. The need to deal with the pain. Things are happening around and to our students lives so quickly they can feel like their lives are out of control. This goes back to knowing the issues, understanding the temptations and being aware of the problems they are facing. Many teens aren't dealing with the pain. They are seeking to numb the pain. This leads to "at risk" behavior which increases the pain. Every month I get between 150-300 internet messages from teens around the world. Many say something like this, "I am sorry to dump all this on you but I don't have anyone to talk with."

"Christ is the answer to sorrow. When Harry Lauder, the great Scottish comedian, received word his son had been killed in France, he said, 'In a time like this, there are three courses open to man: He may give way to despair and become bitter. He may endeavor to drown his sorrow in drink or in a life of wickedness. Or he may turn to God.' In your sorrow, turn to God… Our Christ is more than adequate for sorrow." Billy Graham

I hear these things said over and over again in different ways.
- ➢ "I don't feel like anyone really understands me. No one takes the time to try and understand me."
- ➢ "I am discouraged and depressed."
- ➢ "I am lonely. I've got some party friends but someone who will listen and really care. I don't have that."

Part of our job description should read, "Always listening and seeking to understand." When we do this we give the students hope. Then get them some help for the pain. The pain is like a string on a puppet. We start working with them, they start making progress and then Satan pulls on the string of pain and we are back to square one. We refer them to others who can help with the pain and no longer is the enemy able to manipulate them through their pain. Keep in mind those five basic needs every teen has. Remember, a teen wants to go where their needs are being met.

THINK ABOUT IT:
1. How well are you meeting those five needs?
2. Where are you weakest?
3. What can you do to get more students plugged in?

THOUGHTS FROM OTHERS:
"I am not young enough to know everything." James M. Barrie

"Like its politicians and its wars, society has the teenagers it deserves." J. B. Priestley

"Life is a mission. Every other definition is false, and leads all who accept it astray." Guiseppe Mazzini

"I see no business in life but the work of Christ." Henry Martyn

THOUGHT:
"STAY AWAY FROM WHAT GOD HATES"

"There is a difference between a sinful lapse and a sinful lifestyle, but know that every sinful lifestyle started from a succession of sinful lapses." Scott Brown

Have you ever considered there are things we do that God hates? I mean think about it. Could we be doing something right now He hates? Yes, and this causes me to tremble. I want to stay away from anything that makes Him angry. To do something God hates is to fight against Him and this is a losing battle. Proverbs 21:30 says, "There is no wisdom, no insight, no plan that can succeed against the Lord." When you are doing what God hates, you lose out on His blessing, presence, and power in your life and in your ministry.

If God hates it then stay away from it. Avoid it at all costs, run from it. So, in no particular order, here is what God hates:

Proverbs 6:16-19 says, "There are six things the Lord hates, seven that are detestable to Him: haughty eyes, a lying tongue, hands that shed innocent blood, a heart that devises wicked schemes, feet that are quick to rush into evil, a false witness who pours out lies, and a man who stirs up dissension among brothers,"

1. Haughty eyes. These are the eyes of someone who is proud. They think they are better than others and they look down on those around them. They do not notice or recognize all they are, the gifts, talents, abilities, and even their looks are all from the Lord. God hates this kind of arrogance and He will oppose you. Do you think you're something because a lot of students come to your youth group? Do you think you're something because you get to speak for thousands of teens? Do you think you're something because teenagers like you, think you're funny or think you're cute? I have news for you. Without Jesus Christ you are nothing, He doesn't need you at all. He has chosen to bless you and establish you. But just as quickly He can end your ministry. For some of you this is a word of warning. God is about to humble you and bring your ministry to an end. Unless you humble yourself, (Acts 12:21-23, Daniel 4:24-37, James 4:6, 1 Peter 5:5, Proverb 16:5, Proverb 18:12, Proverb 21: 4, Psalms 101:5, and Psalm 138:6).

"A proud man is always looking down on things and people; and, of course, as long as you're looking down, you can't see something that's above you." C. S. Lewis

Either you get on your knees, with your face to the floor and humble yourselves before God or the Lord will humble you. I have found, through personal experience it is much easier and less traumatic if I humble myself.

2. A lying tongue. I have had first hand experiences with people who lied and it is a terrible sin. People can't trust you anymore. It destroys your character and integrity. All the armor of God falls apart without truth. The first thing you put on is the belt of truth. That is what holds all the rest of the armor together. Without truth, everything else falls apart. What is a lie?
- Saying something you know is false.
- Making something seem worse.
- Making something sound better.
- Telling a half-truth which by definition is a half lie.
- Making up a story, leading others to believe it is true.
- Not taking responsibility and trying to blame someone else when it was your responsibility.
- Using someone else's illustration or talk and not giving them credit.
- Exaggerate numbers of teens involved in your youth group.

"Sin has many tools, but a lie is the handle which fits them all." Oliver Wendell Holmes, SR.

Why is it so important you tell the truth?
- If your word doesn't mean anything, then you don't mean anything because you are your word.
- When you lie, you destroy your trustworthiness. Take a beautiful vase and smash it on the floor, breaking it into hundreds of pieces. Now go ahead and glue it back together

and make it look as good as new. How long will it take you? It will take you a long time. This is what happens to your trustworthiness and character when you lie. You smash it in the eyes of others and it will take you a long time to rebuild that trust. Remember, love is unconditional but trust is earned. How do you earn trust? By consistent behavior over a period of time.

➢ When you are lying you are speaking Satan's native tongue, John 8:44. You speak a language he understands, encourages and likes.

Today teens do not see lying as a big deal. Maybe it's because we haven't seen lying as a big deal. But it is a huge deal and God hates a lying tongue.

3. Hands that shed innocent blood. To be a murderer is horrible and the Lord finds it detestable. I think of abortion doctors and nurses who have killed thousands of innocent babies. I would not want to be in their shoes when judgment day comes. God will not be sympathetic or understanding because He hates hands that shed innocent blood.

4. A heart which devises wicked schemes. Planning something which will hurt, manipulate or use and abuse someone else. You are planning to do something that will hurt others to get what you want. I think of Youth Pastors who have planned how they can take advantage of teenagers or lay staff sexually. You are thinking and planning things that are wrong, evil, wicked, and sin. Catch this, God hates the fact you are thinking about it. Even if you don't do it the Lord still hates the fact you would consider it.

5. Feet that are quick to rush into evil. Webster defines evil as, "Morally reprehensible arising from bad character or conduct." It is your poor character causing you to quickly rush into evil. This is the next step after devising wicked schemes. You aren't just thinking about it anymore. Now you are going to go somewhere that will give you the opportunity to be involved in evil. You rush toward pornographic web sites, bad movies, strip clubs, you can add to this list. Notice the person is rushing toward the evil. There is no hesitation on their part. Their character has been destroyed and their conscience is seared. They don't care anymore. They see the chance to be involved in evil and they rush to it. This behavior appeals to your flesh, feeds your old nature and is valued by Satan, (Romans 12:9). God hates evil and we are to hate evil.

6. A false witness who pours out lies. Here you are called on to give testimony to what you have seen with your own eyes and you lie about it. This is impacting someone else. False witnesses were used against Jesus and they crucified Him. Is there any wonder why God hates a false witness? You are perverting justice.

7. A man who stirs up dissension among brothers. This is someone who is a gossip and causes division within the Body of Christ. They have pet issues that are important to them and they get people on their side to oppose those who think differently. They don't like something which was said or done. Do they talk to the person they are upset at? No, they would rather talk about the person rather then talk to the person.

8. Those who do wrong. Psalms 5:4-5 says, "You are not a God who takes pleasure in evil, with you the wicked cannot dwell. The arrogant cannot stand in your presence, you hate all who do wrong."

We are not talking about those who make mistakes and fall on occasion. We are talking about individuals who set out to do what is wrong and continue in that direction. What is wrong? The acts of the sinful nature. You can check out a list in Galatians 5:12-21...

Sexual-immorality	Witchcraft	Fits of Rage
Envy	Impurity	Hatred
Selfish Ambition	Drunkenness	Debauchery
Discord	Dissension	Orgies
Idolatry	Jealousy	Factions
And the like		

Let me speak with you again about pornography because I think it is one of the greatest evils in the world today. It is responsible for destroying more individuals and families than all the terrorist groups in the world. There are so many good reasons to stay away from pornography and allow me to share a few with you.

- We have more slaves today than at any other time in history and most of them are sex slaves. Children as young as 5 years old being tortured, drugged, kidnapped, raped, forced to pose, made to perform sexual acts and sometimes murdered all to feed our lust. Think about it for a second, how sick, perverted and wrong is that idea? We were never created to be predators, we were created to be heroes of the faith who protect the children and adults from being used and abused.

- Looking at porn is not harmless fun that isn't hurting anyone. When you look at porn you support the sex slave business. Even through some of the men and women have chosen to pose, many have not and there is no way you can tell the difference.

- It is degrading to the opposite sex. You begin to look at them as something rather then someone. They become objects for you to use to gratify your sexual desires.

- You are saying "yes" to something God is saying "no" to.

- It hardens your heart, draws you away from God, then kills you emotionally and spiritually. It causes you to become apathetic toward the things of the Lord and you develop an "I don't care" attitude.

- Pornography does not remain static but always seeks to draw you into darker and more perverted things.

- It is inspired by Satan.

9. Wickedness. Psalm 45:7a says, "You love righteousness and hate wickedness..." Webster defines wicked as, "Morally bad." You find a list of the wicked in 1 Corinthians 6:9-10...

Sexually Immoral	Idolaters	Adulterers
Male Prostitutes	Homosexual Offenders	Thieves
Greedy	Drunkards	Slanders
Swindlers		

The wicked will not inherit the Kingdom of God. Having done these things does not disqualify you from heaven, but continuing to do them does. If you continue to live this lifestyle of sin then you will not inherit the Kingdom of God. 1 Corinthians 6:11 says, "And that is what some of you <u>were</u>. But you were washed, you were sanctified, you were justified in the name of the Lord Jesus Christ and by the Spirit of our God." This means there is hope if you will turn from the sin.

10. Robbery and iniquity. Isaiah 61:8a says, "For I, the Lord, love justice, I hate robbery and iniquity..." Youth Pastors are not always the best paid and there may be the temptation of taking money left over from an activity or part of your youth budget for yourself. That is robbery and God hates it. You can also rob time and energy from your job. To rob someone is to cheat them out of something which belongs to them. You are being paid to do a job and if you are not putting in the hours or effort, that is robbery. Taking home supplies from church to use them personally. Using the church van and its gas to run personal errands without permission. Making copies of CD's and DVD's without permission. Taking petty cash and money collected for events and using it on yourself. Shoplifting the smallest candy bar, newspaper or cup of coffee is robbery. Being given back too much change, knowing it and just keeping it, is robbery.

Webster defines iniquity as, "Gross injustice." One way you might do this is by showing favoritism. Hanging out with, buying things for and giving yourself to the "beautiful people" and ignoring others. Spending a lot of time with the leadership teens and ignoring the fringe kids. I heard of one youth organization has this philosophy...
- ➢ First off you go for the good looking male athletes.
- ➢ This will attract the good-looking girls.

> The good-looking girls attract the other guys.
> And the other guys attract the other girls.

Am I the only one who sees something wrong with this? We are not to show favoritism. I have seen our justice system here in the US show gross injustice. Protecting the guilty and punishing the innocent.

11. Worshipping false gods. Jeremiah 44:2-4, parts of these verses, "This is what the Lord Almighty, the God if Israel says, they provoked me to anger by burning incense and by worshipping other gods...Do not do this detestable thing I hate!" Do not seek any god but the Lord Almighty. Our culture is full of false gods. We worship at the alters of beauty, popularity, fame, and fortune. There is only one God worthy of our time, worship, and adoration and that is the King of Kings and Lord of Lords. Do not put anything or anyone before the Lord.

12. Divorce and violence. Malachi 2:16a says, "I hate divorce, says the Lord God of Israel, and I hate man's covering himself with violence..." Talk about being politically incorrect. We don't like to hear this but it seems pretty clear. God hates divorce, so for you divorce is not an option. Work on your marriage and you take whatever steps you need to take to save it. Get out of ministry if you need to take the step. Some of you wonder why God is removing His blessing from your ministry and why it feels like He no longer responds to your prayers. Malachi 2:13-14 says, "Another thing you do: You flood the Lord's alter with tears. You weep and wail because He no longer pays attention to your offerings or accepts them with pleasure from your hands. You ask, "Why?" It is because the Lord is acting as the witness between you and the wife of your youth, because you have broken faith with her, though she is your partner, the wife of your marriage covenant." God takes your marriage vows very seriously and you better do the same.

Do not allow violence to cover you. It starts on the inside as you cover yourself by what you read, watch and listen to. What you are taking into your life is what is covering you. Then that leads to action. Violence springs from out of control anger. When we become violent towards our spouse, children, teens, or anyone, it is abusive. To become violent toward someone or someone's property is wrong and God hates it. He hates it when we cover ourselves in violence and then make excuses for our behavior.

I have never heard anyone preach on what God hates. Some of you should consider sharing a message like this with your teenagers. When I came to Christ, as a teenager, people told me God loved me. They said I needed to be obedient and they even told me to avoid certain sins. But no one ever told me there were things God hated and I should avoid those things.

Be sure you hate the sin and not the person. Hate pride but not the prideful, hate the lies but not the liar. A teenager's failure is no excuse for us to stop loving them. At times, it needs to be tough love.
- ➢ Hate the sin but not the sinner,
- ➢ Love the sinner and not the sin.

It ought to give you pause, drive you to your knees and cause you to tremble to think you might cross the line. Maybe after reading this you will realize you are doing something God hates. What should you do?
- ➢ Confess it to God, agree it is sin and then ask for forgiveness. I know your sins have been forgiven but asking for it is a good way to humble yourself.

- ➢ Then turn 180 degrees and head in the opposite direction. Begin to do what is right and start making good choices now. God instructs us to stand firm and resist Satan, James 4:7 and 1 Peter 5:8-9, to flee from evil desires, 2 Timothy 2:22.

- ➢ Become accountable to someone or a group so you do not fall back into the traps you were in before. They are a temptation and since you have the enemy working against you, it is a good idea to allow the Body of Christ to work for you. When I was little, my parents taught me it was bad to hate. Now I realize it is good to hate what God hates.

THINK ABOUT IT:
1. Are you doing anything God hates?
2. Do your teens know there are things God hates?
3. Do you find this whole thought of God hating hard to accept? Why?

THOUGHTS FROM OTHERS:
"We are too Christian really to enjoy sinning, and too fond of sinning really to enjoy Christianity. Most of us know perfectly well what we ought to do; our trouble is we do not want to do it." Peter Marshall

"Wise men profit more by fools, than fools by wise men; for wise men avoid the mistakes of fools, but fools do not imitate the good examples of wise men." Cato the Elder

"Sin is cosmic treason." R. C. Sproul

THOUGHT:
"GET INVOLVED IN SHORT TERM MISSIONS"

"The best things are nearest: breath in your nostrils, light in your eyes, flowers at your feet, duties at your hand, the path of God just before you." Robert Louis Stevenson

Where are the William Carey's, Mother Theresa's, Hudson Taylor's, and Jim Elliott's? Right there sitting in your Youth Group. They are waiting for you to cast visions and give them the opportunity to minister on a mission field. They need to be exposed to the needs of the world. To be challenged to take up the call of the Great Commission. I believe this is the generation God is raising up to fulfill the Great Commission. Through all the tattoo's, piercing, problems, and pain, God is going to pour out His Spirit and raise up heroes and champions of the Faith who will travel around the world to share the good news of the gospel of Jesus Christ.

What qualifies a teenager to be a missionary?
- ➢ They love Jesus Christ with all their hearts.

- ➢ They will be obedient to the Spirit of God. A willingness to go where He wants them to go and do what He wants them to do.

- ➢ They will be faithful to use the gifts, talents, and abilities the Lord has given them to bring Him glory.

- ➢ A willingness to sacrifice. This will be the toughest obstacle because the American teen is so affluent and comfortable. We need to help stretch them and move them out of their comfort zone.

Some of our teenagers, as adults, will be martyred for their faith on the mission field. Others will die as a result of sickness or accident. The persecution of Christians will only get worse as time goes by. Is this a waste of their lives? Absolutely not!

Let me tell you what the real waste is; men and women God has called to be missionaries and instead have chosen to be a doctor, nurse, lawyer, banker, teacher, etc., and not answered God's call. They become financially secure, gain recognition, accumulate nice things, and become spiritual failures. They go to a good school, get a practical major that makes sense from the world's perspective, find a lucrative career, have a nice family, and live a comfortable life. But they're not doing what God has called them to do. They miss out on the joy, adventure, and fullness of living in obedience to God. So, we must encourage them to dream-dreams, to not settle for anything less than God's best, to reach beyond their grasp, and to trust God to do the impossible and the miraculous.

How do you do that? Get them on the front lines. Let them experience the mission field. Please get your students involved in short tern missions. There will be few things you do which will have a greater spiritual impact in their lives. Every teenager needs to be given the opportunity to go on an international mission's trip.

As you look to plan mission opportunities for your teens, keep these things in mind.

1. Your mission field starts at home. You need to have a year-round, Great Commission mind set, Matthew 28:18-20. Teenagers are missionaries in their homes, schools, work places, churches, city, state and country and then to the utter most parts of the world. Missions are not just a summer experience, it is a year-round lifestyle. Get them involved in missions in their home town. Sharing their faith and doing service projects allows them times of practice and preparation for what they will do overseas.

God may not call a teen to serve Him full time overseas but He does call all of our teens to be missionaries. To serve Him in their neighborhoods, homes, schools, places of employment, churches, etc.

2. Missions is a form of worship. Missions is all about worshipping

God and giving Him glory. Isaiah 6:1-8 says, "In the year that King Uzziah died, I saw the Lord seated on a throne, high and exalted, and the train of his robe filled the temple. Above him were seraphs, each with six wings: with two wings they covered their faces, with two they covered their feet, and with two they were flying. And they called to one another: 'Holy, holy, holy is the Lord Almighty; the whole earth is full of His glory.' At the sound of their voices the doorposts and thresholds shook and the temple was filled with smoke. 'Woe to me!' I cried. 'I am ruined! For I am a man of unclean lips, and I live among a people of unclean lips, and my eyes have seen the King, the Lord Almighty.' Then one of the seraphs flew to me with a live coal in his hand, which he had taken with tongs from the alter. With it he touched my mouth and said, 'See, this has touched your lips; your guilt is taken away and your sin atoned for.' Then I heard the voice of the Lord saying, 'Whom shall I send? And who will go for us?' And I said, 'Here I am, Send me!'"

As we worship we become open, sensitive, and responsive to what God is calling us to do. Missions is just the result of worshipping God and responding to His leading in our life. Missions is laying your life on God's alter as a sacrifice holy, pleasing and acceptable to Him.

"The Spirit of Christ is the spirit of missions, and the nearer we get to Him the more intensely missionary we must become." Henry Martyn

3. Decide you are going to do a trip. Then decide the time of year, Spring Break or summer. Personally, I think it is pushing it to try to do an international missions trip during Spring Break. You just don't have enough time.

4. What kind of mission trip do you want to do? Will it be task oriented with work projects or relationally oriented working with people? Do you want to primarily do evangelism and discipleship or labor and task? You could try to do a combination of both but I think it's best to focus on one or the other.

5. Where do you want to go? What part of the world do you want your teens to see and experience? Be sure you team up with a church or Christian organization in that country. By doing this you have a system of follow-up in place and you allow your students to get a greater taste of the culture. You might want to consider going somewhere there are missionaries your church supports. Safety needs to be priority number one.

6. "Why recreate the wheel?" Why not team with a teen mission's organization that has already been doing this for years? Make sure you agree with their doctrine, philosophy, and goals. I had a Youth Pastor friend who had one of his girls go with a mission organization that takes non-Christians, teens from cults, as well as Christians. The student came back confused and drawn toward one of the cults. Be careful and check out the organization completely before you trust them with any of your students.

7. What are your goals for the summer? What do you want for your students to get out of the mission experience? Royal Servants International is a mission organization for teenagers and they have four goals for the students.

- For students and staff to fall deeper in love with Jesus Christ and come face to face with the living God.

- They want their hearts to break for the non-Christian. Not just the non-Christian in the country they are ministering in but the non-Christian in their home, neighborhood, school, etc.

- For teens to become unified and to learn what it really means to agape love one another.

- They want teenagers to hear God's still small voice and to catch a vision for what God wants to do through them as individuals and through them as a youth group. For them to know God has a purpose, plan, and destiny for their lives and for the teen to desire whatever God desires for them.

8. How can we serve the missionaries and the Church of the country we are going to? What do you want the mission field to gain from having you with them? What tasks do you want to see accomplished and what ministry do you want to perform? Goals will give you direction and help you in preparing your students.

9. How long of a trip do you want to take? I would suggest you start small and build. Better for students to wish it had gone longer rather than having students thinking, "I wish this would end." If you are heading east or west internationally then you need to build in time to recover from jet lag. You should consider a minimum of fourteen days and I would suggest three weeks. By the time you deal with jet lag, get into the flow of ministry, see some things culturally, and debrief them for home, it doesn't leave a whole lot of time for ministry if you are going for less than three weeks. I understand most church based mission trips last 10-14 days because of a variety of factors, time off for volunteer staff and cost being two of them. You might want to consider teaming with a mission's organization when you head overseas.

The trips I lead usually lasted five to seven weeks. Unless you are teaming with a teen mission's organization, I would not suggest you try to take your teens overseas for that long in the beginning. That would be a good way to have a nervous breakdown.

10. What teenagers can go? You need to set up guidelines and expectations. This should not be, "come one, come all!" If you do, they will begin to view this as a vacation. There should be a process which involves:
- Expectations
- Involvement in the youth ministry ahead of time
- Application
- Interview
- Assignment
- Training

How many teenagers are you going to take? Accommodations will help to determine how many you take. You can only take as many as you can house. Plus, you need to figure staff into the number. I want to take one staff for every four teens. I do this so teens don't fall through the cracks, so there can be significant discipleship and a high degree of accountability.

11. How much will it cost? Keep in mind you never want to be a financial burden to the group bringing you in and housing you. You want to cover all the expenses. It would also be nice, if at the end of the trip, you left them a financial gift for the ministry. Set up a budget and figure flight, food, transportation, lodging, cultural things to see, materials, ministry expense, emergencies, and other surprises. Then divide it by the number going and come up with a cost. It is so much easier to go with an established mission's organization and sometimes it is much cheaper. You need to figure out how the students will raise the money. Set up deadlines for having a certain percentage of the money turned in because you will have deadlines in buying the airline tickets, setting up transportation in country, lodging, etc.

12. Plan ahead. If you are planning to do this on your own, I would highly recommend you fly over to check everything out before you go with the students. This way you will know what you are doing. There will be enough surprises during the summer without wondering where you are and where you need to go next.
- How do you get out of the airport?
- Where do you meet your transportation?
- How do you get to where you are staying?
- Where will you be ministering?
- Is there enough room to minister, to sleep, to teach, etc.?
- Who are your contact people?
- Is everything safe?
- Are they organized and ready for you?

There is no substitute for you being on site, ahead of time and seeing everything first-hand. It will give you confidence and help you to relax and be at peace. Then when you head over, with the teens, you can lead from the knowledge you have already gained.

13. Have the whole time planned out. From the time they get up in the morning till the time they go to bed. Here is a typical schedule

for my time with students in Dunoon, Scotland.
- ➢ 6:00AM - Rise and shine
- ➢ 7:00AM - Breakfast
- ➢ 7:30AM - Clean the building every day so you don't have a mess
- ➢ 8:00AM - Devotions
- ➢ 9:00AM - Small group discussion on devotions
- ➢ 9:30AM - Head to kids' clubs
- ➢ 12:00PM - Lunch
- ➢ 12:30PM - Street theatre and evangelism
- ➢ 3:30PM - Down time to eat fish and chips and relax
- ➢ 5:30PM - Dinner
- ➢ 6:30PM - Worship and prayer time
- ➢ 8:00PM - Small group time
- ➢ 9:00PM - Get ready for bed
- ➢ 10:00PM - Lights out

You want to make sure they are getting at least eight hours of sleep per night. They are on the cutting edge spiritually, emotionally, and physically. If they aren't getting enough sleep they will start getting sick. Everyday is planned out, but you take the rigid stand of total flexibility. Unique ministry opportunities will come up, so you just adjust the schedule.

14. Help students grow spiritually. When you are on the field you want to maximize the spiritual impact. So, keep these things in mind.
- ➢ Keep them focused on Jesus Christ. During the trip, there will be things I will change, but one area I will not change is their personal time with God. Each student will get at least one hour per day to seek the Lord. We want students to study the Word, pray and journal. We will also have corporate times of worship and concerts of prayer.

    I want to keep the focus on God by asking students:
    - What has God been teaching you?
    - Has the Lord been speaking to you?
    - What does He want you to stop doing?
    - How has God been answering your prayers?
    - What does He want you to start doing?

Pray for divine appointments. Nothing is more exciting or more of a spiritual boost than to experience God working through you. I ask God to lead individual students and the team into exciting ministry opportunities.

- Group sharing. We call this "family time." Here they have the opportunity to share and hear what God is doing. Joy is amplified in a group setting. You give them the chance to rejoice with those who rejoice and weep with those who weep. This develops unity as you share, laugh, sing, encourage and pray together.

- Speak to them from the front. Keep the vision, goals, and purpose before them. You are challenging them to lay their lives down, dig deeper, sacrifice, and learn the lessons God wants to teach them. You are encouraging and building them up everyday, you can't do this too much with teenagers. They easily become discouraged, tired, and cranky. Their moods don't just swing from day-to-day but from hour-to-hour. They need to hear you notice when they do a good job. You are there to say, "Well done, I am impressed, Keep up the good work."

- Teachable moments. You are also there to confront the bad attitude, poor choices, and rough edges. You want this to be a life-changing summer for them so you love them by confronting when they blow it. I know this can be hard because the student will usually become upset. But if we are going to love them we need to take this step. I personally enjoy confrontation because it holds the promise and possibility of a changed life. It is exciting to see the Lord chip away at a student and mold them into His own image. You gain their respect, love, and appreciation. They may be upset for awhile, but they usually come back and say "thank you," as long as you follow these simple steps.
    - Calm down emotionally.
    - Bathe it in prayer.
    - If you need to, seek advice. I try to get feedback

    from my staff.
- Think it all out ahead of time, so you can articulate it clearly.
- Do it in private.
- Make sure you do it in love.
- When the confrontation is over be sure you go back and love on them.

They need to know they have the freedom to fail, but you expect them to learn from the failures so they aren't making the same mistakes. I pray God would bring whatever weakness that needs to be worked on to the surface, so the summer becomes life changing.

➢ Care for them physically. We never put teenagers in harms way for the sake of fun or ministry. I understand God may call some to lay down their lives for the gospel in the future. But when they are with you, make sure you do everything you can to keep them safe.

➢ Bring in locals, missionaries and people from the church to speak to your group. Have them talk about cultural differences and ministry in this part of the world. Have them talk about cultural taboos, things the students shouldn't do or say. Give time for your students to ask questions. While on the trip tell them stories about men and women God has used in that country, heroes of the faith God worked through in powerful ways. Ask them, is God giving you a heart for this country? There are three questions you can use to challenge your students.
- If not you, then who?
- If not here, then where?
- If not now, then when?

➢ Give students specific responsibilities. Make sure they know exactly what they are supposed to do. If you don't give them specific instructions, then you will find a bunch of teens standing around. This will eventually lead to frustration on their part. They need to feel like they are an important part of this ministry and they are contributing.

- Set them up to succeed. Place them in areas, responsibilities, and ministries that fit their giftedness. Then be sure to praise, affirm, and support them. You want them to experience success. If they are doing something task related, be sure to allow them to complete the task. What if you are only one of several teams who will be building a church during the summer? Then make sure you set smaller goals within the large project they can successfully complete. If they are doing relational ministry, then give them the definition for successful witnessing. I borrowed this definition from Campus Crusade for Christ, "Share Jesus Christ, by the power of the Holy Spirit, and leave the results up to God."

"Attempt great things FOR God and expect great things FROM God." William Cary

15. Train them before you go. Your preparation time is every bit as important and maybe more important than your time in the field. What are some of your goals in preparing them?
- Make sure they are spiritually ready to go. You want them to be clean vessels for the Holy Spirit to fill and work through.

- Be sure the group is unified and your relationships are right with one another. You do not want to step onto the field with conflict and division. Make sure the students have made restitution and they have a clear conscious before God and man. I find every summer my team goes through these stages.
  - Stage 1 - We all love each other. This is wonderful, exciting, and we get to work together. This is the beginning of the summer.

  - Stage 2 - I can't stand you! You're driving me crazy because...you are a slob, you said something, you did something, you have bad breath, and your feet stink. This usually occurs one to two weeks into the summer as all the newness wears off.

- Stage 3 - Through teaching, confrontation, and prayer, they finally begin to agape love one another. It is a process every group goes through, and I pray stage two comes quickly so we can move to stage three.

➢ Allow them to personally raise a portion of their support. Give them the experience of what a missionary goes through as they prepare to go out. This becomes a faith stretcher as they depend upon God and see Him bring in the finances. At the same time, they are asking people to pray for them. You are allowing each student to develop a prayer base. I cannot emphasize enough how important it is to get your students covered in prayer through the whole mission experience.

➢ Make sure they have an understanding of the culture. What should/shouldn't they do or say? Help them understand what others do in their culture is not necessarily wrong. When I am on the British Isles with students, I remind them they drive on the other side of the road, not the "wrong" side of the road. Different is not wrong, it's just different.

➢ Training. You prepare and teach them all they need to know to effectively minister. That may mean learning street theatre, knowing how to share their faith, basic carpentry skills, etc.

➢ Guidelines. What are the rules for the summer? Teens need to know the "thou shall and thou shall not" before they get overseas. I recommend you write out the guidelines and make sure students and parents sign them. That way they can't say, "I never knew." It also needs to say, if the teen breaks the rules they may be sent home at the parent's expense.

16. Consider having a youth mission's conference at your church. Bring in a speaker who can effectively communicate with teenagers. Why is it some of the worst speakers I have ever heard are missionaries? Maybe because this is not what God has gifted them to do. Do not put them in that role. Invite them to tell a story or give a report for five minutes, but do not make them the key note speaker. When it comes to teenagers it can do more damage than good if you bring in a missionary speaker who is not gifted in communicating. You want to build excitement and anticipation for missions.

17. Address the objections. What about the objections to and complaints about short term missions? Let me address the three main objections I hear over and over again and how I respond to the concern.

> - It becomes a drain on the missionary. Really it is more work then help for them. It takes so much effort and pulls them away from the ministry God has called them to do."
>   - We will only go where we are wanted. You give the missionary an easy out so they don't feel obligated. We are not forcing ourselves on the missionary.
>
>   - Being a mentor, training an intern, doing discipleship, is all draining and more work for you. But it doesn't mean it's not good, right, and profitable just because it's hard.
>
>   - We complain missionaries are retiring and there is no one to take their place. This is why we get teenagers overseas. We expose them to the needs and challenges, then ask them to listen to God's voice. Where do our future missionaries come from?
>
>   - We need to look at the long-term and not the short-term. It may be more work for the missionary for those three weeks but we are raising up missionaries for the future. How many full-time missionaries were exposed to missions through some type of short-term trip while they were in High School or College? I would guess a significant number. Missionaries need to catch the vision they are reproducing themselves in the lives of the teenagers.

- If for three weeks the missionary has a greater work load but God calls three students into fill time missions out of a team of forty, was it worth it? I think everyone would say...YES!

➢ "It costs so much. The money would be better spent if we just sent it to the missionary. Isn't this a waste of money?"
- Again, this argument is looking at the short-term and not the long-term. It is totally worth the cost to see God call students to missions and full-time Christian service.

- You can use the above argument for anything; carpet, choir robes, landscaping and air conditioning is all expensive. Why don't we send the money to missionaries instead? This is why we budget as a church. We definitely need to support our missionaries financially. But we also invest in carpet, robes, landscaping, air conditioning and summer missions.

- You are making an investment in the lives of teenagers and who they are becoming. You are developing leaders now and raising up missionaries for the future.

➢ "Why go overseas when people here in the US need Jesus."
- Because you are being obedient to the Great Commission. God tells us all to "GO." He doesn't put an age requirement on the command.

- I already mentioned we need to have a mission's mind-set for our neighborhood, city, state, and country. I have found students returning from the mission field; have a greater heart for the lost here in the United States.

- Who are we to come between a teen and God? Never object to a teenager wanting to be obedient to a command from God. We want to teach our teens to listen for the voice of God, to be obedient and be willing to go where God is calling them to go. You help them to cement their priorities, develop their spiritual disciplines, and to step out in faith.

- You want to give them a global vision. To be part of what God is going to do in Revelation 7:9-10, "After this I looked and there before me was a great multitude that no one could count, from every nation, tribe, people, and language, standing before the throne and in front of the lamb. They were wearing white robes and were holding palm branches in their hands. And they cried out in a loud voice: "Salvation belongs to our God, who sits on the throne, and to the Lamb." Students who have come with me on short term missions have had a part in Revelation chapter seven. Because of their ministry, people have come to know Jesus Christ as Savior and Lord in...

Scotland	England	France
Germany	Austria	Belgium
Switzerland	Italy	Spain
Republic of Czech	Poland	Hungary
Slovakia	Romania	
and around the world		

During a mission's trip, I have seen students move from being apathetic to dynamic, from knowing all about Jesus Christ to having a passion for Him.

Summer missions is not just about raising up full time missionaries but about touching the lives of teenagers and preparing them to serve Him no matter where He calls them.

THINK ABOUT IT:
1. Do you have a mission program?
2. What can you do to start or improve it?
3. Have you checked out the possibility of teaming with an existing organization?

THOUGHT: "CHARACTER AND TOLERANCE DO NOT MIX"

"With courage you will dare to take risks, have the strength to be compassionate and the wisdom to be humble. Courage is the foundation of integrity." Keshavan Nair

We live in a world that values tolerance and compromise. If you are seen as intolerant then you are labeled as a bigot, prejudiced, judgmental, narrow minded and ignorant! Here is what the world is saying to us and to our teens. "As long as you don't hurt anyone, then it is O.K. If two or more people consent to it, then it is fine. Everything depends on your point of view, there is no black or white, right or wrong or absolutes. Sin is becoming obsolete because it is just a matter of personal choice. It might not be right for you, but it's O.K. for me." Tolerance is the road of compromise, mediocrity, shallow, watered down, lukewarm and ineffective ministry. It is a road that changes from year to year depending on people's opinions. It is a road that will lead you and your teens nowhere.

We become so concerned about making everyone happy we end up making no one happy. We are concerned about offending everyone except God. So, we end up believing everything and nothing. I believe there is a place for narrowness, intolerance and being politically incorrect. That is when we call sin...SIN and refuse to excuse or candy coat it. You cannot be tolerant of sin no matter how politically incorrect it becomes. Being men and women of character means we refuse to compromise on scripture or personal integrity. It is not just knowing the difference between right and wrong but it is choosing to do what is right no matter what the cost. It is not primarily an emotional decision but an act of the will. You have thought it through and have decided, "This is what I will do and this is what I won't do." It isn't easy but it separates someone of character from someone who merely has good intentions.

"Always do right. This will gratify some and astonish the rest." Mark Twain

What is the difference between a moral person and a person of character? A moral person doesn't do what is wrong; a person of character does what is right. A teenager comes to me and says, "A bunch of teens were making fun of Mary but I didn't join in." They are being very moral but did they step in to support Mary and tell the others to stop being mean and cruel? That is what a person of character does. They don't just sit on the sidelines, they aren't spectators but they are participators. That is what it means to be salt and light.

Judah was conquered by Babylonia and many were taken captive. Among them was a young man by the name of Daniel. He had a lot going for him. He came from nobility, had no physical defect, handsome, showed aptitude for every kind of learning, was well informed, quick to understand and qualified to serve in the King's palace. (Daniel 1:3-4)

Daniel 1:5a says, "The King assigned them a daily amount of food and wine from the Kings table..." Now this was a problem because it was probably food and wine dedicated to false gods and the meat, at times, was pork, which Jews were forbidden to eat. So, what is Daniel going to do? He could compromise and say, "I'm only a teenager, in a strange land, and the training is only going to last three years. I will go back to doing what is right after the training. Plus, it seems logical to me. God will understand if I just do it this one time." Things may seem logical but you never honor or glorify God by compromising. After thinking about this and counting the cost, Daniel makes a decision. To refuse to eat the food and drink the wine could cost him his life. He is a prisoner and has no rights. "But Daniel resolved not to defile himself with the royal food and wine, and he asked the chief official for permission not to defile himself this way," Daniel 1:8. Here is a man of character who refuses to eat the food, drink the wine, and doesn't try to hide the fact. He steps forward with an alternative that will honor the Lord, Daniel 1:12-13. He gets permission to eat vegetables and drink water.

Daniel made the decision he would rather die than dishonor God. I remember being invited to a youth speaker's conference by Josh McDowell. He brought in a number or speakers to share with us and I will never forget something Dr. Bill Bright said, "Lord if there is a chance I might ever disgrace you, I don't want to live, just take me home before it happens." This was so powerful for me, as a youth speaker, just starting out, to hear that kind of commitment. Bill Bright lived a life worthy of the calling of Christ, finished well and was promoted to heaven. Daniel and Bill Bright were both men of character who refused to compromise. Like them, we must have purpose in our hearts not to defile ourselves with the things of this world, even if it costs us our lives.

Just because something looks logical or circumstances would seem to dictate we do this, it doesn't mean we ought to do it that way. God is on the throne, He is sovereign and works beyond the circumstances or what might seem logical to us. If Daniel would have done what seemed the most logical and what circumstances were dictating then he would have eaten the food. "Come on God, I can do more for you alive than dead. So, I'll eat the food for a few years and then serve you for the rest of my life." Now that seems logical, but in doing it Daniel would be saying, "God I no longer trust you to be able to take care of me." If you compromise in one area then you are open to compromising in all areas. With each compromise, it becomes easier to do it the next time. Daniel refused to compromise and discovered for God to do the impossible and miraculous was easy.

- ➢ God caused the official to show favor and sympathy to Daniel (1:9).
- ➢ The official agreed to a ten-day test (1:14).
- ➢ After ten days, Daniel looks healthier then those who ate the Royal food from the Kings table (1:15).
- ➢ God then gives Daniel special knowledge and understanding, plus a special understanding of visions and dreams (1:17).
- ➢ The King becomes impressed with Daniel after questioning him (1:19).
- ➢ Daniel becomes ten times better in every matter of wisdom and understanding over all the Kings, magicians, and

enchanters (1:20).

Do you think this would have happened if Daniel had compromised? No, Daniel would have missed out on God's perfect plan for his life. God is in control and we seek His blessing, not man's approval. Your purpose for existing is to glorify Jesus Christ, to fulfill His purpose, plan and destiny for your life-to do His will-to bring a smile to His face. For this to happen you must be a person of character. You must live what you believe, walk by faith and not by sight, and stand for what is good, right, true and pure.

Character and worldly success do not always go hand in hand. Being a person of character doesn't necessarily mean you will have much money, a nice car or big house. Being a Christian of character does guarantee you will succeed spiritually. Compromising to be successful is no success at all because you are failing spiritually.

I spoke for a Family Life Marriage Conference in Southern California. Saturday afternoon a guy walked up to me and asked, "Have you ever done a comedy club?" I said, "No." He replied, "Would you like to?" I sat down and talked with him for awhile. It was a neat opportunity but after finding out about the environment, what goes on in the club, the language of the other comedians, some of their topics they laugh about and what my participation might communicate to others, I decided to turn him down. I am not saying it is wrong for a Christian to do a comedy club. I am saying in the situation he was talking about, it would have been wrong for me to do it. I would have had to compromise and tolerate some stuff that is totally wrong. I had to be obedient to God and say no even though it could have been fun.

"I cannot give you the formula for success, but I can give you the formula for failure-which is: Try to please everybody." Herbert Bayard Swope

Are you a person of character or have you bought into the world's standards of tolerance and compromising? What if every student in the youth ministry was just like you? What kind of group would you have? You are reproducing your life in the lives of these students;

you are teaching them what you have learned and reproducing who you are. You stand before your students and say, "Follow my example, as I follow the example of Christ," 1 Corinthians 11:1. If you can't then there is something wrong with your character.

How do you become or remain a person of character?
- **Love Jesus Christ.** That is the greatest commandment. It is all about being obedient to Him. (John 14:15)
- **Love others.** Love them enough to lead them and not mislead them. Set the example, care about them and be willing to lay down your life.
- **Refuse to compromise on scripture or in your lifestyle.**
- **Guard your heart.** (Proverbs 4:23)
  - Watch what you put into it because out of the overflow of your heart you speak and act. (Matthew 12:33-35)
  - Watch out who you give your heart to.
- **Be strong and courageous.** You must overcome fear of rejection, ridicule, laughter, persecution, etc. (Joshua 1:6-9)
- **Run to win and finish well.** So one day you can hear, "Well done good and faithful servant." (1 Corinthians 9:27)
- **Avoid the traps that will disqualify you.** (1 Corinthians 9:27)

In a world that grows darker, you can either shine brighter or be extinguished. We have been called to be salt and light to the world. You do this by being someone of character. You live the truth, intolerant against sin, refusing to compromise and trusting God with all your heart.

THINK ABOUT IT:
1. Are there any areas in which you are compromising?
2. Are you a moral person or a person of character?
3. Who do you know that is living like Daniel or Bill Bright?

THOUGHT:
"START YOUR YOUTH MINISTRY RIGHT"

"It is a blessed thing that in every age someone has had enough individuality and courage to stand by his own convictions." Robert G. Ingersoll

God has called you to Youth Ministry and that is wonderful. However, He has not necessarily called you to the first church to contacts you. There needs to be a fit. You want to go to a church which emphasizes your giftedness and will allow you to lead from your strengths and not your weaknesses. I know individuals who were very promising and they jumped at the first youth ministry to came along. It turned out to be a dysfunctional church, bad situation, poor fit, discouraging experience and they are no longer in youth ministry. I want you to start your youth ministry right. Here are some things I want you to consider doing.

A church contacts you because you're great, wonderful and the best! Who wouldn't want you? You are interested enough to take the first step. You fill out their application. While you are doing this, ask for written material on the church and youth ministry. They have an information packet but make sure they include in it:
- Doctrinal Statement
- Job Description
- Youth Ministry policy sheets
- A link or CD where you can hear the Pastor preach
- Vision Statement,
- Area and community information, etc.

They like you...of course. So now they want to fly you in for a face to face. You need to be evaluating whether this is where the Lord wants you. Here are some things I want you to do and be aware of as you're meeting with them.

"Ask all your questions now and never assume. Asking now prevents you from regretting later." G S

1. Ask Questions. These questions will give you a start. I want you to add to this list with some questions that are important to you.
- What is your stated vision for the youth ministry?
- Tell me about your present programs and what is the purpose behind each of the programs.
- List the programs from least important to most important. Do this with the search committee, boards, parents, teens, Pastor, lay staff and this will show you what is most important to each group.
- How many volunteer staff work with the teens? Why aren't there more? Are they going to stay if I come? Sometimes you have adults step into leadership to help until the new Youth Pastor arrives, and then they all step aside.
- How many students are on the youth ministry list? How many actually come out?
- How many Youth Pastors have you had in the past ten years? Why did they leave? May I have your permission to talk to them?
- How long has it been since your last youth Pastor? If it has been years, then ask yourself the questions, why has it been so hard for them to fill this position?
- How many people have you considered to fill this position since the last youth Pastor left? This allows you to see whether you are first on their list or just one of many.
- What was the philosophy of the last youth Pastor? Did you like it? Did it work? Do you expect me to have the same philosophy?
- In what area has the youth ministry been most effective? Where are the weaknesses? In your opinion what needs to be worked on first?
- Give me a percent, of how many teens could care less, are lukewarm are champions for Christ? Once you speak to the students and spend time with them you'll be able to tell whether the leadership of the church has a realistic view of the Youth Ministry or whether they are clueless. I am sad to say a lot are clueless.
- How do you measure success?
- Will I be evaluated? Who will evaluate me? How often will I be evaluated?

- Scripture is written in ink and everything else is written in pencil. Do you agree? Is there any area in the Youth Ministry that can't be changed or done away with?
- Please fill in the blank. Make sure you don't_____? What would that be?
- Are teens respectful or disrespectful in large group settings?
- What is the discipline policy?
- What are your views on music? Is there any style of music which would be unacceptable?
- If I came what would your expectations be for the first three months? What would the expectations be of my spouse?
- What will be the youth budget this coming year, not including salaries? Is this an increase over last year?
- What are the biggest barriers to making change here, tradition, church leadership, parents, teens, others and why?
- What are the names of the middle and high schools in the area? What is the student population of each school? How many students do you draw from each school? Do you have a presence at the school?
- How does the worship and church service reflect the needs of teenagers? Are teenagers represented on church boards and committees? Do they have any leadership in the church service?
- What do the teenagers think about the church services?
- Is there a janitorial staff to help with set-up, tear-down and clean-up?
- Is there a youth ministry secretary/administrative assistant?
- Do I have office space?

If you decide to come to the church I would suggest you get the responses to the next nine questions in writing. It is amazing how things change after you have accepted a position.
- How many and what kind of meetings is the Youth Pastor expected to attend?
- What is your policy for professional conferences, continuing education, sabbaticals?
- How many hours am I expected to work each week? How many of those hours am I expected to be in the office?
- How much vacation time is there? Does this increase with

time?
- Do you give a book allowance?
- Is it OK to take a full work day off each month to pray and listen to God?
- Will I have responsibilities outside of youth ministry?
- How do you handle future raises?
- What is the church policy when you hire a new Senior Pastor? Some churches want all the Pastors to resign and then allow the new Senior Pastor to decide who stays and who goes.

If you get a chance to sit down with the Senior Pastor here are some questions for him.
- How involved do you want to be in Youth Ministry? You do not want to work under a micro manager!
- How do you see Youth Ministry? Did you used to be a Youth Pastor? If yes, then tell me about your ministry and philosophy when you worked with teens. Do you want me to do the same thing?
- What are your expectations for me and the Youth Ministry?
- How often do you meet as Pastors and for how long?
- How long do you expect to be here at this church?
- Are there Pastor Retreats? What is the purpose?
- Do Pastor/wife couples get together?
- How will you decide whether I am being successful or not?
- What will you do if parents come to you to complain about me? What I want to hear is, "I would ask them if they had talked to you first. If they hadn't, then I would stop the conversation and send them to you."

It is important you feel like you connect with the Senior Pastor. Will you grow personally under their ministry? This needs to be someone God will use to feed you and your entire family. Ask the church to send you CD's from the last four messages so you can hear them preach. If you don't connect with their speaking then do you want to spend the next ten years sitting under their ministry? Plus, if you are not connecting, then how do you think the teens are responding? Do you want to serve at a Church where the teens do not like the Senior Pastor's preaching and teaching?

How important is it for you to be involved in the leadership of the church as a whole? For me it wasn't important but I have friends in Youth Ministry who find it very important. If it is important, will you sit on the board, will you have a vote, do you get to preach on occasion, are they going to seek input from you when it comes to policy and direction of the Church?

Keep in mind this whole process is kind of like a first date. You are both on your best behavior attempting to positively impress the other person. A big problem is you are usually going from first date right into marriage. We all know marriage is much different from dating. So, ask as many questions as you can up front and do not assume anything.

2. Red Flags. During this process, you need to be looking for red flags. Is there anything God might use to cause you to slow down or remove your name from consideration? In the past, there have been four churches that have contacted me about being their Youth Pastor and I ended up stopping the process and removing my name from consideration because of red flags. Beware if they…

- Can't keep a Youth Pastor. This can mean they are abusive toward their Youth Pastors.

- Don't want you to talk to past Youth Pastors. Now there could be a legitimate reason. For example, if they were fired for sexual immorality. But if there is no good reason then I wonder, "what are you trying to hide?"

- Have a Senior Pastor or Pastor you report to that is a micro manager. Do not go there, because they will drive you insane.

- Have a poor pay package. They aren't looking to take care of you. If they don't care about your material needs, then will they really care about your emotional or spiritual needs?

- Have little or no Youth budget. This can say youth ministry is not really a priority or they have no vision in this area.

- Have few lay staff. People are not interested in serving in youth ministry. Maybe there are problems in the ministry. Maybe lay staff haven't felt like they were valued in the past or teens are out of control or the ministry was disorganized, etc.

- Have crazy job descriptions. Responsibilities two full time staff couldn't handle.

- Have a job description that makes you responsible of things outside of youth ministry. Do you really want to do those things? You run the risk of them giving you more responsibilities outside your calling after you have been around awhile.

- Have a job description calling for giftedness and strengths in areas where you are not gifted. If so, you become drained and the church will be frustrated and upset. Don't do it to yourself. Also, your job description should include something like, "Maintain a close personal relationship with Jesus Christ." Do you want to work for a church that assumes you will do it but doesn't see it as absolutely crucial for the success of the youth ministry? If they did, they would write it down.

- Have no job description. You open yourself to being used and abused.

- Provide vague promises about the future. Do not count on any promises. Like we can pay you more money a year from now or after awhile we will move you to Youth Ministry exclusively but right now we need you to head up senior citizen ministry. Can you live with things as they are? Because chances are things will not change like they said it would. Remember, "When all is said and done…more is said then done." Get the promises in writing.

- Do not give you a strong vote of confidence. Some churches only require a majority vote. 51% vote for you; how nice, but it means 49% voted against you, not so nice. I would not accept a call with less than a 90% vote. I am talking about the original vote. Because sometimes the church will have a motion from the floor to make the vote unanimous after the majority has voted yes. I was the candidate at a church and told the Senior Pastor I would not come for less then a 90% vote. The vote was 85% and I said no. That doesn't have to be your stand but keep this in mind, if a thousand people are voting and 85% say yes, it means 150 people are saying no for some reason and for me that is a significant number of people who do not want me from the very start. Even if it is a church of one hundred you still have 15 voting against you.

- Concerns about the Senior Pastor. Not feeling like you can grow under their ministry or feeling there is some kind of clash. Maybe personality conflict, different view of youth ministry or just a gut feeling this isn't a fit. I was told this story. A guy goes through the process to be a Youth Pastor and everything is going great. It is a big church and he now has a short meeting with the Senior Pastor. The Senior Pastor asks him one question and it goes something like this. "You are driving on a country road and you come across a serious crash involving several cars. Your cell phone doesn't work, people are badly hurt, what would you do?" The guy says, "I would stop and see what I could do to help." The Pastor says, "Wrong, you need to go for help."
He dismissed him and they don't hire him because he didn't answer the Pastor's question correctly. Now, I think he was better off not working with this guy, he did get another position as youth pastor. Who would want to work for some idiot who based his entire impression of a person on one question? If I was the youth guy I would have said, "What if one of the victims was your daughter, who was bleeding to death, and if I didn't stop and help her she would die?" Now what do you want me to do?"

- ➤ The Holy Spirit does not give you confirmation. There are times when everything looks good on the outside but you will lack peace or the Holy Spirit will say no.

- ➤ Beware if your spouse has concerns. God will speak to you through your spouse. If they do not feel comfortable about going then do not go. I would never drag Bonnie somewhere she didn't feel at peace about. If God is calling me then He will confirm it through my wife. You are a team and God will call you as a team.

- ➤ Beware if Godly family and friends have concerns. If you have people who love you and know you, saying they don't think you should go, why wouldn't you listen to them?

THINK ABOUT IT:
1. Have you asked all the questions you need to ask?
2. Have you seen any red flags?
3. Have you listed all the pros and cons about this church and ministry?

THOUGHT: "START STRONG"

"All the way my Savior leads me; What have I to ask beside? Can I doubt His tender mercy, who through life has been my guide?"
Fanny J. Crosby

Now you are looking to take the next step, what do you need to keep in mind? Be sure you focus on what is really important and don't get sidetracked by the tyranny of the urgent. You want to seek God, build relationships and keep your priorities straight.

Get off on the right foot. Congratulations! Everything has worked out and you have accepted the call to serve as Youth Pastor. You have a wealth of knowledge because you have graduated from_____, the leading school for Youth Ministry. Or you may have been doing this for awhile and you are coming in with years of successful ministry. That is why they hired you, because of the experience, or knowledge, or both. So, you start and you stick with what you know, or what has worked in the past, and you work very hard, then you fail and fall flat on your face. What happened? This is a different church, different part of the country, different teens, different needs, and what worked at your past church or theoretically in the class room will not necessarily work here and now.

What do you need to do? Let me suggest some things you can do to help you get off on the right foot and to start strong.

> **Seek God first.** Take all the books and put them back on the shelf. Take all your past experiences and lay it on the back burner. Now pull out the Bible and let God speak to you through His word. Then pray and ask God what He wants you to do. Commit your life to Him. Be willing to do whatever He wants you to do. Be willing to put everything you have learned and all your past experience aside to step out in faith. You are seeking to join God and do what He wants to do rather than asking Him to join you and your

plans and ideas. Who knows more about Youth Ministry, you or God? Then who should follow who?

Ask God to give you favor in the eyes of the students, parents, staff, etc. Spend time in worship. Praise Him as King Of Kings and Lord Of Lords. Then take a prayer walk through the building. Warfare pray and clear it of all enemy activity. Ask God to make it Holy ground. Ask the Lord to be present and active. Set up a prayer calendar and divide the number in your youth group by 28 and then each day pray for those students and staff. Every month you are praying for each student and staff specifically.

> **Set your priorities at the very beginning.** The number one priority needs to be your walk with God. This should be in your job description and if it isn't then you need to be a little concerned about the church's priorities.

Your second priority is your spouse. You have moved to a different part of the country and neither of you have established relationships. You are able to jump into the ministry, meet people, make friends and stay busy. Your spouse can't find a job, they are home with the children and they aren't making friends. You start working more hours and you come home exhausted. In a relatively short amount of time your spouse feels alone and neglected. What happens next? Conflict begins to arise. You say to me your spouse doesn't understand but the person who doesn't understand is you! Your priority must be your spouse over the ministry. This shows itself in the amount of time you spend with them. It also shows itself in the quality of the time you spend together. Are you exhausted and non-communicative? If they have spent all day alone or with the kids then they need you. Not just your physical presence but being there emotionally and spiritually.

The third priority is your children. Remember they spell love T - I - M - E. Be sure they are not feeling neglected by you. They need attention from you, being in a new place can add fear, insecurity and loneliness.

Then the fourth priority is your job, the ministry. Be sure you control your schedule or you schedule will control you.

➢ **Know your job description.** Now this seems obvious but it is so important. This defines what they expect of you. They will evaluate you on how well you are fulfilling what is spelled out in the job description.

➢ **Build relationships.** So many Youth Pastors set themselves up to fail because they skip or neglect this step. If you do not build relationships, then they do not see or understand your heart and they can begin to resist you and your ideas. You need to spend time with students and lay staff. Ask questions and listen. You can't learn if you aren't listening. Ask questions like...
- What can help me to get to know you as a person?
- What do you like best about this youth ministry?
- What would you like to see changed or improved?
- What would you like me to do?
- How are you and Jesus doing?
- What can I do to encourage you?

People want to know you care about them. I had spoken for a middle school retreat; the church had just hired a new high school Pastor. Some of the middle school staff were going to be seniors in high school. I was asking how they liked the new Pastor and it wasn't pretty. He was a young guy, twenty-eight, who came from a large, successful church. He had a lot of ideas and was making a number of changes. The changes can all be great and even necessary but he hadn't been taking the time to build relationships. He was with a group of his seniors and said to them, "I am going to observe you for the next few days to see if you'll be leaders in the Youth Ministry." You know how the teens responded to this? They basically said, "What? You don't even know me, you have been here less then a month and now you will watch me to see if I qualify, in your mind, to be staff? Forget it!" This would have been totally different if he had first taken the time to build relationships and love on these students. Skip this priority and you are doomed to failure.

➢ **Do what God is calling you to do.** Doing what you read in a book or what worked at your last ministry is not as important as doing what the Lord is leading you to do. Find that out and then do it with excellence. Focus on the priority areas of the ministry and don't try to do everything at once. All of sudden you have 100 things on your plate and you feel overwhelmed and stressed to the max. What begins to happen? You do everything half way and you achieve mediocrity instead of excellence. Break down everything you need to do into four categories. I learned this from John Maxwell.

- High need and should be done now. There are your high priority items which have to get done now if the ministry is going to continue to grow. Things like:
  ✓ Recruitment and training of lay staff.
  ✓ Relational time with students.
  ✓ Message preparation.

- High need but can be done later. Here are things you need to set deadlines for and look to get done in the near future. Delegate as much as possible. Things like:
  ✓ Youth room painting and decorating.
  ✓ Getting the budget ready for next year.
  ✓ Meet with parent advisory board.

- Low need but should be done now. These are things you are tempted to put off but really need to get done right away. Things like:
  ✓ Returning phone calls.
  ✓ Anything your Senior Pastor asks you to do.
  ✓ Getting your report done for the board meeting.

- Low need and can be done later. Here are things you want to delegate. Get them off you plate but make sure

they get done. Things like:
- ✓ Refreshments for the next meeting.
- ✓ Signing church up for basketball league.
- ✓ Picking the color of outfit for the Christmas musical.

"The value of life lies not in the length of days, but in the use we make of them." Michel de Montaigne

Remember to focus on what only you can do, like preparing your message for Wednesday night. No one can do that for you. It is very important to the health and growth of the youth ministry. Then delegate out as much as possible, it allows more people to be involved and own the ministry.

When you first arrive, be a listener and observer. What is working and what isn't working? Do not make a bunch of changes at the very beginning. People will resist this because they don't know your heart and you have not given them a part in the process of change. They will not own it. "Let the wise listen and add to their learning, and let the discerning get guidance," (Proverbs 1:5). You start out by listening and observing. When you do this, you add to your knowledge and understanding. "He who answers before listening- that is his folly and his shame," (Proverbs 18:13). A Youth Pastor who makes changes before really understanding what is going on, what teens are feeling, and developing relationships is a fat head.

Do you know what the traditions and sacred cows are? These can be deeply rooted and you probably don't want to change those at the beginning of your ministry. Like the Youth Pastor who decided to pull the youth group out of their usual camp because he knows one that is nicer and cheaper. Yes, the camp was nicer and cheaper, but he didn't know the teenager's grandparents had gone to the camp. There was a wonderful, spiritual tradition of God showing up at camp. They had gone to camp for over forty years and the youth pastor decides, on his own, to end this tradition. Everything hit the fan. When he tried to go back to the old camp they were already booked. What a shame, folly and maybe, ministry death because he started making changes before he listened and understood.

At the beginning make small and easy visual changes, to build enthusiasm. Things like:
- ➢ Change the look of the room. Color, how it is decorated, and the direction the chairs face.
- ➢ Put together a solid worship band
- ➢ Really good multi media
- ➢ More students, who are Godly, up front in leadership.

Small changes can make big impressions. You are doing things the students can see. You want the teens to begin to think and say, "This is better, I like this." You are building expectation, excitement and momentum.

- ➢ **Accept responsibility.** God has called you to this ministry; you are in charge, the buck stops with you, so take leadership. In accepting responsibility for the youth ministry, you are going to:
  - Set the example. If you haven't yet, now is the time to grow up. You are an adult leader, not a kid. You may still want to be a kid but you can't be a kid because you are in charge. I am all for having fun but you can't get carried away. Lose your temper, be overly competitive, prank others, lead cabin raids at 3 AM, acting like a teen will come back to bite you.

  - Listen to godly advice from individuals who are living for Jesus now and not living off past spiritual experiences. Otherwise you will be listening to advice out of tradition, the business world, human understanding and sometimes the world's values. Keep in mind your final authority is the Word of God. If anyone contradicts the Word of God then they're wrong.

  - Delegate things you are not gifted to do. There is stuff that must get done which you are not good at doing. Be willing to delegate and do not micro manage. You need to make sure it gets done, but don't be looking over their shoulder, giving advice and breathing down their neck. Let them do it differently than you would have done. If you micro manage you will drive others insane and they will quit on you. Be aware of your weaknesses, you can't do it all. For you to think you can do it all is either arrogance, pride or stupidity.

- Make the difficult decisions. You must make the difficult decisions that will make a difference. These are not easy, you don't want to do it but you have to do it. I was on a mission's trip in Scotland and three of my guys decide to go up into the highlands to smoke cigarettes. This is stupid and a bad choice but I wasn't going to send them home. I wanted them to come clean and apologize. But the three had agreed they would deny it and lie if they were confronted. I separated the three guys and brought them into my room one at a time. The first guy came in and the conversation goes something like this:
    - ✓ Me: "What were you doing up in the highlands today?"
    - ✓ Him: "We were just throwing rocks and hanging out."
    - ✓ Me: "Were you doing anything else while you were hanging out?"
    - ✓ Him: "No."
    - ✓ Me: "Look at me. If you lie to me I am going to send you home. Do you understand?"
    - ✓ Him: "Yes."
    - ✓ Me: "Repeat for me what I just said."
    - ✓ Him: "If I lie to you then you'll send me home."
    - ✓ Me: "What were you doing today up in the highlands?"
    - ✓ Him: "We were smoking."

I said thank you very much and I sent him to bed without talking to the other guys. The second guy came in and we have the same conversation. He lied till the very end and then finally breaks and says, "I was smoking." He goes to bed and the third guy came in and lied like the other two. We get to the end and it went like

this:
- ✓ Me: "If you lie to me I will send you home. Do you understand?"
- ✓ Him: "Yes."
- ✓ Me: "Repeat what I just said."
- ✓ Him: "If I lie to you, you'll send me home."
- ✓ Me: "What were you doing up in the highlands?"
- ✓ Him: "Nothing, were just hanging out and throwing rocks."
- ✓ Me: "Thank you very much" and I sent him to bed. The next morning the three got together and the last guy realizes the other two told the truth. So, he came to me right before breakfast.
- ✓ Him: "Greg, I couldn't sleep all night because I lied to you."
- ✓ Me: "I know you lied."
- ✓ Him: "I am really sorry."
- ✓ Me: "I appreciate that."
- ✓ Him: "So what are you going to do?"
- ✓ Me: "I am going to send you home."

He begged and pleaded and cried, but I sent him home because it was the right decision, even though it was a very difficult decision. When he left it was like a breath of fresh air. The entire team did better and the two other guys shaped up right away. The right choice is not always the easy choice. But it must be made.

- Over communicate. I know I said this before but let me say it again, parents, teens, lay staff, your secretary all need to know what is going on. They need to understand the vision, goals, and purpose of the ministry. You all have to be on the same page. If not, there will be frustration and confusion.

Get off on the right foot and it will save you a lot of heartache down the road. Take some of the simple steps we have talked about. Do it right from the beginning. You are building expectations and laying a foundation for your ministry.

THINK ABOUT IT:
1. Do you have your priorities straight?
2. Are you building relationships with students, staff and parents?
3. Are you asking for and listening to advice?

THOUGHT:
"ALWAYS ASK, HOW ARE WE DOING?"

"Being at peace with yourself is a direct result of finding peace with God." William M. Evarts

It is important you are asking yourself and others how things are going. If we are going to take the steps we need to take, then we have to evaluate. What are we doing well and what needs to be changed? This is how we stay on the cutting edge. Be a listener and hear what God and others are saying to you about the Youth Ministry.

1. Evaluate the Youth Ministry. You have been there for awhile. You have listened and observed. Now where do you see the Youth Ministry? I hope and pray you have known what you were walking into. Now you are ready to pick one of four directions.

- Start. This is a church plant; never had a youth group or they have never had Youth Pastor. You are going to be starting everything.

- Change. This is a dysfunctional and dead group. It needs major help and changes.

- Realign. The ministry has some good direction but there are some glaring weaknesses and need for some significant changes.

- Sustain. Great ministry and you need to ask yourself, "What's the next step we can take?"

If this was a car you would look at it this way.
- Start - You are getting a brand new car
- Change - You need to junk the old car and get a new one
- Realign - It needs an overhaul but you keep the car
- Sustain - Just give it a tune up.

Each direction you take has a distinct set of challenges to will keep you dependent upon the Lord. The overall goal for each group is the same. To glorify God and produce fully devoted followers of Jesus Christ. But how you get there will be very different. Here are some of the challenges.

- **Start.** You are responsible for starting and creating everything. Developing lay staff, attracting teens, establishing your vision and direction, putting together program and dealing with limited resources. You might not have money for a youth budget and you could be working out of a rented facility.

- **Change.** Where do I start and what are my priorities? Do I begin by working with teens, parents, and lay staff that are discouraged and frustrated? What about working with people who feel betrayed and may not trust Youth Pastors? Do I try to encourage teens who are apathetic and carnal?

    Is my focus dealing with entrenched traditions, programs and activities which are no longer working or relevant? Keep in mind just because teens are showing up doesn't mean things are going well. Maybe they are forced to come by their parents or they come to see their friends and for no other reason.

- **Realign.** What do we change and what do we sustain? Because things are going O.K. people may not see the need for change. You will have some people loving programs in desperate need of change.

- **Sustain.** It can be difficult living in the shadow of a former Youth Pastor who was deeply loved, the transition is not easy. It takes time to win the hearts of the teens and staff. You may be dealing with complacency which will strongly resist change or a sense of disloyalty to the former Youth Pastor if we change. But we remind them it was evaluation and change that got you on the cutting edge and it is what will keep you there, healthy and vibrant. We must be sensitive to the Holy Spirit and let Him birth the vision in our hearts to see the next step and understand where the ministry needs to move next.

As you get to know your ministry, you can start doing more evaluation and you will be able to break down and place your different programs into these four general areas. For example:
- Start - Missions program and parent meetings
- Change - Retreats and Sunday School
- Realign - Small groups and discipleship
- Sustain - Evangelism and mid week meetings

This way it becomes manageable and you see which areas need immediate attention. By doing this kind of evaluation you make it easier for yourself and others to see the next steps to be taken and establish your priorities for change.

"Thinking is the hardest work there is, which is probably the reason why so few engage in it." Henry Ford

2. Be realistic. What is really happening? We all get together as Youth Pastors and talk about how everything is great but not everything is great. I know because I have been there and done that. What can help you to be more realistic?

> It is O.K. to have weakness in your Youth Ministry. When you first start at the church it is easier to see all the problems because you don't feel responsible for them. But it becomes harder after you have been there a year because now you feel the weight of responsibility. The ministries failures become your failures. Youth Ministry runs in cycles and what could have been a strength last year has all of a sudden become a weakness. Last year you had a strong senior class with a heart to reach their non-Christian friends. This year the senior class is carnal and doesn't really care about the unsaved. So, what are the weaknesses? Be realistic and honest. You can't fix it if you can't see it. The problem areas will not disappear if you ignore them, they will only get worse.

➢ Be careful. If you go into a youth ministry where the person before you has had a long, fruitful, successful ministry, then you can become the sacrificial lamb. You become the Church's number one trivia question! "Who was the Youth Pastor that served between our two favorite Youth Pastors?" It may not sound spiritual but you need to be realistic and make sure enough time has passed between the former Youth Pastor's resignation and when you begin to candidate. Otherwise you will face:
- Teens and parents who love the other Youth Pastor.
- Lay staff loyal to the other Youth Pastor.
- People who resist change.
- Juniors and seniors who don't see the value of getting to know you.
- Individuals still sad the Youth Pastor left.
- Teens who will compare you and not like the fact you have a different personality, sense of humor, strengths and weaknesses.
- People who don't feel like they need you.

If you aren't realistic and don't go into this with your eyes wide open, it can be one of the most frustrating and discouraging times in your life. You had big dreams, high expectations and no sense of reality.

➢ There will be opposition. No matter how great the candidate process went, and how strong the vote was, there are still those who oppose you. Being realistic is just being aware of this. There isn't always a lot you can do about it. There is the honeymoon time when everything seems great but then some opposition starts to surface. Why?
- Their allegiance to the former Youth Pastor.
- They voted against you. There can be this sick attitude which hopes you fail so   they can say, "See I told you so and that is why I didn't vote for them."
- You did or said something they didn't like. Many times, they won't talk to you but they will be happy to talk

about you.
- You are bringing change and for whatever reason they are uncomfortable with the direction things are going.
- You've become a threat to what they value. You are doing things that do not fit with their traditions or expectations.
- Lay staff can see you as a threat to their popularity and power base. Teens really liked them but now they are starting to like you. No longer do they have the control and authority like they did before.

A ship in harbor is safe, but that is not what ships are built for."
William Shedd

Deal with the fact some people will not like you, is a reality. Youth Ministry is not a popularity contest. We are not in it to be loved but to love. We realize because it is an effective door for ministry there will be opposition. Through the years I have experienced plenty of opposition and I am such a nice guy. Let me give you some examples.

- A group of individuals were upset because I was not teaching what a famous speaker, at the time, was saying. They were upset because I was not teaching his materials and I was not taking groups of teens to his seminars.

- Some parents who were upset with me because so many non-Christians were coming out on Wednesday night. They did not want their children impacted in a negative way by these students. They did not like the sound of the music. They didn't think I should be teaching on topics like sex. They were upset I wasn't teaching topics like length of hair, tattoos, piercing, evils of Christian rock, etc. They pulled their teens out of the youth ministry and started their own home school youth group.

- Some people were upset with me because our youth ministry was not as big as the one across the street.

- I had to let a staff member go because of lying. He had his supporters and there were a number of people who were upset with me. But it was the right decision.

- Parents of teens who are spiritually dead. These people were just negative. Their teens aren't doing well and they want to blame you rather than take responsibility.

- A lay staff member became jealous after I arrived. He was the teen's favorite but he felt his popularity slipping.

It is a mystery to me why people want to assume the worst rather than the best. Why don't they think a Youth Pastor loves Jesus and wants what is best for the students? Why can't they give him the freedom to fail without making a big deal out of it? Why don't they think a Youth Pastor has feelings? How come they can be very disrespectful and down right mean and expect you to just take it? I am always amazed at how a person can claim to be a Christian and at the same time be cruel and insulting. Youth Ministry is not for cowards. Face it, no matter who you are or what you do there will be some people who don't like you. Jesus faced it and so will you.

➢ **People are evaluating you.** This will happen from day one and first impressions are hard to break. Parents, teenagers, staff and others will be asking themselves questions. They don't all ask the same questions but the questions they ask themselves are what they use to form their opinion of you. Here are some of the questions.
  - Do they love Jesus?
  - Are they approachable?
  - Do they care about me?
  - Do they care about my children?
  - Are they a person of character?

- Do they know what they are doing?
- Are they fun?
- Can they make tough decisions?
- Do they share my values and standards?

If you worry about what others are thinking, then you will drive yourself insane. Take the steps you need to take, honor the Lord and then trust Him with your reputation. "Let love and faithfulness never leave you; bind them around your neck, write them on the tablet of your heart. Then you will win favor and a good name in the sight of God and man. Trust in the Lord with all your heart and lean not on your own understanding; in all your ways acknowledge him, and he will make your paths straight." (Proverbs 3:3-6). God has raised you up and He will strengthen and guide you.

THINK ABOUT IT:
1. Have you been evaluating the Youth Ministry?
2. Where are the strengths and where are the weaknesses?
3. Put your programs in four different categories: start, change, realign and sustain.

THOUGHT: "DON'T JUST DO SOMETHING, TO DO SOMETHING"

"Am I doing activities for activities sake or am I doing activities to accomplish ministry purposes in the lives of my students?" Brian Float

In the past, we have done things just to do them, something to fill the time and entertain the students. There is no real purpose or plan involved but it seemed like a good idea at the time. This happens when we are shooting from the hip and not planning ahead. It is time we stop and start thinking things through. There needs to be a purpose and plan behind what we are doing.

Programs. You will have a variety of programs taking place within your ministry. As you are putting them together keep these things in mind.

> - **What is the purpose?** Why are you going to do this? Everyone needs to know the purpose. You, your staff and all the teens need to be on the same page. This helps the student decide whether they want to be there and shapes the expectations of those who do come. Break your programs down into three categories.
>   - Discipleship. This is a growth level program where we want to deepen a student's walk with Jesus Christ.
>   - Evangelistic. This is a program where we want to expose students to the good news of the Gospel of Jesus Christ.
>   - Pre-Evangelistic. This is something for the non-Christian that will attract them and get their foot in the door.

"When we accept tough jobs as a challenge and wade into them with joy and enthusiasm, miracles can happen." Arland Gilbert

- **Define your goals.** What do you want to see accomplished? This will help you to put together a plan and reveal all the specifics for the program. What do you want them to leave with? What is the theme? What do you want to communicate? Keep the main thing the main thing. Defining your goals will help you to focus in on what is most important.

- **Who is in charge?** Someone needs to be responsible for the program. If you don't have a "buck stops here" person then everyone and no one is in charge. This will lead to frustration and conflict. Be sure you delegate and then let the person who is in charge of the program delegate too.

- **What are the different elements that will make up the program?** Make a list. Things like greeting, announcements, Power Point, drama, music, games, mixers, multi-media, teaching, worship, prayer, etc. Make different people responsible so you get as many people involved as you can.

- **What will be your priorities as you look at the different elements?** You tend to establish priorities by the amount of time you give to them. If you give 20 to 30 minutes to games and 5 to 10 minutes to teaching then what are you communicating is most important? The priorities will differ depending on the purpose. During the fall, after the football games, we would have "5th quarters". This was pre-evangelistic and included games, refreshments, fellowship and no teaching at all.

- **Evaluate.** If you are going to stay current and effective you need to be evaluating. When you look back at a specific program, ask yourself these three questions.
  - What went well? Be sure during this step you are very complimentary. Build up those in the room. Write some thank you cards, make some phone calls. Remember, the worst thing you can do is be silent. People work hard, you don't notice and they give up.

- Where do we need to improve? As we pursue excellence there will always be ways we can improve. Do not be threatened by this process. It is hard to improve if we do not acknowledge the areas we need to work on. Keep a written record of your evaluation. You think you will remember everything for next time but you won't remember!
- What will we do next time? What's the next step we need to take? We look at fifteen things that need to be improved, become overwhelmed and end up doing nothing. Instead, pick one thing, the next step and take it.

Programs are great but don't just do something because you don't know what else to do. Have a purpose behind what you are doing. Think things out ahead of time and know what you are doing.

THINK ABOUT IT:
1. What is the purpose for each of your programs?
2. Are you balanced between discipleship, evangelistic and pre-evangelistic?
3. After each program are you evaluating?

THOUGHTS FROM OTHERS:
"Start by doing what's necessary, then what's possible and suddenly you are doing the impossible." Saint Francis of Assisi

"You decide what it is you want to accomplish and then you layout your plans to get there, and then you just do it. It's pretty straightforward." Nancy Ditz

"Success is simple. Do what's right, the right way, at the right time." Arnold Glasow

THOUGHT: "DO NOT FEAR"

"You may laugh out loud in the future at something you're eating your heart out over today." Charles Swindoll

"For God did not give us a spirit of timidity, but a spirit of power, of love and of self discipline," (2 Timothy 1:7). That is the truth but we don't always feel the power. Honestly, for many of us, more times then we want to admit, we are gripped by worry and fear. Sometimes it seems like fear is more real to us than God. Fear is a dream killer that paralyzes us from doing what we need to do, being what we need to be and stepping out to follow the Holy Spirit's leading. We emotionally curl up in a ball, put up walls, shrink back and give up. We become confused; lose confidence in God and His ability to work through us. I am not sure what to do, so I do nothing. It is hard to have a vision for the future when we find it hard to get out of bed and face the day.

We all struggle with different kinds of fear. I have an irrational fear of large sharks that can eat me. If I am in the ocean and I can't touch the bottom, it freaks me out because I don't know what is underneath me. My wife Bonnie and I were in the Caribbean and I went snorkeling. That was hard; I kept listening for the music warning me Jaws was approaching. But this kind of fear doesn't really impact my ministry to teenagers, especially living in the Midwest. There is a fear I struggle with which does impact my ministry and that is the fear of failure. I am happy to succeed for Jesus and to have Him work through me in great and powerful ways. But failure scares me to death. It can cause me to seek what is comfortable, safe and familiar rather then something God is calling me to do which might be spiritually, emotionally or even physically risky. Being on the cutting edge spiritually is not always safe, even though you are secure in the arms of Jesus. Am I willing to put my reputation in the hands of God? Am I willing to seemingly fail in the eyes of man, so I ultimately succeed in the eyes of God? Intellectually I can say yes but I still struggle in my heart. I have to remind myself God's purpose for my life is the process and not just the outcome.

"Never be afraid to trust an unknown future to a known God." Corrie ten Boom

Fear has to do with your feelings and those feelings can lead you in the opposite direction of what God is calling you to do. If you waited to act until you weren't afraid then you might not get anything done. You must know what is true, do what is right and not depend on you feelings. We all fail at times. I had my worst public assembly ever in Georgia. It was optional at the end of the day and with very little supervision. It was a disaster! They didn't like me, I couldn't capture their attention and they were rude the whole time.

In California, I was invited to do a series of three evening evangelistic outreaches for teenagers. They didn't like my style of teaching, didn't like my humor, sound effects, illustrations, nothing. But they really liked the musician. So, as the days went by they liked the musician more and more and disliked me more and more. When they introduced him, the crowd roared and when they introduced me, it was the sound of one hand clapping. It got so bad the musician was trying to give me tips on speaking.

This is all part of the process of keeping me humble and close to Jesus. These times can be some of my greatest times of learning. Life experiences are used by God to teach and shape us. Even though I would not be excited about going through those experiences again, I am thankful for everything God taught me

What are some things that will cause us to fear?

- ➢ Comparison. Not feeling like we are as talented or effective as the other person or comparing our ministry to another ministry.

- ➢ Focus. Being focused on you rather than Christ. Peter got out of the boat, which is more than the other disciples, or some of us are willing to do. As long as he focused on Jesus he was fine, but when he took his eyes off Jesus and focused on the waves, storm and deep water, he sank. We are fine when we focus on Jesus Christ but when we take our eyes off Jesus to focus on ourselves, problems, situations and circumstances, then we can begin to sink into fear.

- ➢ Negative thinking. Sometimes we have a negative perspective towards life. The cup is always half empty and nothing is going right. It's the kind of attitude that says, "Life stinks and then you die." Your thinking is saying, "I can't, it won't work, nobody, everybody, I'm just a failure." Faulty thinking will lead you to fear and despair.

- ➢ The past. Failure, mistakes, and problems can cause you to fear the future. We think, "Better to play it safe than to step out in faith." Once does not mean always. You struggled last week with your speaking. This does not mean you will always struggle with your speaking. Do not allow the past to rob you of the future.

- ➢ The enemy. The enemy will attack us with fear so we don't do what God is calling us to do. Fear, deception and doubt are three of his main weapons he attacks me with and pretty soon I am focused on the fear and not the Father, I became unproductive and ineffective. I get to the point where I want to give up.

Growing up, we had a peeping tom in our neighborhood. One evening, late, I was lying on my bed, not able to sleep. I turned on my light to read. It was summer and my windows were open but the curtains were closed. All of a sudden, I heard footsteps out on the road. Then I could hear them move into our yard. I am starting to get scared. We had small rocks that edged our grass and I could hear them walking through the rocks and onto the porch by my window. Slowly and quietly I got out of bed and moved to the window. I could almost hear their breathing on the other side of the screen. I began to pull back a corner of the curtain to peek outside. This person and I were only separated by inches. As I was pulling back the curtain ever so slowly...BAM, BAM, BAM! This guy pounded on the window. I fell straight back onto the floor, I heard footsteps running away from the house, our dog was going crazy barking, my heart was pounding and I couldn't move. I was absolutely frozen by fear. It woke my dad up and he was mad because he thought I was messing around. Me? Mess around? Come on! You become frozen by fear. Your heart pounds, you feel sick to your stomach and you can't do what you need to do. I wanted to get up off the floor and chase the guy but I couldn't move. The feelings are real but if you let fear grip you then it leads to avoiding, escaping and giving up.

How can you begin to conquer fear in your life?

> ➤ Hold onto Jesus. God is greater than all your fears. You need to put your focus back on the King of Kings and Lord of Lords. He is all powerful, all knowing and in control. There is nothing you can't face with God. Greater is Jesus in you, than anyone or anything. When my children were little, they would have a bad dream and be scared. I would hold them in my arms and they would be safe and secure. When one of those huge Midwestern thunderstorms would roll through they would all run into our bedroom and climb into bed with us and there they would feel protected and loved. This is what you need to do. Rest in the arms of Jesus, climb into His lap and let Him care, protect, love and restore you. Remember the old saying:
> - No God - Know Fear
> - Know God - No Fear

"Anxiety does not empty tomorrow of its sorrows, but only empties today of its strength." Charles Spurgeon

> ➤ Claim the promises of God's Word. His promises are true and you can depend upon His word. Study the Bible, memorize His Word and claim those promises. The Holy Spirit will apply the Word to your life to teach, rebuke, correct, and train you, 2 Timothy 3:16. Now read these verses and claim the promises now. This is God speaking to you and what He says is true no matter how you feel.
>
> | | |
> |---|---|
> | Joshua 1:9 | Luke 12:32 |
> | Psalm 37:5-6 | John 14:1 |
> | Psalm 55:22 | 2 Corinthians 12:9-10 |

Proverbs 16:3
Isaiah 26:3-4
Isaiah 41:10&13
Jeremiah 17:7-8
Jeremiah 29:11-12

Philippians 4:4-7
Philippians 4:13&19
Hebrews 4:15-16
Hebrews 13:5-6
I Peter 5: 6-7

- ➢ Be obedient. Now you know the truth, you need to step out in faith, and do what God is calling you to do. I know it may be very hard, but if it was easy you might not need God. Allow the Lord to work miracles in your life. As you step out, you will see Him work, which will strengthen your faith, and cause you to trust Him for even greater things. Cast all your cares upon Him, tell Him exactly what you need and then step out in obedience. What is impossible for you is possible for God.

- ➢ Let others love you. Let those you can trust into your heart and life. Be open and vulnerable with them. They need to know fear has gripped you. Allow them to listen, love and pray for you. You need to let the Body of Christ do what it is supposed to do. Weep with you, rejoice with you, encourage you and pray for you. Let them serve you in this way. If you don't let them, you rob them and yourself. You rob them of God's blessing as He works through them and you rob yourself of the comfort, support, wisdom, and direction.

- ➢ Name the fears. Sometimes, we are afraid but we haven't really processed what we are scared of. Naming the fears brings them into the light, allows you to get a handle on them and gives others the opportunity to speak truth into your life. Naming them can help turn mountains back into mole hills.

- ➢ Don't compare. You are unique and unlike anyone else. You have different gifts, talents, and abilities. Be content with what God has called you to do and how He has equipped you to do it. It's O.K. if I am not a teenager's favorite speaker. I have been called to be faithful with the gifts God has given me and not to compare myself with anyone.

- Arm yourself. Put on the full armor of God every single day, Ephesians 6:13-18. To go into a battle unarmed is suicide. But some of us do this on a daily basis. We are in the middle of a huge war unprotected. We become an easy target for fear.

- Remember the blessing of failure. Now, that even sounds wrong to me. But I see the truth of it in my life. Failure has caused me to draw near to God. It has kept me dependent upon the Holy Spirit. It has taught me lessons of what to do and what not to do. Erwin Lutzer wrote a book, "Failure, Back Door to Success." It is true. In the midst of the failure there are lessons to learn that will become blessings in our life, ministry, and future.

Be strong and courageous! Now get out there and live for Jesus!

THINK ABOUT IT:
1. What fears do you struggle with?
2. What causes your fear?
3. What do you need to do to conquer your fear?

THOUGHTS FROM OTHERS:
"Fear imprisons, faith liberates; fear paralyzes, faith empowers; fear disheartens, faith encourages; fear sickens, faith heals; fear makes useless, faith makes serviceable." Harry Emerson Fosdick

"Fear is faithlessness." George MacDonald

"There is much in the world to make us afraid. There is much more in our faith to make us unafraid." Frederick W. Cropp

"Deep faith eliminates fear." Lech Walesa

"I will not fear, for you are ever with me, and you will never leave me to face my perils alone." Thomas Merton

FINAL THOUGHT:

Well there it is, like it or hate it, keep it or toss it. I have tried to share some of my experiences and thoughts on youth ministry. I have loved the ministry God has given me, the different opportunities to work with teenagers. Being a Youth Pastor, caseworker, youth specialist and missions leader have given me unique experiences and insights into working with teenagers. It hasn't always been easy but it has never been boring. God has taught me so much over the years. Too much of what I learned, I learned the hard way. I wanted this book to be an encouragement and guidepost for those who come after me. For those who are called by God to the greatest ministry there is…youth ministry.

If I have offended you it was not my intention and I am sorry. I have found within the Body of Christ people are too easily offended. We need to be able to disagree and dialogue with each other. At least think about some of the things I have said and consider what God might say to you, even through my foolishness.

"How long will you continue to work with teenagers?" I get this question all the time and my answer is, "As long as God gives me favor in the eyes of teens." There is nothing I would rather do or be involved in than the lives of teenagers.

I would be happy to correspond with you. You can E-mail me at gregospeck@gmail.com and I would invite you to check out my web site at www.gregspeck.com. Be patient, I do my best to respond to all the notes I receive.

I love to laugh so I leave you with some final thoughts to think about that made me laugh and think. God bless you.

> ➢ "No man knows his true character until he has run out of gas, purchased something on the installment plan and raised an adolescent." Mercelene Cox

> ➢ "You can learn many things from children. How much patience you have, for instance." Franklin P. Jones

- "A critic is a legless man who teaches running." Channing Pollock

- "There is nothing more pathetic as a forgetful liar." F. M. Knowles

- "Never let a fool kiss you or a kiss fool you." Joey Adams

- "Grandchildren don't make a man feel old; it's the knowledge he is married to a grandmother." G. Norman Collie

- "Back of every achievement is a proud wife and a surprised mother-in-law." Brooks Hays

- "You can be sincere and still be stupid." Charles F. Kettering

- "Many peoples tombstones should read, 'Died at 30. Buried at 60'." Nicholas Murray Butler